THE ROAD MAP TO NOWHERE

THE ROAD MAP TO NOWHERE

Israel/Palestine since 2003

Tanya Reinhart

VERSO

London • New York

First published by Verso 2006
© Tanya Reinhart 2006
All rights reserved

The moral rights of the author have been asserted

1 3 5 7 9 10 8 6 4 2

Verso
UK: 6 Meard Street, London W1F 0EG
USA: 180 Varick Street, New York, NY 10014–4606
www.versobooks.com

Verso is the imprint of New Left Books

ISBN-13: 978–1–84467–076–5
ISBN-10: 1–84467–076–7

British Library Cataloguing in Publication Data
A catalogue record for this book is available from the British Library

Library of Congress Cataloging-in-Publication Data
A catalog record for this book is available from the Library of Congress

Typeset in Perpetua by Hewer Text UK Ltd, Edinburgh
Printed in Germany by GGP Media GmbH, Pössneck

Contents

Figures

Introduction[1]

IN THE PRESENT POLITICAL ATMOSPHERE in the US and Europe, anybody who expresses criticism of Israel's policies is immediately silenced as an anti-Semite. Part of the reason why the pro-Israel lobbies have been so successful in their use of this accusation is the massive lack of knowledge about what is really happening in Israel–Palestine. Without the facts, the dominant narrative remains that Israel is struggling to defend its very existence. Attention focuses mainly on the horrible, despicable Palestinian terror; hence critics of Israel are often accused of justifying terror. My aim in this book is to provide the facts, as they unfold – openly – in the Israeli media.

This book covers the history of the Israeli occupation of Palestine since 2003; it is framed against my previous book *Israel/Palestine*,[2] which covers the period between 1999 and 2002. At the opening of *Israel/Palestine* I wrote:

> The state of Israel was founded in 1948 following a war which the Israelis call the War of Independence, and the Palestinians call the *nakba* – the catastrophe. A haunted, persecuted people sought to find a shelter and a state for itself, and did so at a horrible price to another people. During the war of 1948, more than half of the Palestinian population at the time – 1,380,000 people – were driven off their homeland by the Israeli army. Though Israel officially claimed that a majority of the refugees fled and were not expelled, it still refused to allow them to return, as a UN resolution demanded shortly after the 1948 war. Thus, the Israeli land was obtained

through ethnic cleansing of the indigenous Palestinian inhabitants.

This is not a process unfamiliar in history. Israel's actions remain incomparable to the massive ethnic cleansing of Native Americans by the settlers and government of the United States. Had Israel stopped there, in 1948, I could probably live with it. As an Israeli, I grew up believing that this primal sin our state was founded on might be forgiven one day, because the founders' generation was driven by the faith that this was the only way to save the Jewish people from the danger of another holocaust. But it didn't stop there.[3]

Since 1967 Israel has occupied the Palestinian territories in the West Bank and the Gaza Strip (as well as the Syrian Golan Heights). Today, over three and a half million Palestinians still live in these two areas under Israeli occupation. In 1993, it seemed that the occupation was reaching its end. Many believed that the Oslo Accords, signed in Washington that year, would lead to Israel's withdrawal from the occupied territories and the formation of a Palestinian state. But this is not how things turned out. As I discussed in *Israel/Palestine*, the political leadership of the Israeli peace camp turned the Oslo spirit of reconciliation into a new and more sophisticated form of maintaining the occupation. But during all these years Israel's official line has been that the situation is temporary. According to this line, the Oslo Agreements were just interim agreements – necessary steps in the long process required for working out the details of a final agreement. At least the Labor governments kept pledging that at the end of the so-called "interim period" Israel would eventually withdraw, dismantle settlements and end the occupation. In July 2000, a Labor prime minister – Ehud Barak – led the Israelis and the world to believe that Israel was, finally, willing to start this new era of peace. Instead, however, his premiership marked the end of the Oslo period and the return of direct Israeli military control of the occupied territories.

In *Israel/Palestine*, I described the period between 2000 and 2002 as the darkest years in the history of the Israeli occupation of the Palestinian territories. But in the period since, under the leadership of Ariel Sharon, it became even worse. Sharon started a massive project of ethnic cleansing in the areas of the West Bank bordering Israel. His wall project robs the land from the Palestinian villages in these areas, imprisons whole towns, and leaves their residents with no means of sustenance. If the project continues, many of the 400,000 Palestinians affected by it will have to leave and seek their livelihood in the outskirts of cities in the centre of the West Bank, as has already happened in the northern West Bank town of Qalqilya. The Israeli settlements were evacuated from the Gaza Strip, yet the Strip remains a big prison, completely sealed off from the outside world, nearing starvation and terrorized from land, sea and air by the Israeli army.

Nevertheless, as this book goes to press, in April 2006, the Western world seems still under the spell of the legend of Ariel Sharon and the supposed great change he brought about in Israeli policy – from expansion and occupation to moderation and concessions. Since the evacuation of the Gaza Strip settlements, the dominant Western narrative runs that Israel has done its part towards ending the occupation and has declared its readiness to take further steps, but now it is the Palestinians' turn to show that they are able to live in peace with their well-intentioned neighbour.

How did it happen that Sharon, the most brutal, cynical, racist and manipulative leader Israel has ever had, should end his political career as a legendary peace hero? The answer in this book is that Sharon has never changed. Rather, the birth of the Sharon myth reflects the present omnipotence of the propaganda system, which, to paraphrase a notion of Chomsky, has reached perfection in manufacturing consciousness.

As has become commonplace in the recent history of the occupation, the period covered here opened with a new peace initiative – the Road Map. The Palestinians accepted the plan and declared a ceasefire, but, as we shall see, while the Western world was celebrating the new era of peace, the Israeli army under Sharon intensified its policy of assassinations, maintained the daily harassment of the occupied Palestinians, and eventually declared all-out war on Hamas, killing all its first-rank military and political leaders. Later, as the Western world was once again holding its breath in an eighteen-month wait for the planned Gaza pullout, Sharon did everything possible to fail the newly-elected Palestinian president, Mahmoud Abbas, and turned down his offers of renewed negotiations.

I argue that, contrary to the prevailing assumptions, Sharon did not evacuate the Gaza settlements of his own free will. He cooked up his disengagement plan as a means to gain time, at the peak of international pressure that followed Israel's sabotaging of the Road Map. Yet still, at every moment since then, up until the very moment of disengagement, he was looking for ways to renege on this commitment, as he had done so many times previously. But this time he was forced to follow through with the Gaza pullout by the Bush administration. Though it was kept fully behind the scenes, US pressure on Sharon was massive, and included military sanctions on Israel.

At the same time, what Sharon has brought to perfection is the manufacturing of consciousness, showing that war can be always marketed as the tireless pursuit of peace. He proved that Israel can imprison the Palestinians, bombard them from the air, steal their land in the West Bank, stall any chance for peace – and yet still be hailed by the Western world as the peaceful side in the Israel–Palestine conflict.

As the book ends, Sharon had retired from political life, and is currently unconscious in a Jerusalem hospital. But this alone does not portend any change: Sharon may have gone, but his legacy is very much alive. It has been nurtured for over a decade in the Israeli military, which is in effect the dominant factor in Israeli politics.

In *Israel/Palestine* I survey the role of the military in the Israeli democracy. I argue that the current escalation of hostilities that started at the end of September 2000 was not a spontaneous outburst of violence, but rather a calculated and well-prepared move by the Israeli military, which was at the time gaining enormous political power with the appointment of its former chief of staff, Ehud Barak, as prime minister. (The book surveys in detail the close relations of Barak and Sharon both before and during that period.) I contend that the Oslo Accords in 1993, and the agreements that followed, were in effect the realization of Labor's long-standing Alon plan, by which Israel would keep about forty per cent of the West Bank's land and in the rest, the Palestinians would be allowed to have a functioning autonomy. But in the eyes of the military and the hawks in the Israeli political system even that was too much, because, from a longer-range perspective, it risked leading to the loss of Israel's control of the territories. Both Barak and Sharon had expressed vociferous opposition to the Oslo Agreements from the outset.

On the eve of Oslo, the majority of Israelis were tired of war. In their eyes, the fights over land and resources were over. However, the ideology of the "redemption of land" never died out in the army and the circles of political hawks. In their eyes, Sharon's alternative of fighting the Palestinians to the bitter end and imposing a new regional order most likely failed in Lebanon in 1982[4] because of the weakness of a self-indulgent Israeli society, but with Israel's massive military superiority, it might still be possible to crush Palestinian resistance and gain more land through the use of force. When Barak took power in 1999, the road opened to undo the Oslo Agreements. In order to achieve this, it was first necessary to convince the spoiled Israeli society that the Palestinians were not willing to live in peace and were in fact threatening Israel's very existence. Barak succeed in doing this with his "generous offer" in the July 2000 Camp David summit, which, as I show in detail in *Israel/Palestine*, was nothing but a fraud.[5] Under

Sharon, the process of restoring direct military control of the occupied territories was completed.

The military is the most stable – and most dangerous – political factor in Israel. As an Israeli analyst stated in 2001, "in the last six years, since October 1995, there were five prime ministers and six defense ministers, but only two chiefs-of-staff".[6] Israeli military and political systems have always been closely intertwined, with generals moving from the army straight to the government, but the army's political status was further solidified during Sharon's premiership. It is often apparent that the real decisions are made by the military rather than the political echelon. Military seniors brief the press (they capture at least half of the news space in the Israeli media), and brief and shape the views of foreign diplomats; they go abroad on diplomatic missions, outline political plans for the government, and express their political views on any subject and occasion.

In contrast to this military stability, the Israeli political system is in a gradual process of disintegration. In a World Bank report of April 2005, Israel was found to be one of the most corrupt and least efficient in the Western world, second only to Italy in the government corruption index, and lowest in the index of political stability.[7] Together with his sons, Sharon personally was associated with severe bribery charges that have never reached the courts.[8] The new party that Sharon founded, Kadima, which now heads the government, is a hierarchical agglomeration of individuals with no party institutions or local branches. Its guidelines, published on 22 November 2005, enable its leader to bypass all standard democratic processes and appoint the list of the party's candidates to the parliament without voting or approval of any party body.[9]

The Labor party has not been able to offer an alternative. In the last two Israeli elections, Labor elected dovish prime-ministerial candidates: Amram Mitzna in 2003 and Amir Peretz in 2006. Both were initially received with enormous enthusiasm, but were immediately silenced by their party and campaign advisors and by self-imposed censorship, aiming to situate themselves "at the center of the political map". Soon, their programs became indistinguishable from those of Sharon. Peretz even declared that on "foreign and security" matters he will do exactly as Sharon, or later Olmert, do, differing from them only on social matters. Thus, these candidates helped convince the Israeli voters that Sharon's way is the right way. In recent years, there has been no substantial left-wing opposition to the rule of Sharon and the generals, since after the elections, Labor would always join the government, providing the dovish image that the generals need for the international show.

A prevailing explanation as to why the Israeli political leadership has made no progress on resolving the Israeli–Palestinian conflict is that in Israeli society there exists no majority backing for sweeping concessions. Hence, even the most well-intentioned and dovish of Israeli leaders have to restrain themselves and offer only what the majority can swallow. This may have been true in the past, but since at least the early 1990s this claim has had no basis in reality. In fact, there is a wide consensus in Israeli society that peace with the Palestinians and other Arab neighbours requires withdrawal from the occupied territories and the evacuation of settlements. The first Palestinian uprising or *intifada* (1987–93) brought about a substantial change in Israeli public opinion. Israeli society discovered that its military occupation of Palestinian land came with a heavy price attached. Many could no longer accept the occupation on moral grounds; others were just unwilling to pay its economic and human cost. This shift of view was reinforced by a parallel change in Palestinian society. Since the first *intifada*, the Palestinian struggle for independence was also based on explicit recognition of Israel's right to exist in its pre-1967 borders. The *intifada* meeting of the Palestine National Council in Algiers in 1988 called, for the first time, for the partition of the historical Palestine into two independent states.[10]

Since the early 1990s, Israeli public opinion has formed a clear pattern. About one third is firmly against the occupation and the settlements on moral and ideological grounds; another third believes in Israel's right over the whole land and supports the settlements; the middle third is people with no fixed ideological view on the matter – people whose sole concern is their ability to lead a normal life. At the time of the Oslo Accords, the middle third joined the end-the-occupation camp: two thirds of Israelis supported Oslo in all polls, though it was conceived as leading to an eventual Israeli withdrawal from the occupied territories and the evacuation of the settlements. This pattern has remained essentially unchanged in the years since, with all polls showing that close to two thirds of the Israelis support withdrawal and evacuation of West Bank settlements.[11] Nevertheless, this majority has not been able to enforce its will. Since 1999, all Israeli leaders (including Sharon, as we shall see) have promised huge concessions for peace in their election campaigns, only to do the opposite when elected.

With the collapse of the political system, the army remains the body that shapes and executes Israel's policies and, as is already obvious in the few months since Sharon left office, is determined to implement his legacy, together with Sharon's successor, Ehud Olmert. This legacy, as it unfolds in the period covered in this book, is eternal war, not just with the Palestinians, but with what the Israeli army views as their potential network of support, be it Iran now, or Syria tomorrow. The book ends close to where it started, with a new "peace plan" promoted by Olmert. As we shall see in Chapter 7, the goal is to obtain international approval for Israel to annex unilaterally 40 per cent of the West Bank. But Olmert is Israel's new man of peace.

Nevertheless, the period covered here was not just a chronology of victories for the politics of power and the manufacturing of consciousness. From the perspective of maintaining Israel's occupation of the Palestinian territories, evacuating the Gaza settlements was a defeat, forced on Israel by international pressure. In Chapter 5, I argue that the reason the US exerted pressure on Israel for the first time in recent history, was because at that time it was impossible to ignore the widespread global discontent over Israel's policies and unswerving US support of them. For example, despite the apparent success of pro-Israel lobbies in silencing any criticism of Israel in Europe, in a comprehensive European poll the majority viewed Israel as the country most threatening to world peace. The US had to yield to public opinion.

This turn of events shows the limits of propaganda – it appears possible to manufacture silence or compliance, but it may be impossible to manufacture consciousness. Basic concepts of justice, international law and solidarity with the oppressed have disappeared from mainstream political discourse, but they are present in people's minds. Chapter 8 is devoted to some of the history of the struggle to keep these concepts alive.

The story of the Gaza evacuation also shows that international pressure can lead Israel to concessions. I believe that this provides hope both to the Palestinians and to the Israelis. Israel's policies threaten not just the Palestinians but also the Israelis themselves. In the long run, this war over land is suicidal. A small Jewish state of seven million residents (5.5 million Jews), surrounded by two hundred million Arabs, is making itself the enemy of the whole Muslim world. There is no guarantee that such a state can survive. Saving the Palestinians also means saving Israel.

* * *

My major source of information in constructing the history of this period is the Israeli media. In the Israeli newspapers much more information is available about what is happening and what is being planned than appears in any foreign coverage. One often hears statements interpreting this as signifying that the Israeli media is more liberal and critical of Israel's policies than other Western media. This, however, is not the explanation. With the notable exception of courageous and conscientious journalists like Amira Hass, Gideon Levi and a few others, the Israeli press is as compliant as elsewhere, and it faithfully recycles military and governmental messages. But part of the reason it is more revealing is its lack of inhibition. Things that would look outrageous in the Western world are in Israel considered natural daily routine.[12]

While the Israeli media remains the best source for government and military plans, a change I have noted since the writing of *Israel/Palestine* is that its reporting of the Israeli army's actions in the territories has substantially shrunk. Often, daily atrocities are either ignored, or pushed to the back pages with minimal coverage. A reliable alternative source of information during this period has been the British *Guardian*. But to get a full picture of the daily reality of the occupation one also needs to read the Palestinian internet media.

Of the Israeli Hebrew papers, only *Ha'aretz* has an internet English version, which I have used for most quotes from *Ha'aretz* in this book.[13] For the other Israeli papers, the quotes are my translation of the original Hebrew. In a few cases, where I could not find the English version of a piece that appeared in *Ha'aretz* in Hebrew, the quote is marked as 'author's translation'. I try to bring as much of the story as possible in the direct voice of the media sources I use, because often the tone is no less revealing than the content. I also try to give some of the stage to alternative critical voices in the Israeli and international media.

I

Spring 2003: The Road Map Era

O N 29 APRIL 2003, the Palestinian Legislative Council approved a new Palestinian Authority cabinet under Prime Minister Mahmoud Abbas, popularly known as Abu Mazen. This followed a long period of pressure on Palestine to reform by the US and Israel; they appeared to extend support to Abbas, whom they considered a moderate. While presenting his ministers and his political vision, Abu Mazen stated: "We reject the terror on either side and in any form, in keeping with our tradition and moral values . . . We stress that terror and its various forms does not help our just cause, but rather destroys it, and will not bring the peace we want."[1]

Israel welcomed Abbas's announcement with a new assassination the same day. An Israeli air force Apache helicopter gunship fired several missiles at a car driving in a residential neighbourhood south of Khan Yunis, killing local PFLP (Popular Front for the Liberation of Palestine) commander Nidal Salameh and another PFLP member, Awani Sarhan. *Ha'aretz* reported that "in response to criticism over the timing of Salameh's killing (on the day that a new, reform-minded Palestinian government was being approved), IDF Chief of Staff Moshe Ya'alon said that . . . Salameh's assassination will actually strengthen the new Palestinian prime minister, Mahmoud Abbas (Abu Mazen)."[2] The following day, two suicide bombers from the Gaza Strip blew themselves up at Mike's Place, a Tel Aviv beachfront pub, killing three Israelis and wounding about sixty.[3]

It was against this setting that the 'Road Map' document was ceremonially presented to both sides, on 30 April 2003. US

Ambassador Daniel Kurtzer brought the document to Prime Minister Ariel Sharon's Jerusalem office, while European representatives presented it to Palestinian Mahmoud Abbas at the Department for Negotiations that he had established in Ramallah.[4]

The Road Map has its roots in a speech made by US President George W. Bush on 24 June 2002, which outlined a vague two-state solution and called for the replacement of the then Palestinian leadership, headed by Yasser Arafat. On 15 July, the foreign ministers of the Quartet – the United States, European Union, United Nations and Russia – met to detail the principles of the Road Map, which were formulated in the US State Department under the direction of William Burns. In October 2002, the first draft of the document was presented to Sharon on the eve of his meeting with Bush at the White House, whereupon Sharon appointed his chief of staff, Dov Weisglass, to coordinate Israel's comments and corrections. On 20 December 2002, the final version of the plan was drawn up; in the following months, however, Weisglass's team submitted about a hundred corrections to it.

The Road Map's stated aim was "a final and comprehensive settlement of the Israeli–Palestinian conflict by 2005",[5] a goal to be achieved in the plan's third stage, after two preparatory phases. In considering whether the Road Map offers any concrete solutions to the conflict it is necessary first to refresh our memory regarding what the conflict is about. From Israeli discourse since the failure of the Camp David negotiations in 2000, one might get the impression that it is about Israel's right to exist. This view holds that the Palestinians are trying to undermine the very existence of the state of Israel in their demand that Palestinian refugees be allowed the right to return to their original dwellings before 1948, a goal they are trying to achieve through terror.[6] However, this viewpoint seems to forget that in practice this is a simple and classical conflict over Palestinian land and resources – particularly water – that have been under Israeli occupation since 1967. The Road Map document as well manifests a complete absence of any territorial dimension.

In the Road Map's text, the demands made of the Palestinian side in the first two preparatory stages of the plan are clearly spelled out. The Palestinians must establish a government that is defined by the US as democratic; form three security forces which will be defined by Israel as reliable; and crush terror. Once these demands have been fulfilled, the third stage can begin: at this point the Israeli occupation will miraculously end. Crucially, however, at this third stage the document doesn't make any explicit demands of Israel regarding how it will end the occupation. Most Israelis understand that there is no way to end the occupation and the conflict without the Israeli army leaving the territories, and the West Bank settlements being dismantled. But these fundamental issues are not even hinted at in the document, which only mentions freezing the building and expansion of settlements and dismantling new outposts, which should be carried out already at the first stage of the plan: "GOI [Government of Israel] immediately dismantles settlement outposts erected since March 2001. Consistent with the Mitchell Report, GOI freezes all settlement activity (including natural growth of settlements)."[7]

Apart from this reference to the old US demand to freeze settlement expansion, the plan is remarkably unspecific as to how its final stage is to be implemented: "Phase III objectives are consolidation of reform and stabilization of Palestinian institutions, sustained, effective Palestinian security performance, and Israeli–Palestinian negotiations aimed at a permanent status agreement in 2005 . . . leading to a final, permanent status resolution in 2005, including on borders, Jerusalem, refugees, settlements; and . . . progress toward a comprehensive Middle East settlement between Israel and Lebanon and Israel and Syria, to be achieved as soon as possible."[8]

The proposed first phase, however, is more substantial,

because it repeats the ceasefire plan proposed by then CIA head George Tenet, in June 2001. The essence of the Tenet plan was that in order to restore calm, the Palestinians should cease all terror and armed activity, and Israel should pull its forces back to the positions they held before the second Palestinian uprising or *intifada* in September 2000. This was a substantial demand to make of Israel, because in September 2000 large swathes of the West Bank were under Palestinian control. Restoring the conditions that existed before September 2000 would mean lifting the many roadblocks and army posts that Israel subsequently imposed on these areas. The first phase of the Road Map reiterates the Tenet plan: Israel shall "withdraw from Palestinian areas occupied from Sept 28 2000 . . . [and restore] the status quo that existed then".[9]

There is no doubt that fulfilment of this demand would contribute greatly to establishing calm. But was there any basis for the hope that Tenet's plan would be finally implemented in this round of negotiations? The previous negotiating round, which I examined in *Israel/Palestine*,[10] was what appeared to be an American ceasefire initiative in March 2002, for which the US special envoy, Anthony Zinni, and Vice-President Dick Cheney were sent to the region. At that point Sharon stated emphatically that he would not agree to a ceasefire, but only to goodwill gestures, such as easing the conditions for the population in areas in which quiet will be preserved – in some unspecified way.[11] Yet Sharon's refusal did not prevent the US from pointing the finger at the Palestinians as the side responsible for the failure to agree to a ceasefire. With the end of this initiative, Israel embarked on the spree of destruction labelled "Defensive Shield," with the blessing of the United States.

Was there any chance that things would turn out differently with the presentation of the Road Map in April 2003? On the face of it, this time circumstances seemed potentially more favourable to negotiations. Since 2001 Israel, backed by the US, had argued that the real obstacle to restoring calm was the continued leadership of Yasser Arafat, who it said orchestrated terror from behind the scenes. Israel demanded the appointment of a different Palestinian prime minister, favouring Mahmoud Abbas for the role. Furthermore there were at the time many reports of Abbas and others negotiating a comprehensive cease-fire or *hudna* with the various Palestinian organizations, during which they would agree to refrain from any attacks on Israeli civilians and soldiers. What could be more suitable for a new peace initiative than starting with a period of calm – for the Israelis, a period of cessation of terror, and for the Palestinians, a period without the constant presence of the Israeli army in their midst?

This, however, was not how the Israeli authorities viewed it. As soon as Abbas was elected, they changed their tone. On the day he was sworn in it was reported that ''Military Intelligence told the political echelon at the beginning of the week that the new Palestinian government headed by Prime Minister Mahmoud Abbas has no intention of uprooting the terrorist infrastructure. 'According to what we know now, Abu Mazen plans to speak with the Hamas and Islamic Jihad leaders, and not clash with them.' ''[12]

The background for this dissatisfaction with Abbas lies in a demand posed by Israel as a condition for accepting the Road Map. Israel stated that the Palestinian Authority's successful halting of terror would not be sufficient in itself. A reliable Palestinian Authority, said Israel, should go further, engaging in an actual clash with the various armed organizations with the aim of destroying them. This demand was later reiterated in the resolution the Israeli cabinet passed when it approved the Road Map on 26 May 2003: ''In the first phase of the plan and as a condition for progress to the second phase, the Palestinians will complete the dismantling of terrorist organizations (Hamas, Islamic Jihad, the Popular Front, the Democratic Front, Al-Aqsa Brigades and other apparatuses) and their infrastructure.''[13] The dismantling should involve ''arrests, interrogations, prevention and the enforcement of the legal groundwork for investigations, prosecution and punishment".[14]

From the Palestinian perspective, carrying out this Israeli demand would in essence mean civil war. The list of groups whose dismantling Israel demanded comprises most Palestinian political organizations; Israel demanded not only that their military wings be dismantled, but their ''infrastructure'' – which is to say the political and social organizations that support them, organizations that also provide welfare and education. Furthermore, Israel stated that this long and fraught process of dissolution should take place as a precondition to any further progress towards the goals of the Road Map – all this at the very start of the process, and before any Israeli concessions would be made. There could be no reason to assume that the various organizations would simply obediently dismantle, or let their members be imprisoned or killed by the new security forces that Israel expects the Palestinian Authority to form. Rather, the process will involve armed clashes with these organizations. As I have discussed elsewhere, certain Palestinian organizations (most notably Hamas) were warning as early as the start of the Oslo peace process in 1993 that Israel is trying to push the Palestinians into a civil war, in the process of which Palestinian society would turn in on and destroy itself.[15] One of the achievements of Arafat's leadership, in collaboration with virtually all segments of Palestinian society, has been to avoid civil war. The new prime minister, Mahmoud Abbas, was neither able nor willing to risk civil war – he was, however, able to offer a cessation of terror and attacks on Israel. As Khalil Shikaki, a Palestinian political analyst, explained to the British *Guardian*, ''a ceasefire and the dismantling of groups like Hamas and Islamic Jihad were in contradiction . . . Why would Hamas continue a ceasefire if it was merely cover for its destruction? And if Abbas had the infrastructure to dismantle these groups, he wouldn't need the ceasefire in the first place.''[16]

The Israeli leadership viewed the cessation of terror offer as a threat, rather than progress. As Aluf Benn summarized in *Ha'aretz*: "As the Abu Mazen confidence vote drew closer, the tone changed in Jerusalem. At first Israel presented his election as a large celebration, as Israel's fruit of victory in the *intifada*. Now the prime minister, foreign minister and defense establishment are warning of another trick of those cunning Palestinians. The Israelis' position, supported by an intelligence analysis of Abu Mazen's statements in various conferences, is that the new [Palestinian] prime minister will try to push Israel to concessions by means of *hudna*, an agreed cessation of attacks among the Palestinian organizations . . . Jerusalem sources warn that the international community is deaf to . . . nuances and, as soon as a false calm prevails, will demand from Israel withdrawals and settlement freezes. Israel is demanding a Palestinian 'Altalena',[17] no less than a confrontational showdown between Abu Mazen and Mohammed Dahlan[18] on the one hand and Hamas, Jihad and the Al-Aqsa Brigades on the other."[19]

To mark the beginning of the Road Map era, a ceremonial summit between Bush, Sharon and Abbas was scheduled to take place in Aqaba, Jordan, at beginning of June 2003. As the date of the summit approached, Hamas leaders started to openly declare their willingness to enter into a ceasefire or *hudna* with Israel, for the first time since the movement's establishment in 1987. *Ha'aretz* reported that "a senior Hamas spokesman in Gaza, Abdel Aziz Rantisi, who usually represents movement hardliners, said on Friday: 'The Hamas movement is prepared to stop terror against Israeli civilians if Israel stops killing Palestinian civilians . . . We have told [Palestinian Authority Prime Minister] Abu Mazen in our meetings that there is an opportunity to stop targeting Israeli civilians if the Israelis stop assassinations and raids and stop brutalizing Palestinian civilians."[20]

Sharon immediately rejected this proposal. On the eve of the Aqaba summit, *Ha'aretz*'s front-page headline declared: "Prime Minister: A Palestinian ceasefire is not enough." The accompanying article went on to explain that "in his meeting with U.S.

president George Bush at the Aqaba summit, Prime Minister Ariel Sharon will seek U.S. backing of his demand that the Palestinian authority use forceful [military] means against the terror organizations and their infrastructure in the territories, as a precondition for any diplomatic advance. Sharon will tell Bush that it is not acceptable to settle just for agreements between the Palestinian organizations to a ceasefire (*Hudna*) . . . In return Sharon will promise Bush that Israel will evacuate illegal out-posts in the West Bank.''[21] Two weeks later, on 10 June, came the Israeli army's explicit reply to Rantisi's ceasefire offer. Two helicopter gunships fired seven missiles at his car in Gaza City, setting it ablaze, killing two people and wounding twenty. Rantisi escaped this assassination attempt, and survived another year until he was killed by the Israeli army on 17 April 2004.

Still, none of this seemed to have registered in Western – and certainly not in Israeli – consciousness. The collective perception of the events was informed solely by the generalized and abstract declarations coming from Israel's leaders. The Road Map document requires that ''at the outset of Phase I . . . the Israeli leadership issue an unequivocal statement affirming its commitment to the two-state vision of an independent, viable, sovereign Palestinian state living in peace and security alongside Israel, as expressed by President Bush''.[22] This, in fact, is the only clause in the Road Map with which the Israeli leadership complied. Sharon declared on several occasions that he ''accepts Bush's vision of two states,'' and on 26 May the Israeli cabinet, following a ''stormy'' six-hour debate, approved the Road Map (along with fourteen reservations that deprived it of content, although these did not attract much media attention).[23] At the level of declarations, Sharon was willing to go even further and utter the taboo word ''occupation''. At a meeting of the Likud Knesset faction on 27 May he said: ''I think the idea that it is possible to continue keeping 3.5 million Palestinians under occupation – yes it is occupation, you might not like the word, but what is happening is occupation – is bad for Israel, bad for the Palestinians, and bad for the Israeli economy."[24] This was sufficient to arouse a storm in right-wing circles, and to give Sharon complete credibility in the eyes of the Israeli doves. The idea that this might in fact be yet another piece of Israeli deception – that Sharon might be offering empty words in order to bolster his image as a "man of peace" – did not seem to cross anybody's mind.

Israeli public discourse immediately focused on "Sharon's revolutionary change of mind," provoking an extensive debate on whether he had undergone a personal Damascene conversion, or whether it was all the result of US pressure. Either way, Sharon had suddenly turned into the beloved leader of the Israeli "peace camp". The furious right wing and the celebrating peace camp were agreed on one thing: Sharon's Israel had already taken an irrevocable, historical step: it had committed itself to ending the occupation. "In Aqaba, the State of Palestine was founded!" declared the headline of *Yediot Aharonot* on 5 June. Following the tradition since the 1993 Oslo Accords, the mere declaration of a possible willingness to give away something at some future time is itself seen in Israel as the most painful and crucial of concessions. As Labor MP Abraham Burg, in an excited address of appreciation to Sharon, declared: "even if you regret this later; even if you will not be able to stand the pressure of your own party, you have already made your contribution, because you said occupation, you said evacuation, you said peace: you started to believe."[25]

In the Israeli consciousness, it is not the test of actions that matters, but the test of words – the complex art of the simulation of peace, which so eased the liberal conscience during the years of the Oslo Agreements. In this view, Bush and Sharon are the indubitable proponents of world peace. Who, then, would stop to notice what actually occurs in the real world?

It was, in fact, possible to learn from the Israeli newspapers at the time that nothing whatsoever had changed in the daily reality of the occupation. The Israeli army continued to arrest, shoot and assassinate Palestinians. Even during the week of the Aqaba summits, when in the world of simulation the headlines heralded an easing of the closure, the Israeli army made sure to signal that nothing would change. On the contrary, restrictions on Palestinian movement were increased. Here is how Arnon Regular described it in *Ha'aretz*: "The Palestinians might have heard about Israel's easing conditions for travel, but they haven't seen this on the ground. In fact, there are signs that nothing at all has changed . . . The picture that emerged yesterday after a day of driving up and down and back and forth across the West Bank is of tens of thousands of people who have seemingly been thrown back into the Middle Ages, when the only mode of transport was by foot."[26]

The diabolical aspect of Sharon's US-backed deception was that, from this point on, the finger of blame would only be pointed at the Palestinians for any and all future violence that occurred. From the Aqaba summit onwards, any Palestinian resistance to the army's continued brutality could not be tolerated because, in the eyes of Israeli public opinion, Israel had already fulfilled its part of the bargain when Sharon declared that he had had enough of the occupation. Now it was the turn of the Palestinian Authority to fulfil its part of this ostensibly generous agreement, and to prove that it was capable of controlling terror – even though there had been no actual change in the situation on the ground.

Nevertheless, the Palestinian Authority and the various Palestinian organizations fulfilled their side of the bargain, declaring a complete ceasefire for three months, during which they would halt all attacks in Israel and the occupied territories, as stipulated in Phase I of the Road Map. The first announcement that the Palestinian organizations had reached a ceasefire agreement came on 25 June 2003. Hamas spokesmen observed that "it was noteworthy that they had accepted the three-month lull without receiving any guarantees from Israel that it would cease its military activities against them in exchange for the ceasefire."[27]

The Israeli immediate reaction was instantaneous and decisive. Within minutes of the Palestinian announcement, "Israeli helicopters fired missiles at two cars near the southern Gaza city of Khan Yunis, killing two people, including a woman. The Israel Defense Forces said the helicopters fired the missiles at a Hamas cell that was about to fire mortar shells at an Israeli settlement."[28] In Jerusalem, "Prime Minister Ariel Sharon and Defense Minister Shaul Mofaz decided . . . that Israel will ignore any agreements on a *hudna*, or ceasefire, reached by the Palestinian organizations, and will instead insist that the Palestinian Authority disarm militias in any area in which it assumes security responsibility . . . The Foreign Ministry . . . instructed foreign legations to prepare for a Palestinian propaganda assault that will blame Israel for violating the 'ceasefire' while ignoring the PA's [Palestinian Authority's] responsibility for continued terrorist activity by 'local' cells."[29]

With perfect coordination, US reaction ran along the same lines: "President George W. Bush reacted skeptically yesterday to the reported [Palestinian] agreement on halting attacks against Israelis for three months. 'I'll believe it when I see it', Bush said. Bush demanded that Hamas and groups like it be taken out of business . . . 'It's one thing to make a verbal agreement', he said. 'But in order for there to be peace in the Middle East, we must see organizations such as Hamas dismantled, and then we'll have peace, we'll have a chance for peace.' . . . Bush said he did not know details of the reported deal, but was dubious about it, 'knowing the history of the terrorists.' During the meeting with Romano Prodi, president of the European Commission, and Greek Prime Minister Costas Simitis, the outgoing head of the EU . . . Bush pressed for the EU to outlaw Hamas in European countries, where a distinction is made between the movement's military and political wings."[30]

Although both Israel and the US made their intentions clear, even they could not keep pursuing this line publicly once it was evident that the Palestinians would pursue their ceasefire despite considerable Israeli provocation. On 29 June, the ceasefire was officially declared[31] – and this time, Israel appeared partially to cooperate. The Israeli army pulled out its forces from one town in the northern Gaza Strip and opened the main road in the Strip (the "Tancher" route) to Palestinian traffic. Sharon promised to consider the release of Palestinian prisoners. Later, in July, Israeli forces pulled back from the West Bank town of Bethlehem in the West Bank and three checkpoints were removed in the central West Bank Ramallah district, as "goodwill gestures to the Palestinians to coincide with Prime Minister Ariel Sharon's trip to Washington, where he is expected to face pressure from the U.S. to ease humanitarian conditions in the territories".[32]

But this more or less exhausted Israel's "goodwill" measures. For about six weeks, as the Palestinians fully kept to the Road Map's first phase, Israel did nothing to implement its side of the bargain. As I have mentioned, Sharon had already emphatically stated his refusal to comply with the fundamental requirement in the Tenet plan, reiterated in stage one of the Road Map, that the Israeli army should pull back to the positions it held before the 2000 *intifada*. Still, one might at least have expected that Israel would freeze military activity in these areas during the ceasefire. In fact, the Israeli army maintained – indeed increased – its level of operations in all Palestinian towns and villages; arrests, shooting, house demolitions, closures and blocking exits continued as usual.

Although the ceasefire was proving increasingly one-sided, the Palestinians continued to adhere to it (with one exception, on 7 July). Israeli society was both relieved and hopeful, yet this very optimism was apparently a cause of concern for those "Jerusalem sources" who, right from the start, "warned that the international community is deaf to . . . nuances and, as soon as a false calm prevails, will demand from Israel withdrawals and settlement freezes".[33] And indeed, after six weeks of the fully observed Palestinian ceasefire, Israel resumed its policy of assassinations, mainly targeting leaders of Hamas.

On 29 July, the day the Palestinian ceasefire was announced, some of the assessments of the Israeli security forces were shared with the public: ''The IDF's intelligence units believe that, of the three organizations that declared a suspension of attacks yesterday, Hamas activists will most closely adhere to the deal. Hamas is considered strictly hierarchical and relatively disciplined, and it seems that the group's leaders will do all they can to enforce the *hudna*.''[34] In this light, it is hard not to interpret the steps Israel subsequently took in August 2003 as an attempt to break Hamas's resolve and provoke it back to arms.

On 9 August, a squad of naval commandos killed two leading Hamas figures, Hamis Abu Salam and Faiz al-Sadar, in the Askar refugee camp near the West Bank town of Nablus. In the riots that erupted at the Askar camp following the assassination, two more Palestinians were killed. Three days later, two suicide bombers, both from the Askar refugee camp, blew themselves up in two terror attacks on the West Bank Ariel settlement and the Israeli town of Rosh Ha'ain, killing two Israelis. Following this, the Hamas leadership in Gaza finally made the slip for which the Israeli security forces had been waiting. It announced that although it was still committed to the ceasefire, the conditions were now changed so as to permit responses to Israeli aggression.[35] Israel immediately seized the opportunity to provoke local Hamas cells into action. Against this setting of growing frustration on the part of the Palestinian organizations that tried to stick to the ceasefire, Israel proceeded to target Mohammed Sidr, the head of Islamic Jihad's military wing in Hebron, killing him on 14 August. As always, Israel claimed that such killings were necessary to prevent terror – but Amos Harel, a senior security reporter and analyst in *Ha'aretz*, raised some doubts. Reporting the security forces' claim that ''recently, new intelligence has indicated that some of the Islamic organizations'' field operatives have tired of the ceasefire and have resumed planning near-term attacks,' he noted: ''If this is indeed what happened, the facts should be presented in full. As long as Israel makes do with generic statements about 'ticking bombs' and 'an attack the wanted man was planning in the near future', there will always be those who suspect it is Israel that is stirring up trouble in order to free itself of the yoke of the concessions demanded by the Road Map.''[36]

On the day of Sidr's assassination, security sources were already informing the Israeli media that the ceasefire was about to end. One Jerusalem source said, ''We must assume that everything is going to fall apart, and if so, it had better fall apart on the neighbor's side rather than on ours.''[37] It was obvious that the failure of the ceasefire would deal a mortal blow to Mahmoud Abbas's new government. By this time, however, the Israeli leadership was openly no longer interested in maintaining his rule. Abbas, whose appointment was hailed less than four months previously as a victory for Israel's tireless pursuit of peace, had fallen out of favour with the rulers; apparently, Israel had also managed to convince the Bush administration that the time had come to replace him. The same day, it was reported that ''Jerusalem received indications that the White House too is becoming increasingly disappointed with Abbas. The Americans had pinned many hopes on him, believing that his weight and authority would grow with the job, but they learned that his cabinet is not making the necessary changes and is not fighting against terrorism . . . Israeli sources assume that if the Americans despair of Abbas, they will threaten to cut the PA's funds off, thus leading to the collapse of its government and the rise of an alternative leadership.''[38]

Israel had often applied the assassination policy before in the full awareness that it would be bound to stall any Palestinian attempt at restoring calm.[39] As on many previous occasions, ordinary Israelis paid the price for this strategy. On 19 August, a suicide bomber belonging to a Hamas cell in Sidr's hometown of Hebron blew himself up on a Jerusalem bus, killing twenty people, including six children, and wounding about a hundred. The ceasefire was on life support, but at this stage it was still possible to save it. Abbas was quick to react: "Overnight he had secured the endorsement of Yasser Arafat to crack down on Hamas and Islamic Jihad for violating the ceasefire with the Jerusalem bombing. The tentative plan called for the arrest of the militants involved in the bombing, shutting Hamas mosques, and disabling its patronage network of schools and hospitals."[40] Foreign media reported that the White House had been informed that this crackdown operation on Hamas, in both the West Bank and Gaza, would begin on 21 August.[41] But Israel did not wait to find out the results of Abbas's initiative; on that day, it struck the final blow to the ceasefire.

As senior *Ha'aretz* analyst Ze'ev Schiff reported, it was known that the Jerusalem bombing was planned locally, and did not involve any coordination with the Hamas leadership. "The Hamas leadership in the Gaza Strip," noted Schiff, "had no advance knowledge of the Jerusalem bus bombing. Hamas leaders in Gaza, like members of Islamic Jihad, were sure that it was an operation carried out by Islamic Jihad."[42] Nevertheless, on 21 August, Israel chose to retaliate against the Hamas leadership in Gaza in a strike aimed not at Hamas's military wing but at one of its most moderate political leaders. Here is how the *Guardian* described it: "Five Israeli missiles incinerated Ismail Abu Shanab in Gaza City yesterday, killing one of the most powerful voices for peace in Hamas and destroying the ceasefire that Palestinian leaders believed would avert civil war . . . Ariel Sharon could not have been in any doubt that killing Abu Shanab would wreck the ceasefire. He was widely seen as more pragmatic than his fellow leaders. He broke a taboo within Hamas by recognising that there would have to be a Palestinian state alongside Israel, not in place of it."[43]

Abu Shanab's death prompted tens of thousands of Palestinians to take to the streets of the Gaza Strip. Hamas activists launched mortars at Israeli settlements within the Strip, while

Hamas's leadership and other organizations announced that the ceasefire was over. At that point, the Israeli army was already in the process of launching raids on Palestinian cities in the West Bank, and was amassing forces around the Gaza Strip in readiness for a large-scale operation. The Road Map initiative, which had ignited so much hope for so many Israelis and Palestinians, was over.

Just as in the previous rounds of apparent US attempts to broker a ceasefire along the lines of the Tenet plan, the US administration had extended Israel its unequivocal support. When, after the Aqaba summit in early June, Colin Powell apparently attempted a hesitant denunciation of Israel's continuation of its liquidation operations as the Palestinians were working to enforce a ceasefire, he was soon called to order. Some weeks later, following the killing of Abdullah Qawasmeh, head of military operations for Hamas in the Hebron region on 22 June, Powell was again reportedly ''critical of the operation and said . . . that he 'was sorry for the killing of Abdullah Qawasmeh', which he considers to have been unnecessary and 'a possible impediment to progress [for peace].' '' Yet the Bush administration quickly moved to reassure Israel that Powell had not in fact condemned the killing: ''U.S. ambassador to Israel Dan Kurtzer called the Prime Minister's Office and said that Powell had expressed sorrow over the fact that the situation in the Middle East leads to such measures being taken.''[44]

Subsequently, there were to be no further such slips of the tongue during the Palestinian ceasefire. The US administration moved solidly behind Israel's liquidations policy, referring to it repeatedly as ''Israel's right to defend itself''. Even when it was clear that the ceasefire was on the brink of collapse, ''the [US] administration avoided asking Israel to restrain itself and rein in its forces following the Jerusalem attack, instead placing all the responsibility for the crisis on the Palestinian side. The Israel Defense Forces'' operations in Nablus and Hebron in the West Bank [prior to the Jerusalem attack], in which Hamas and Islamic

Jihad militants have been killed, have been met with American understanding. The U.S. sees these operations as justified in order to stop 'ticking bombs' . . .'[45] It is hard to avoid the conclusion that the US was no more interested in the actual implementation of the first phase of the Road Map than was Israel.

As anticipated by the "Israeli sources" above, Mahmoud Abbas's government collapsed following the failure of the ceasefire. On 7 October 2003, he was replaced by Ahmed Qureia (also known as Abu Ala), who on the day of his inauguration offered to renew the ceasefire. Like his predecessor, however, Qureia was given no chance to restore calm: "Foreign Minister Silvan Shalom . . . rejected Ahmed Qureia's ceasefire offer, and labeled it a deceitful trick. An Israeli government source said . . . that Qureia's new government, which was sworn in earlier in the day, is 'a long tentacle of Arafat.' "[46] Israel hastened to clarify that it "will not establish official ties with the Qureia government, before it proves in deeds its intention to fight terror and to dismantle the terror infrastructure."[47]

On the day of Abu Shanab's assassination, Israeli security sources had announced that all Hamas leaders were now considered fair targets. The next day, Israel's *Ma'ariv* newspaper published a deck of thirty-four cards, each depicting a top Palestinian leader, in imitation of the cards issued by the US military to soldiers in Iraq showing the faces of wanted Iraqis from Saddam Hussein's deposed government. In *Ma'ariv*'s pack, the ace of hearts was Sheikh Ahmed Yassin, the founder and spiritual leader of Hamas. The joker was Yasser Arafat. In the following months, the Israeli army started its manhunt. It focused specifically on Hamas, targeting its military and political leadership as well as its middle-ranking and grassroots activists. As *Ha'aretz* reported, in the first half of September, fourteen Hamas middle-ranking activists were assassinated, while unsuccessful attempts on the life of higher-ranking leaders, including the paraplegic Sheikh Ahmed Yassin, had also been made.[48] Hamas issued a plea to the Arab world and Europe to condemn Israel's assassinations, but at the same time, the European Union decided to place Hamas's political leadership on its list of terrorist organizations: Israel could continue its assassinations undisturbed.[49]

Some months later, on 22 March 2004, the Israeli army decided that Sheikh Ahmed Yassin's time had come.[50] At 5.20 a.m., Israeli helicopter gunships fired rockets at the car of the wheelchair-bound Yassin as he was leaving a mosque in Gaza city after morning prayer. What was inconceivable even a year earlier had become reality.[51]

According to international law, the execution of any person in an occupied territory is illegal. The fourth Geneva Convention, born out of the horrifying experience of the Second World War, imposes limitations on the use of force even in times of war. The Convention distinguishes between war and a state of occupation. Its fundamental principles are, first, that occupied people should be "protected". and that the occupier is responsible for their safety. Second, it determines that occupied peoples have the right to fight for their liberation.

International conventions are one of the means people have developed for self-preservation. Without them, there is a danger that the human race would annihilate itself – first the strong would wipe out the weak, and then each other. During its thirty-seven years of occupation, Israel has already violated every article of the Geneva Convention. But the brutal killing of Sheikh Yassin was an act of unprecedented magnitude. As Robert Fisk stated in the British *Independent*, "no one has begun to work out the implications of all this. For years, there has been an unwritten rule in the cruel war of government-versus-guerrilla. You can kill the men on the street, the bomb makers and gunmen. But the leadership on both sides – government ministers, spiritual leaders – were allowed to survive."[52] Even when the leaders advocate the use of violence and terror, the norm has been that they might be imprisoned, but not killed.

Again, the US refrained from condemning the assassination. As Suzanne Goldenberg wrote in the *Guardian*, "with the November election approaching [Bush is] mindful of keeping the support of evangelical Christians, who have lined up on the Israeli side of the debate and criticised the White House for not doing enough to support the Israeli prime minister, Ariel Sharon. The result has left America out of step with the rest of the world. Washington alone has failed to condemn the assassination of Sheikh Ahmed Yassin. President Bush . . . insisted that Israel had the right to defend itself. There was no move to cancel meetings with the Israeli foreign minister, Silvan Shalom, who was in Washington, or to postpone a visit to the White House by Mr Sharon scheduled for April 14. Instead, the Bush administration has clung to the view that Mr Sharon is a valued ally in the war on terror."[53]

As I wrote at the time, "since September 11, as part of its 'war against terror', the U.S. has been pushing to destroy all defenses provided by International Law. But even the U.S. has not yet dared to publicly execute a spiritual-religious leader (for example, the Taliban in Afghanistan). Now Israel has determined, with U.S. blessing, that even this is permitted. Under the rule of the military, Israel has become a leading force in the destruction of the very protections that humankind has established for its own preservation."[54]

2

Winter 2004: The Disengagement Plan

On 2 FEBRUARY 2004, Sharon shook Israel and many throughout the world with the announcement of his "disengagement" plan. In an interview with *Ha'aretz*, Sharon stated that "this vacuum for which the Palestinians are to blame, cannot go on forever. So, as part of the disengagement plan, I have ordered an evacuation . . . of 17 settlements with their 7,500 residents, from the Gaza Strip to Israeli territory . . . The aim is to move settlements from places where they cause us problems or places where we won't remain in a permanent arrangement. Not only settlements in Gaza, but also three problematic settlements in Samaria [in the north of the West Bank]."[1]

The evacuation of these settlements took place eighteen months later, over a three-week period in the late summer of 2005.

The evacuation of the three isolated settlements in the north of the West Bank was hardly a significant move. They were problematic in any case, as Sharon had pointed out. Their residents had begged for years to be given compensation so that they could leave, and in two of them (Ganim and Kadim), about half the occupants had already left, long before the announcement of the disengagement plan. But the evacuation of the Gaza settlements was a different matter – a dramatic move, unprecedented in the history of the Israeli occupation of Palestine. It established Sharon's status as a hero of peace in Israel and the West. In the dominant Western discourse, the disengagement's announcement was clear evidence that Sharon, for so long the mastermind of the Israeli occupation, had had a fundamental change of heart. According to this interpretation of events, although the plan would take some while to implement, it was proof of the sincerity of the words Sharon had uttered almost a year previously: "I think the idea that it is possible to continue keeping 3.5 million Palestinians under occupation . . . is bad for Israel, and bad for the Palestinians."[2] In this view, the evacuation of Gaza was just the first step in Sharon's metamorphosis into a "man of peace," who had also resolved to end the occupation in the West Bank. Despite the persistence of this viewpoint, in reality there was, as we shall see in the coming chapters, no evidence whatsoever that it had any basis in fact.

A prevailing alternative view contended that Sharon had decided to relinquish Gaza in order to focus his efforts on the main goal of keeping the West Bank under Israeli control, and expanding its settlements. From this perspective, the continued occupation of the heavily populated Gaza Strip was becoming too costly, absorbing military and other resources. The situation in Gaza was, then, analogous to the Israeli occupation of Southern Lebanon, which was such a drain on resources that it led eventually to a decision to withdraw.

There is no doubt that Sharon openly used the Gaza disengagement plan to expand and strengthen Israel's grip of the West Bank. But there is no evidence that he decided to give Gaza up because the occupation proved too costly. The occupation of Gaza has, of course, always been maintained at a high price – and even in the eyes of the most committed Israeli expansionists, it is clear that Israel does not benefit from this piece of land, one of the most densely populated areas in the world, and (unlike the West Bank) lacking any natural resources.

Nevertheless, the problem with letting Gaza go is that one cannot let Gaza be free, if one wants to keep the West Bank. A third of the occupied Palestinian population inhabits the Gaza strip. If Gaza were to be given independence its population would become the focus for the Palestinian liberation struggle, with free and unfettered access to the Western and Arab world. It would undoubtedly use these contacts with the world politically, to keep the Palestinian cause alive in world consciousness, and possibly also militarily, to build Palestinian armed resistance to the Israeli occupation of the West Bank. In order to control the West Bank, therefore, Israel had to commit to its occupation of Gaza. In this, the Gaza settlements were of crucial importance, providing both a support system for the Israeli army, and the moral justification for the soldiers' brutal job of occupation; portraying their presence in Gaza as a mission to protect the homeland. In Southern Lebanon, by contrast, where there were no settlements, soldiers felt alienated and frustrated, which contributed to its occupation becoming impossible.

I shall return to the history of Gaza's occupation in the following chapter. But for now it is worth emphasizing that the settlements in the Gaza Strip, just like those in the West Bank, were used as a major justification for Israel's continued control of the occupied territories. Since Oslo, the settlements have been conceived both locally and internationally as a tragic problem that, despite Israel's desire to find a way to end the occupation, cannot be solved. Even if it was acknowledged that the previous generation of Israeli leaders made a mistake in settling in the territories, so this story went, the result was a human tragedy: tens of thousands of Israeli families, with children who grew up in the settlements and had never known another home. Uprooting them would not only be cruel; it would in practice be completely unworkable. According to this argument, the Israeli army therefore needs to stay in the territories and protect the settlers, despite Israel's stated wish to pull out. This rather convenient myth was broken with the evacuation of the Gaza settlements in August–September 2005, which showed in fact how easy it is to evacuate settlements, and what considerable support there is in Israeli society for doing so.

From the perspective of Israel's continued occupation of the territories, the evacuation of Gaza was a defeat; moreover, it was not something Sharon himself wanted, but that he was in fact forced to undertake. In Chapter 5, I argue that there is, moreover, good reason to believe that Sharon originally hoped to find a way to avoid implementing the disengagement plan, just as had been the case with his previous commitments. Be this as it may, the plan seemed to be a calculated risk, sacrificing the Israeli settlements in Gaza in order to tighten and expand Israel's grip in the West Bank. Let us turn now to how this decision came about.

Sharon disclosed that the disengagement plan was conceived in November 2003, three months before it was publicly announced, in a meeting in Rome between Sharon and Elliot Abrams, US deputy national security advisor, head of Middle East affairs at the National Security Council, and at the time a key advisor to Bush and Rice on Israel–Palestine.[3] The meeting had been convened against a backdrop of mounting international pressure and criticism over the way Israel handled the Road Map, its construction of the West Bank wall, and the expansion of settlements there. In interviews on the eve of Rosh Hashana (the Jewish New Year) in September 2004, some months after he announced the disengagement plan, Sharon explained why he had to propose some new plan.

> I didn't think it would be possible to continue the current situation the way it is. This would have brought heavy pressure on Israel to come up with solutions, and there were all kinds of suggestions for various solutions. I don't think the US, dealing with all its problems, would be able to stand there all the time and prevent the presentation of plans that could be dangerous to Israel.[4]

Around the same time, Dov Weisglass, Sharon's aide and chief negotiator with the White House reiterated this explanation:

[In] the fall of 2003 we understood that everything is stuck. And even though according to the Americans' reading of the situation, the blame fell on the Palestinians and not on us, Arik [Sharon] grasped that this state of affairs would not last. That they [the US] wouldn't leave us alone, wouldn't get off our case. Time was not on our side. There was international erosion.[5]

As we have seen, the US stood firmly behind Sharon as Israel obstructed any chance of implementing the Road Map.[6] But by November 2003, the US was coming under pressure from its allies in the EU for its stance on Israel–Palestine. The most notable signs of frustration came from UK Prime Minister Tony Blair, who had been a driving force behind the now defunct Road Map. Sidney Blumenthal, formerly a senior advisor to President Clinton, described British sentiments when President Bush visited London in November 2003:

Tony Blair, about to welcome George Bush to London with pomp and circumstance, has assumed the mantle of tutor to the unlearned president.

Bush originally came to Blair determined to go to war in Iraq, but without a strategy. Blair instructed him that the *casus belli* was Saddam Hussein's weapons of mass destruction, urged him to make the case before the UN, and . . . convinced him to revive the Middle East peace process, which the president had abandoned. The road map for peace was the principal concession Blair wrested from him.

The prime minister argued that renewing the negotiations was essential to the long-term credibility of the coalition goals in Iraq and the whole region. But within the Bush administration that initiative was systematically undermined . . . The key to the road map's success was US support for the Palestinian prime minister, Abu Mazen, indispensable as a partner for peace, but regarded as a threat by both Sharon and

Arafat . . . On September 6, Abu Mazen resigned, and the road map collapsed.

Blair provided Bush with a reason for the war in Iraq, and led him to express his plan for peace for the Middle East, preventing Bush from appearing a reckless and isolated leader. In return, the teacher's seminar on the Middle East has been dropped.[7]

At the time, the main bone of contention between the EU and the US was the West Bank wall that Israel had started constructing, and which it described as "a separation fence". The issue of the wall came to the fore in October 2003, with a series of discussions in the UN security council and general assembly. On 15 October, the US vetoed a UN security council resolution condemning the construction of the wall, but a similar resolution was passed in the general assembly six days later. The vote was carried 144 to 4, with 12 abstentions. As the *Guardian* noted at the time, "Unlike the 15–nation security council, the general assembly does not have the power to make its resolutions legally binding under the UN charter. However, it is an important indicator of international opinion. The resolution was backed by the EU, one of the sponsors of the current road map peace plan."[8] Preparations began for a resolution authorizing the UN to refer the issue to the International Court of Justice (ICJ) in The Hague, a move that "Israeli diplomats termed 'most dangerous' ".[9] The resolution was passed in December 2003, with hearings of the ICJ scheduled to begin on 23 February 2004.[10]

Although the US continued to back Israel in the UN, it issued statements objecting to certain aspects of Israeli policy. During his London visit, Bush criticized "continued expansion of Jewish settlements and construction of the fence, which he said prejudiced final negotiations for a Palestinian state . . . Washington has also been pressing Mr Sharon to fulfill the promises made to Mr Bush to dismantle Jewish outposts in the West Bank ".[11] Secretary of State Colin Powell had previously made even more assertive comments, referring to the fact that the fence is not being built on the Israeli 1967 border, but rather deep inside the Palestinian land: "As the president has made clear, the fence is a problem. If you want to put a fence on something that is a recognized border of a Green Line, then put a fence on your property line."[12] Later in November 2003, the US announced that it would penalize Israel for going ahead with the construction of the "security fence," and for its continued expansion of Jewish settlements, by cutting nearly $300 million in loan guarantees – a symbolic gesture, given that US loan guarantees to Israel totalled $1.4 billion. As Chris McGreal observed in the *Guardian*, "The size of the cut – $289 million – is equivalent to the amount Israel spent on construction of the fence and new infrastructure for settlements in the occupied territories this year."[13]

It was obvious that a revival of the peace process was required to allay international concerns. At the time, Sharon objected to the idea of resurrecting the Road Map. As he later explained in one of his September 2004 Rosh Hashana interviews, "This would have placed us in a very difficult situation. To this I did not agree. Even now we are not going to the Road Map. To this I do not agree."[14] Some other initiative was therefore needed.

According to Sharon, what Elliot Abrams proposed in their November 2003 meeting in Rome was a renewal of peace negotiations between Israel and Syria: "He wanted to talk with me then on the Syrian issue," Sharon said in his Rosh Hashana interview with *Ha'aretz*. "He spoke about what the Syrians were trying to do, that they would enter into negotiations with Israel." But Sharon rejected this proposal. "It was immediately taken off the agenda and they [the US] are not raising it any more," Sharon asserted.[15]

If Abrams did indeed propose reviving the Syrian track in that meeting, such a suggestion could not have been driven by any animus against Israel; according to Blumenthal, Abrams was one of Israel's staunchest supporters: "In the internal struggle over peace in the Middle East, the neo-conservatives within the administration prevailed. Elliot Abrams, chief of Middle East affairs at the NSC [National Security Council], was their main man. During the Iran–contra scandal, Abrams had helped set up a rogue foreign policy operation. His soliciting of $10m from the Sultan of Brunei for the illegal enterprise turned farcical when he juxtaposed numbers on a Swiss bank account and lost the money. He pleaded guilty to lying to Congress and then spent his purgatory as director of a neoconservative thinktank, denouncing the Oslo Accords and arguing that 'tomorrow's lobby for Israel has got to be conservative Christians, because there aren't going to be enough Jews to do it'. Abrams was rehabilitated when George Bush appointed him to the NSC. In his new position, Abrams set to work, trying to gut the text of the road map. He was suspicious of the Europeans and British, considering them to be anti-Israel, if not inherently anti-Semitic."[16] Now that Abrams had been sent to solicit some commitments from Sharon, he was probably looking for some "creative solution" that would enable international attention to be diverted from the failure of the Road Map.

Throughout the history of Israel's occupation of the Palestinian territories, the "peace process" would occasionally shift focus from the Palestinian to the Syrian channel, and vice versa. Former Israel prime ministers Yitzhak Rabin and Ehud Barak both carried lengthy and highly publicized negotiations with Syria, which led nowhere; they did however prove a useful delaying tactic, diverting international attention from the continued occupation of the Palestinians.[17] In fall 2003, Syrian President Bashar Assad sent numerous signals of his willingness to renew peace negotiations with Israel. About two weeks after the Sharon–Abrams meeting, Assad made a public overture to resume the negotiations in an interview with the *New York Times*, in which he called for renewed talks and spoke of the "normalization" of Syrian–Israeli relations.[18]

Sharon rejected this move outright. Israel's reaction to

Assad's *New York Times* statement came swiftly the following day, when Foreign Minister Sylvan Shalom issued a statement using precisely the same language that Israel used in response to Palestinian offers of a ceasefire: "Positive remarks about peace are always encouraging, but words are not enough. We want to see action. Syria must put an end to terror activities that begin on its territory, and curtail arms shipments from Iran to Hezbollah. Should Syria do this, and if it is prepared to engage in talks with Israel without preconditions, there's no doubt the government of Israel will seriously consider this option."[19]

Sharon could not have possibly accepted the Syrian route. Since becoming prime minister in February 2001, Sharon had focused his efforts on constructing an image of Syria as an enemy of the Western world. Following 9/11, it had been widely reported in the Israeli media that "since the September 11 attacks in the U.S., Israeli officials have stressed in talks with American counterparts that the Syrians have been deeply involved in sponsoring terror activity. The Israeli officials have been hoping that the American-led war against terror will widen in scope, to encompass groups whose terror activity has been targeted primarily against Israel."[20] In the process of constructing their case against Syria, Israeli security officials started producing what they labelled evidence that the Lebanese Hizbollah – and by extension Syria – was behind the terror attacks carried out in the West Bank by Palestinian Islamist organizations (although the nature of this evidence has never been shared with the public). In Sharon's frequent meetings with Bush, he constantly stressed his anticipation that "Syria will be one of the targets in America's campaign against terror".[21]

In April 2003, just two weeks before the formal announcement of the Road Map, Ed Vulliamy reported in the UK *Observer* that Sharon would not accept the plan until his final demand was fulfilled:

Washington has promised Israel that it will take 'all effective action' to cut off Syria's support for Hizbollah – implying a military strike if necessary, sources in the Bush administration have told the *Observer*. The new US undertaking to Israel to deal with Hizbollah via its Syrian sponsors has been made over recent days during meetings between administration officials and Israeli diplomats in Washington, and Americans talking to Israeli Prime Minister Ariel Sharon in Jerusalem. It would be part of a deal designed to entice Israel into the so-called road map to peace package . . . Prime Minister Ariel Sharon has so far rejected the road map initiative . . . The undertaking dovetails conveniently into 'phase three' of what President George Bush calls the 'war on terror' and his pledge to go after all countries accused of harbouring terrorists. It also fits into calls by hawks inside and aligned to the administration who believe that war in Iraq was first stage in a wider war for American control of the region. Threats against Syria come daily out of Washington.[22]

Seven months later, by the time of Sharon's November 2003 meeting with Elliot Abrams in Rome, there were clear signs that the White House was implementing commitments made to Sharon regarding Syria on the eve of the Road Map. On 3 October, the Bush administration had given Congress the go-ahead to approve legislation to bring sanctions against Syria, scheduling the first step in this procedure – a vote by the House International Relations Committee – for 8 October.[23] The legislation, named "The Syria Accountability and Lebanese Sovereignty Restoration Act," had already been drawn up before the Iraq war, but had at that time been blocked by the White House. Tracing the Act's history, Brian Whitaker observed that the legislation was originally "inspired by an alliance of Israelis, American neo-conservatives and wild-eyed Lebanese Christians, and originally put to Congress in 2002 by Senator Rick Santorum, a self-caricaturing anti-abortion, anti-gay, pro-guns Republican". At the time, however, Whitaker continues, "President Bush was less enthusiastic and his secretary of state, Colin Powell, declared the sanctions plan 'unhelpful' . . . Legislation of the kind proposed against Syria, he said, would 'have a negative effect on our efforts to bring down the violence, avoid the outbreak of regional war, and help the parties back to a path to comprehensive peace'.'' This, Whitaker notes, was not the only consideration. ''The Syrian regime, for its own reasons, had always kept a close watch on Islamic extremists and was quietly passing information about them to the Americans . . . In addition, American sanctions would be at odds with EU policy, which favoured cajoling Syria towards reform through 'critical and constructive engagement'. This was one area where the British prime minister, Tony Blair, did not diverge from his European colleagues . . . In the run-up to war with Iraq, the congressional plans for sanctions against Syria were quietly shelved.''[24] In October 2003, however, Bush put them back on the agenda.

On Sunday 5 October, two days after the White House gave the green light to the legislation against Syria, Israel launched an unprecedented airstrike deep in Syrian territory, fifteen miles from its capital, Damascus. The attack was aimed at what Israel defined as a training camp of Islamic Jihad – although according to witnesses quoted in the *Guardian*, it had been abandoned years before[25] – and was Israel's response to a suicide bombing in Haifa, carried out by the West Bank Islamic Jihad, which killed nineteen people. Israel's strike on Syria prompted a wave of anger in the Arab world, but Bush was fully supportive: ''For the second time in as many days, Bush said Israel was justified in bombing deep into Syria on Sunday, the first such attack since the 1973 Middle East war . . . 'The decisions he (Sharon) makes to defend [Israel's] people are valid decisions', Bush told reporters after a Cabinet meeting. 'We would be doing the same thing.' ''[26]

The Syria Accountability Act passed the House International Relations Committee as scheduled, and progressed smoothly, with a vote of 398 to 4 in the House of Representatives on 15

October. On 11 November, the week of the Sharon-Abrams meeting, it was finally approved by the US Senate.[27] For Sharon, therefore, Abrams's proposal regarding diplomacy with Syria was not an option; entering into even superficial negotiations with Syria at this time would have potentially undermined Sharon's long-term project of making Syria one of the principal targets in America's war against terror. Instead, as he subsequently disclosed, Sharon surprised Abrams during their meeting "when he brought up for the first time his proposal for a unilateral move consisting of withdrawing from the Gaza Strip and evacuating the settlements there".[28]

There were further reasons for Sharon to announce a big initiative at this particular time. Dov Weisglass explained that along with the "international erosion," there was also "internal erosion":[29]

> Domestically, in the meantime, everything was collapsing. The economy was stagnant, and the Geneva Initiative garnered broad support. And then we were hit with letters of officers and letters of pilots and letters of commandos [letters of refusal to serve in the territories]. These were not weird kids with green ponytails and a ring in their nose who give off a strong odor of grass. These were people like Spector's group [Yiftah Spector, a renowned air-force pilot who signed the pilots' letter]. Really our finest young people.

In the runup to the Israeli election on 28 January 2003, following which he was elected prime minister for a second term, Sharon had promised "painful concessions" for peace, including hints at the evacuation of settlements. According to opinion polls conducted during the campaign, about 70 per cent of Israelis believed that Sharon would start to dismantle settlements.[30] He had had to make election promises of this sort in order to garner widespread support: since Oslo, a stable majority of over 60 per cent of Israelis have approved the dismantling of settlements and withdrawal from most of the occupied territories.[31] The general recognition that Israel's ongoing occupation is costly and that it is ruining Israel not only Palestine spread in the second year of the Palestinian uprising. Before his demise Sharon, fully aware of the results of the polls, repeated the same tactics in his 2006 election campaign, dropping widespread hints of concessions. I have already noted the euphoric Israeli reaction to the Road Map summit, and the amount of enthusiasm the words 'end of occupation' managed to arouse in the media.[32] For many, Israel's apparent acceptance of the Road Map was interpreted as Sharon cashing in on his election-campaign commitment in early 2003. When this new mirage of hope faded, there was a substantial amount of frustration. A rally on Rabin Memorial Day in November 2003 turned into a huge protest against Sharon, drawing over 100,000 people chanting slogans such as "Leave the Territories – Save the Country, 'Sharon Go Home!' and "The Geneva Accord – New Hope".[33] Although past experience has shown that Israeli public opinion can always be appeased by vague promises, by the end of 2003 more concrete steps seemed to be required.

The disengagement plan, then, was unveiled to the public in February 2004.[34] Although the headlines presented it as a plan for an immediate unilateral Israeli withdrawal from the Gaza Strip, modelled on Israel's withdrawal from Southern Lebanon, Sharon had already emphasized that "the process will take one to two years". He warned that a long process of negotiation lay ahead – not with the Palestinians, who would be excluded from any discussions regarding the plan – but with the US, with whom "agreement is needed on both the evacuation and the matter of the fence".[35]

One might well wonder why such a long process of negotiations would be needed for an essentially internal Israeli process. (As we shall see, the actual preparations for the evacuation only started about four months before it took place.) Weisglass explained that the plan's chief attraction was that it enabled the freezing of the dangerous process that started with the Road Map, which if left to run its course might have led to withdrawal from the West Bank and evacuation of its settlements. For this, of course, the longer the disengagement process took, the better:

> The disengagement is actually formaldehyde. It supplies the amount of formaldehyde that's necessary so that there will not be a political process with the Palestinians . . . After all, what have I been shouting for the past year? That I found a device, in cooperation with the management of the world, to ensure that there will be no stopwatch here. That there will be no timetable to implement the [West Bank] settlers' nightmare. I have postponed that nightmare indefinitely . . . That is the significance of what we did. The significance is the freezing of the political process. And when you freeze that process you prevent the establishment of a Palestinian state and you prevent a discussion about the refugees, the borders and Jerusalem. Effectively, this whole package that is called the Palestinian state, with all that it entails, has been removed from our agenda indefinitely. And all this with authority and permission. All with a presidential blessing and the ratification of both houses of Congress.[36]

More specifically, the crucial factor informing the disengagement plan was to gain the necessary time to advance Sharon's project of the West Bank wall, which would also enable the expansion of the central settlement blocks. Recall that the plan was hatched at the peak of international criticism of the wall's construction, with the hearings at The Hague International Court of Justice scheduled to begin on 23 February 2004, just a couple of weeks after the plan's announcement. There was considerable concern in Israel that the forthcoming ruling of the International Court of Justice would build pressure on Israel to stop the construction of the wall – and that the US might yield to this pressure.

Three days after the disengagement plan was made public, full details were given of Sharon's demands of the US in return for his concessions on Gaza. They included "shifting the separation fence to the east, with U.S. approval, to a temporary security line that will surround more settlements than the present path of the fence". Sharon also sought US permission "to expand the big settlement blocks in the West Bank, which are to be annexed to Israel in the permanent agreement".[37] At this time, the route of the wall was the focus of intense Israeli–US negotiations. As Nachum Barnea, one of the most well-briefed Israeli journalists, reported: "Israel does not ask for money to finance the evacuation, although it will be glad to get it. It mainly seeks support of the fence route."[38]

One of the earliest crises to hit Sharon's disengagement plan came when Finance Minister (and ex-Prime Minister) Benjamin Netanyahu expressed scepticism over whether Sharon would get US consent for rapid advancement on the West Bank wall. This crisis was settled following Sharon's visit to Washington, in April 2004, when "Netanyahu announced that he intends to support the disengagement after the three conditions he posed were met . . . [including] completion of the fence before the evacuation".[39] Subsequent discussions of the evacuation's timing revolved around the completion of the barrier: "The prime minister took a commitment that the separation fence will be completed before evacuation starts . . . Security spokesmen estimate that the fence can be completed at the earliest towards the end of 2005. In other words: It is possible that Israel will not be able to complete the evacuation at the date that was promised to the U.S."[40]

When Bush and Sharon met at the White House in April 2004, Sharon received Bush's public approval for his plan. In appreciation of Sharon's declared intention to pull out of Gaza, Bush declared that "in light of new realities on the ground, including already existing major Israeli populations centers, it is unrealistic to expect that the outcome of final status negotiations will be a full and complete return to the armistice lines of 1949 [the 1967 border]."[41] This was widely interpreted as an acknowledgement of Israel's right to eventually annex the big settlement blocks in the West Bank. Israel also received tacit backing for the wall's construction, which, as we shall see in Chapter 7, essentially delimits the areas it wants to annex in the future. However, the real development in the Bush–Sharon agreement was not to be found at the level of declarations. Also in previous plans, such as Clinton's and Beilin-Abu Mazen's, it was evident that Israel was not offering a return to the precise line of the 1967 borders, nor an acceptance of the Palestinian right of return.[42] However, these were bases for negotiation, in which the Palestinians would in theory have at least some input. In the new disengagement era, it had become clear that the Palestinians were not even to be included in negotiations: Israel and the US alone would determine the facts on the ground. Israel would demarcate the land it wanted, and would build a wall to surround it.

As far as Sharon's West Bank ambitions were concerned, therefore, the disengagement plan had proved a great success. For eighteen months, as the world held its breath in anticipation of the Gaza evacuation, Sharon pursued the wall project almost undisturbed, continued construction in the settlements, devastated the Palestinian neighbourhoods around Jerusalem, and expanded the road system which would form the basis for Israel's control of Palestinian land.[43]

However, Sharon has now lost the Gaza settlements. As previously mentioned, I believe that when he declared his disengagement plan, Sharon gambled, not knowing exactly how it would end. Almost to the end of the Gaza process – certainly until April 2005 – he hoped that at the end of this pressure-free eighteen-month period, he would find a way of reneging on his commitment, and that the US would continue to turn a blind eye, as it had done up to that point. I return to this issue in Chapter 5, where I argue that in early 2005, the pendulum began to swing the other way. The United States was stuck in the Iraq quagmire, incurring defeats and casualties, and becoming more heavily dependent on international opinion. Freed from the pressure of the Jewish vote after the presidential elections in November 2004, the second Bush administration trapped Sharon in his words and forced him, behind the scenes, to carry out the evacuation of the Gaza settlements.

In any event, when Sharon gambled on the disengagement plan he must have taken into account the possibility that he would have to implement it. We should note that at no stage did Sharon make a commitment to give up the full Israeli control of the Gaza Strip. Immediately after Sharon received Bush's public approval for the plan on 16 April 2004, the full text of the disengagement plan was published in the Israeli press.[44] It specified that, with the evacuation of the Israeli settlements, the occupation of the Gaza Strip would be declared to be over. But in every other aspect, the situation there would remain as is. The Palestinians in Gaza would be effectively imprisoned from all sides, with no connection to the outside world except through Israel: "Israel will supervise and guard the external envelope on land, will maintain exclusive control in the air space of Gaza, and will continue to conduct military activities in the sea space of the Gaza Strip".[45] Regarding the crossing point with Egypt, Gaza's only international border, then under Israeli control, "the existing arrangements will remain in force".[46] Israel also "reserves the right" to occasional military presence inside the Strip: "Israel reserves for itself the basic right of self-defense, including taking preventative steps as well as responding by using force against threats that will emerge from the Gaza Strip."[47]

According to the disengagement plan, then, the status quo of the Gaza Strip would be largely unaltered; it would continue to remain effectively a big prison. At the same time, however, the plan opened up new prospects for the future maintenance of the prison – for example, shifting responsibility for feeding the prisoners. Under the fourth Geneva Convention, the occupier is responsible for the welfare of the occupied people. Israel's policy since the Oslo Agreements has been to attempt to pass this responsibility to the international community, under the pretext that the Palestinians are on their way to independent statehood. But, as Sharon revealed in the interviews describing the international atmosphere that pushed him to towards the disengagement plan, Israel was beginning to face difficulties in this area as well: "There was also a problem with organizations that help the Palestinians. There are today 1.8 million Palestinians supported solely by aid from various international organizations. These organizations told us clearly that if we continue to hold on to the territories and run everything, they can't give that aid."[48]

But the published disengagement plan neatly resolved this issue, stating that "the disengagement move will obviate the claims about Israel with regard to its responsibility for the Palestinians in the Gaza Strip".[49] In other words, since the Strip will no longer be defined as an occupied territory, Israel will not be subject to the fourth Geneva Convention, and will therefore not be responsible for the occupied people. National Security Advisor Giora Eiland, who supervised the full composition of the disengagement plan, discussed this openly in a meeting of the security establishment with Sharon. As Israel withdraws from the Gaza Strip, he explained, "it would no longer be responsible for what happened there. 'Let the world worry about them', he said. 'I will no longer be the occupier in Gaza, so it will be as much the Egyptians' and Europeans' business as mine." [50]At the time of writing, six months after the evacuation of the Gaza settlements, the situation in the Gaza Strip remains precisely as outlined in the disengagement document. Let us turn now to some history of the Israeli occupation of the Gaza Strip, and the present realities of Gaza.

3

Israel's Plans for Gaza

TO GET A GRASP OF why the occupiers needed the Gaza Strip, let us go back to the previous time in history that Israel had a seemingly visionary peace leader, Yitzhak Rabin, who was widely believed to be determined to end the occupation and who, like Sharon, declared "let us start with Gaza first".

Before the September 1993 Oslo Accords, the Gaza Strip had become the subject of substantial consensus in Israeli society. With (then) one million people living in one of the most densely populated and poorest areas of the world, with little water or natural resources, many Israelis started wondering what the rationale was behind maintaining the Israeli occupation of Gaza. A plan based on the idea that ending the Israeli occupation should start with Gaza, initially known as "Gaza first," was gaining substantial support in both Israeli and Palestinian society at the beginning of the 1990s.[1]

Nevertheless, during the Oslo negotiations, Rabin insisted that Israel would not dismantle any settlements in Gaza during the "interim period" that would be in place for five years, until a permanent peace agreement with the Palestinians could be achieved. In previous discussions about the "Gaza first" plan, the local Palestinian delegation headed by Dr Haidar Abd-el Shafi[2] insisted that it would not accept any agreement that did not include an immediate dismantling of the Israeli settlements in the Gaza Strip. However what finally enabled the Oslo Agreement to be signed was that in another round of negotiations, conducted behind the back of the local Palestinian delegation, Arafat and his team ceded this point accepting Israeli's condition that the settlements should remain in place.

Méditerranée

Point de passage d'Erez

Bayt Lahyia

Nissanit

Camp de Shâti'

Bayt Hanoun

Gaza-ville

Camp de Jabâliya

Netzarim

Point de passage de Karni

Camp de Nusayrât

Camp de Burayj

Camp de Deir al-Balah

Camp de Meghazi

Deir al-Balah

Kfar Darom

Kfar Yam

Katif

ISRAËL

Camp de Khân Younis

Khân Younis

Névé Dekalim

Morag

Camp de Rafah

Rafah

Point de passage de Sûfa

Point de passage de Rafah

Frontière de 1967 (Ligne verte)

ÉGYPTE

GAZA

ISRAËL

▲ Colonie juive
✳ Point de passage
☙ Camp de réfugiés
♧ Zone construite
● Ville ou village

0 km   6

Israel's Plans for Gaza   49

The Palestinian negotiators agreed to this condition when they signed the Oslo Accords at the White House. Worse was to follow. In negotiations held in Taba, just a month after the Oslo Accords ceremony had been held at the White House, Israel unveiled its actual maps for the division of Gaza, which left much more than the settlements under full Israeli control. Israel insisted that the settlements be grouped in three blocs, which would also include the lands between the individual settlements; these, combined with a network of bypass roads, amounted to nearly one third of the land in the Gaza Strip. The Palestinian negotiators responded with apparent shock and anger and left the negotiations in protest.[3] But only two weeks later, in talks in Cairo on 18 November 1993, the Palestinian negotiators fully accepted all the Israeli demands. This is how the situation in Gaza was determined and maintained for the next twelve years.

Why did Rabin insist on maintaining the Gaza settlements, which also entailed full Israeli control over the Gaza Strip? It was not driven by popular pressure. The evacuation of Gaza had comprehensive support among the Israeli public at the time (comparable to the support for the evacuation twelve years later). Most Israelis believed that the Oslo Accords would lead eventually to the dismantling of settlements in both Gaza and the West Bank, and the price of housing in central Israel rose in expectation of a new wave of evacuated settlers. Nevertheless, two thirds of Israelis supported the Accords in all polls. Many of the inhabitants of the more isolated Gaza settlements wanted to leave at the time, and demanded compensation for alternative housing. In April 2004, the settlers of Dugit (in the north of the Gaza Strip) camped for a whole month in front of the government offices in Jerusalem, demanding to be evacuated with compensation.[4] But Rabin refused, and the settlers were forced to return to their homes in Gaza. Other settlers would undoubtedly have opposed evacuation, just as they did twelve years later, but in 1993 it would certainly have been possible, given the favourable climate of public opinion, first to let those who wanted to leave do so, and then evacuate the remaining settlers.

Neither can Rabin's insistence on maintaining the Gaza settlements be explained by the simple land greed and expansionism that has underlain much of Israeli policy in the West Bank.[5] In the Oslo period, Rabin was striving to realize the Labor party Alon plan, which unlike the plans of Sharon and the hawks in the 1980s did include some compromise over land. (Under this initiative, Israel would eventually annex about 40 per cent of the occupied territories, and the rest would return to Jordanian rule or, in a later development of the plan, would be under some form of Palestinian self-rule.) When the plan was first formulated by Yigal Alon in 1967, the Gaza Strip was included in the areas for eventual annexation, because of its strategic location on Egypt's border; the plan envisaged that all Palestinian refugees living in Gaza should be "relocated".[6] But as the initiative developed, and particularly following the peace accords with Egypt in 1979, proponents of the Alon plan seemed increasingly willing to give up their claim on Gaza; Rabin himself had already declared his willingness to do so in 1983.[7]

But the Alon plan was not openly on the table during the Oslo period. The Palestinians have always rejected it, depriving them as it does of 40 per cent of what remains of their land – no Palestinian leadership would have accepted that plan at the time of Oslo. At that point, the Palestinians had been led to believe that Israel under Rabin had undergone a real change of policy, and was genuinely considering the eventual evacuation of all the West Bank after the aforementioned five-year "interim period", during which negotiations over a final agreement should take place, as specified in the Oslo Accords. But the Accords were based on deception; as it turned out, the occupation was far from over in the eyes of the Israeli army and even the Labor Israeli leadership.[8] Given that Israel was not ready to concede the West Bank and dismantle its settlements, there was no choice but to keep the Gaza Strip under full Israeli control.[9] Keeping the Gaza settlements intact would guarantee this control.

This was how the status quo in Gaza was determined for the next twelve years. The settlements occupied 54 square kilometres of the Strip's total area of 365 square kilometres, while their no-go areas – roads for Jews only flanked by wide security strips, together with other "security zones" and army checkpoints – narrowed further the land remaining for the Palestinians. All in all, about a third of Gaza was reserved for the sole use of half of 1 per cent of its population. (In 2004, there were 1.4 million Palestinians and 8,000 Israeli settlers in Gaza, a similar proportion to 1993.) This situation did not appear tenable in the long term, and Israeli policymakers have long had to face the question of how to guarantee that the anger and frustration generated by such conditions would not boil over and disrupt the daily life of the occupiers.

The Israeli solution – its model for control of the Gaza Strip – had already been established during the "Oslo years" (1993–2000). The concept of a wall sealing in the Palestinian enclaves was not in fact Sharon's invention, but had already been fully road-tested in Gaza. In 1994, during Yitzhak Rabin's administration, a fence was constructed, enclosing the Strip along its border with Israel. The 52-kilometre (30-mile) barrier consists mainly of a wire fence with posts, sensors and buffer zones, augmented by an open observation area 300 metres wide on the Gaza side. Moving from Gaza to Israel is possible only through a few heavily monitored crossing points in the barrier. On the Strip's southern border with Egypt, a steel wall was erected, punctuated by several large armoured posts along its length. Inside the Gaza Strip, an Israeli-patrolled security strip known as the "Philadelphi Road," ran along the wall, preventing any direct Palestinian movement to or contact with Egypt. The Mediterranean seashore – the only remaining potential exit – was (and still is) heavily guarded by the Israeli navy.

This sealing of the Gaza Strip was carried out undisturbed; on the contrary, the construction of the fence was even hailed by many, because it was packaged as marking the borders of a future Palestinian state. But the fact of the matter is that during the Oslo years, over a million people became prisoners in their own land, with movement in or out permitted only through Israeli security gates – and mostly not permitted at all. Surrounded by electric fences and military posts, tightly sealed from the outside world, Palestinian Gaza was converted into a prison ghetto. The living standards in the Strip, already among the lowest in the world, deteriorated sharply after Oslo. Until that time, it had been possible for Palestinian Gaza residents to obtain exit permits. After the Oslo Accords, they were not even allowed to visit their relatives in the West Bank, while only a lucky few carried exit permits for work in Israel.

In Gaza, Rabin thus paved the way for what would later become Sharon's model for the occupation of the West Bank: turning the Palestinian enclaves into huge prisons. The Palestinians in the sealed Gaza Strip were divided further into internal enclaves, fully controlled from outside by the Israeli army, which would enter the enclaves at will. If the prisoners tried to rebel, as happened during the second Palestinian *intifada*, the internal roads were blocked and the area divided into smaller prison units, each surrounded by Israeli tanks. The Palestinian prisoners could be bombarded from the air, with nowhere to escape to, while their food supply, electricity and fuel were – and remain – all controlled by Israel and cut off at the will of the prison guards. Israel gave the Palestinians in Gaza one choice: accept prison life, or perish.

Despite all this, during the Oslo years the sealed Gaza Strip still enjoyed some degree of autonomy in the running of its internal affairs. But from September 2000, the beginning of the current wave of Israeli oppression, the prison conditions worsened substantially. From mid-2001 onwards, the Israeli army was beginning to undo the Oslo Arrangements and re-establish direct Israeli military rule. Alex Fishman, senior security analyst for *Yediot Aharonot*, explained in March 2001 that in the Oslo years, "the IDF [Israel Defence Force] regarded the occupied territories as if they were one territorial cell," and that "this placed some constraints on the IDF and enabled a certain amount of freedom for the PA and the Palestinian population".[10] Israel's new plan was a return to the concept of the military administration during the pre-Oslo years. The occupied territories would be divided into dozens of isolated "territorial cells," each of which would be assigned a special military force. Fishman added that the Israeli army had already completed the division of Gaza into territorial cells, although "so far there has only been isolation, and not yet treatment inside the cells".[11] In the months to come, the Israeli army took direct control over policing the occupants of the "territorial cells," entering at will any neighbourhood targeted for "operation". Everything seemed to indicate that the army was gearing up for a long period of direct military rule in Gaza.

In the period between the start of the second *intifada* and the disengagement in September 2005, one of the Israeli army's chief projects in Gaza was the expansion of the physical distance between the Palestinian residents and the Israeli occupiers, thus further narrowing the prison cells. This was achieved through the steady eradication of houses, agricultural land and orchards along the margins of the Israeli settlement blocs and the roads that Israel defines as their "security strips". The Palestinian Centre for Human Rights in Gaza reported that between the end of September 2000 and the end of April 2004, a total of 1,710 houses in the Strip were completely demolished, while 1,474 others were partially demolished.[12] According to an Amnesty International report of May 2004, some 18,000 Palestinians, mostly refugees, have been made homeless by the destruction carried out in the Gaza Strip by the Israeli army.[13] The area where most homes have been destroyed is the Rafah refugee camp. In this area, more than 1,000 homes have been demolished, and hundreds of others partially destroyed or very seriously damaged since 2000. As Amnesty reported, "the Rafah refugee camp, in existence since 1948, is very densely populated, with rows of houses separated by narrow alleyways. In late 2000 the Israeli army began the massive destruction of houses in the camp. Until then, houses had stood only a few meters from the border with Egypt: now houses are reduced to rubble for up to 300 meters from the border. The destruction has targeted row after row of houses, contrary to claims by the Israeli authorities that they only destroy houses used by Palestinians to attack Israeli soldiers patrolling the border, and houses used as cover for tunnels."[14]

Controlling over a million people struggling for their liberation in prison conditions may seem unrealistic. The Israeli concept of how this might be done was based not only on policing, but on systematic destruction of the society, its infrastructure and its prospects for development. As Harvard scholar Sara Roy writes: "there is no doubt that the destruction wrought by Israel over the last five years – the demolition of homes . . . schools, roads, factories, workshops, hospitals, mosques and greenhouses, the razing of agricultural fields, the uprooting of trees, the confinement of the population and the denial of access to education and health services as a consequence of Israeli roadblocks and checkpoints – has been ruinous for Palestinians, especially those in the Gaza Strip."[15] Israel has been forcing the Gaza Strip into poverty and despair, in an attempt to break the Palestinians' spirit and force them into accepting prison life.

A chief method of control has been economic strangulation. Israel's economic siege of the territories, which I have discussed at length in my *Israel/Palestine*,[16] only increased in the period since 2002. Two thirds of households in Gaza live below the poverty line, many relying on UNRWA and other relief agencies for their livelihood. Economic strangulation is also used as a collective punishment. Following Palestinian attacks on soldiers, the crossing points connecting Gaza to Israel are closed – crossings on which the feeble local economy crucially depends for the transfer of goods. As Amira Hass explains, "the closing of the border crossings causes a chain reaction of economic damage within just days. Since the middle of March [2004], when Karni [crossing] was operating only on a partial basis, there was an immediate drop in both the private and public construction sectors until they were completely paralyzed due to a lack of gravel, cement and iron. Food and drink factories went on strike, meaning thousands of workers were left without income. The impact was immediately felt by a drop in consumer traffic in stores and the cancellation of bank credit lines."[17] By these means, the Israeli army effectively holds the Palestinian population hostage in its fight against Palestinian militants.

At the beginning of June 2004, Deputy Prime Minister Ehud Olmert announced that the industrial zone at the Erez crossing was to be shut down as part of the disengagement plan, and that Israeli investors would be compensated. This was the only aspect of the disengagement that Israel did not procrastinate in implementing: two months later, the zone had essentially been closed. According to *Ha'aretz*, ''the Erez industrial zone, established 30 years ago, was always seen as a model of coexistence. Israeli and Palestinian business owners employed Palestinian workers, sometimes jointly. Today it appears that Erez's only raison d'etre was the minimal labor costs there: since their companies were not located within Israel, industrialists there employed laborers at virtually no cost and were not required to pay national insurance, transportation, vacation or overtime . . . Despite the exploitation and low pay, the real losers will be the Gazans: the 4,500 workers at Erez were the economic base for an estimated 50,000 people in the Strip. The unemployment rate there, according to UNRWA [United Nations Relief and Works Agency], is about 75 percent, so the Erez workers' chances of finding other jobs near home are nonexistent.''[18] This was the real face of the Israeli disengagement: it planned to maintain full military control of Gaza from the outside and prevent its contacts with the outside world. At the same time, it substantially cut its means of livelihood.

As the strangled Gaza Strip came to depend increasingly on UNRWA's aid, Israel moved to obstruct UNRWA's effective operation. On 1 April 2004, UNRWA issued a desperate press release: "The United Nations Relief and Works Agency for Palestine Refugees today stopped distributing emergency food aid to some 600,000 refugees in the Gaza Strip, or approximately half of the refugees receiving UNRWA food aid in the occupied Palestinian territory, following restrictions introduced by Israeli authorities at the sole commercial crossing through which the Agency is able to bring in humanitarian assistance. Stocks of rice, flour, cooking oil and other essential foodstuffs that UNRWA provides to refugees reduced to poverty, or otherwise affected by a humanitarian crisis now in its 42nd month, have been fully depleted." The press release went on to specify that "UNRWA is not alone in facing chronic obstacles to the flow of humanitarian assistance. These have been experienced by all UN agencies operating in the West Bank and Gaza, whose Agency heads in a joint statement on 26 March called, without success, on the Government of Israel to loosen the restrictions currently in force in Gaza." UNRWA Commissioner General Peter Hansen emphasized that "The suspension of UNRWA's emergency food aid in the Gaza Strip will further distress communities already struggling to cope with unrelieved economic hardship and malnutrition. If the new restrictions in Gaza continue, I fear we could see real hunger emerge for the first time in two generations."[19]

Peter Hansen's insistence on UNRWA's fulfilment of its mission eventually cost him his position. In January 2005, at the end of his third term as UNRWA Commissioner General, UN Secretary-General Kofi Annan decided not to reappoint him, in the face of Israeli and US pressure. "Political sources in Jerusalem . . . confirmed the reports . . . and said Hansen's dismissal was the direct result of diplomatic activity. The campaign to oust Hansen was directed by Foreign Minister Silvan Shalom."[20] According to Reuters, "the Bush administration made clear it would be hard to keep up the $120 million annual U.S. contribution to the agency if Hansen were reappointed due to unhappiness over him in Congress, the officials said. "It was clear that he wasn't renewed because of U.S. and Israeli calls for his head," said one official familiar with the deliberations, speaking on condition of anonymity. The United States was the only member of the advisory board opposing Hansen's reappointment, the official said, adding that European Union and Arab nations backed him for a new term.[21]

The intensity of the military operations inside Gaza increased substantially following Sharon's announcement of the disengagement plan in February 2004. In February and March there were several Israeli raids on Palestinian communities in the Strip (reported on 12 February, 8 March and 17–21 March). Israel then carried out two full-scale military offensives. "Operation Rainbow," in May 2004, concentrated on the vicinity of Rafah, and left dozens of houses demolished. "Operation Days of Penitence" in October 2004 was similar – in both scale and horrors – to April 2002's "Operation Defensive Shield" in the Jenin refugee camp in the West Bank. The Israeli army estimated the number of Palestinians killed at 130; about 500 others were wounded.[22] According to UNRWA, 91 houses were fully destroyed, and 101 others damaged.[23] Remarkably, this massive spree of destruction received hardly any attention in the Western media. Events in the Gaza prison had often passed largely unnoticed, but following Sharon's declaration of disengagement, the army was given a free hand to kill and destroy, assured that whatever it did would be perceived as necessary for the coming pullout.

These operations were punctuated by the arbitrary killing and destruction that had become the daily reality in Gaza since September 2000. As Amira Hass wrote in January 2005, the army "controls Gaza through its fortified positions, which dominate densely populated residential areas; it controls Gaza with its airborne drones and their unceasing buzzing; the bulldozers that have not ceased demolishing, flattening, exposing, uprooting for the last four years; the helicopters that fire missiles; the military orders that turn roads and farmlands and half the coastline into areas "prohibited to Palestinians" so that any Palestinian using them ends up dead; orders that close all the passages into Gaza; the tanks that fire into civilian neighborhoods with . . . tank shells and other forms of munitions with a frequency that makes it impossible to count them, as opposed to the Palestinian Qassams [mortars], which fired one by one are counted one by one.'[24]

Israel describes its acts of devastation in Gaza as self-defence, necessary to counter Palestinian reliance on arms and violence. According to international law, the Gaza Strip is occupied territory, and the fourth Geneva Convention recognizes the right of an occupied people to carry out armed struggle against the occupying army – as opposed to terror against civilians, which is not defended by international law. It is possible to question the wisdom of the Palestinian resort to armed struggle, but it is no less necessary to ask what other way Israel has left open for the Palestinian people to struggle for their liberation. In both Gaza and the West Bank, any form of civil struggle is brutally quashed by the Israeli army, which often fires on non-violent demonstrations.

In one of the most flagrant instances of military violence against non-violent demonstrations, the Israeli army shelled, and launched missiles against, an unarmed demonstration of 3,000 people in Gaza on 19 May 2004, during the Operation Rainbow in Rafah. At this time, the Tel al-Sultan neighbourhood was under siege; there were widespread accounts of army brutality, and families were unable to bury their dead. A solidarity march was organized at Rafah town, which progressed along the Beach Road towards Tel al-Sultan. According to numerous witnesses and photographs, there were no armed men among the demonstrators. "We were marching down the road shouting "We need help" as a message to the world, and "No to occupation," Hussam Mustafa, a civil engineer, told the *Guardian*. "There was a missile and then people started running back and then there was another missile right into the crowd."[25] Israeli security sources explained that "the IDF feared a mass march toward its troops in the Tel Al-Sultan quarter in Rafah. The forces were ordered to take escalating measures to keep the hundreds of demonstrators . . . from confronting the soldiers.''[26] Images of the attack were broadcast around the world, and the Israeli army hastened to "express its sorrow". But the message to the Gaza Palestinians was blunt and unequivocal – no form of protest would be allowed.

The complete closure of the Gaza Strip behind walls and barriers has proved effective in preventing militants from infiltrating Israel from the Strip; indeed, it has become impossible to reach Israel at all through the prison walls. During the current Palestinian uprising, virtually all suicide bombers trying to leave Gaza have detonated their explosives at the barrier's crossing points, or were stopped while trying to cross the barrier elsewhere. A rare exception was on 14 March 2004, when two eighteen-year-olds from the Jabalya refugee camp managed to hide in a secret compartment constructed behind a false wall in the rear of a container filled with marble and ceramic tiling. The container was then loaded onto a Palestinian truck heading to the Israeli port of Ashdod and transported through the Israeli Port Authority-run Karni crossing. The two detonated their explosives in Ashdod, killing ten Israeli port workers.

But the imprisoned Gaza Palestinians found another way to disturb the life of the Israelis in the vicinity of the Strip, by launching rockets and home-made Qassam mortars across the wall against the settlement blocks in Gaza, and against Israeli towns bordering the Strip. These primitive rockets lack the precision to focus on a target, and have rarely caused Israeli casualties; they do however cause physical and psychological damage and seriously disturb life in the targeted Israeli neighbourhoods. Though substantially less advanced technologically, their effect is reminiscent of the Katyusha mortars launched by the Hizbollah against northern Israeli towns prior to Israel's withdrawal from Southern Lebanon. In the period after the two Israeli military operations in 2004, and before the second Palestinian ceasefire was declared in February 2005, there was a substantial escalation of mortar attacks. According to Israeli military sources there were some hundred attacks per week in January 2005.[27]

Israel tries to portray mortar attacks as on a par with terrorist attacks. The reason is obvious: terror is inexcusable. Terrorists are not protected by international law, and any punitive acts are therefore viewed as justified. But from the Palestinian perspective, the firing of mortars and rockets constitute acts of war, not terror. As we have seen, according to international law the Gaza Strip is an occupied territory – but Israel has been systematically pushing to redefine the situation as one of war. Israel has been sending its air force and tanks to bombard residential areas, something only permitted in war. In war, it is accepted that there may be civilian casualites – "collateral damage," in military language. But if this is war – a process where each side defends itself by attacking the other – shelling the enemy is considered acceptable. So from this perspective, one articulated by Hamas in particular, Palestinians have the right to defend themselves by launching mortars. It is of course no contest: mortars with no precision and a range of maximum 9 km are pitted against a country with one of the strongest armies in the world. Nevertheless, in Hamas's eyes, it is a legitimate response to the war Israel has declared on the Palestinians.

During the military reoccupation of Gaza in 2001, it became clear that these mortar attacks would prove the most difficult problem encountered by the army, against which neither Israel's military superiority, nor its most sophisticated methods of surveillance and control from the air could be of much use. It remained a serious concern after the disengagement plan was announced. The evacuated Gaza settlements of course no longer represent targets for the Palestinian mortars, but as long as the occupation of the West Bank continues and Gaza is controlled by Israel from the outside, the Negev Israeli neighbourhoods will continue to be attacked. The army sought to solve this problem by restricting the Palestinian ability to obtain mortars and similar weapons, a major channel for which is the Gaza–Egypt border. Over the years, the Palestinians managed to build tunnels under the border wall, which are used, among other things, to smuggle weapons and rockets.

To control millions of desperate people, it is necessary to guarantee that they cannot find aid in neighbouring countries. The army's aim in the aforementioned destruction of dwellings in Rafah was to expand the "Philadelphi Road," the security zone separating the Strip from the Egyptian border; this, the army hoped, would prevent the construction of smuggling tunnels. As Alex Fishman of *Yediot Aharonot* observed in March 2004, "in the Gaza battalion, they keep executing gradually but systematically the old dream: to widen the "Philadelphi" road to at least one kilometer in width . . . The realization of this dream has been happening for two years already. Every time the IDF spokesman announces that our forces are operating in the area of Rafah to expose tunnels, a few rows of houses are erased in the refugee camp. In some of the segments of the road, the width is already a few hundred meters, and their hands are still outstretched.'[28]

The army's preparation and research for what it calls "tunnel warfare" is meticulous – and chilling. Amir Oren reports a conversation with Major Moshe Huli, the head of an urban warfare section, who "encountered the problem of the Rafah tunnels . . . Huli investigated tunnel combat in the world wars, in Vietnam, in Afghanistan, in Chechnya and even in the Warsaw Ghetto."[29] Major Huli, like all Israelis, has probably grown up with the stories of the courageous Jewish resistance in the Warsaw Ghetto, where tunnels were built to smuggle weapons, and establish communication with the outside world. Now he studies the same stories, to learn how resistance can be most efficiently crushed.

Following the announcement of the disengagement plan, the Israeli army started preparing for what would effectively become a new phase in the occupation of Gaza. As outlined in Chapter 2, under this plan the Strip will remain fully sealed from the outside world and the Israeli army will continue its external military control, entering when necessary to take "preventative measures" as well as "responding by using force against threats that will emerge from the Gaza Strip".[30] The bulk of policing work will be done from the air, through surveillance, precision missiles for so-called "targeted killings" or more "traditional" methods of aerial bombardment. As Ze'ev Schiff explained after the pullout, "the objective will likely be pursued . . . with troops entering the area only for tactical purposes. Fire from IDF artillery and Israel Air Force helicopters will increase, including into populated areas, after residents are warned to get out "in order to avoid getting hurt".[31] Since the pullout in September 2005 all these measures have been put into effect.[32]

In the original disengagement plan, Israel also insisted that its control over the Philadelphi security zone remains under any future "final arrangement". Clause VI of the plan specified that "Israel will continue to maintain a military presence along the border line between the Gaza Strip and Egypt ("Philadelphi Route"). This presence is an essential security need, and in certain places, it is possible that there will be a need for the physical enlargement of the area in which the military activity will be carried out.'[32] This is the same concept that underpins Israeli plans for the West Bank, in which Israel demands that the Jordan Valley, bordering Jordan, should be a permanent security zone controlled by Israel.

In its vision for a watertight seal around the Gaza Strip, the Israeli army was planning before the pullout to expand the "security zone" along the Philadelphi route. In January 2005 Ha 'aretz reported that "the Israel Defense Forces have asked Attorney General Menachem Mazuz for permission to clear completely a 300-meter-wide strip along the Gazan–Egyptian border. This would require the demolition of hundreds of Palestinian houses in Rafah."[34] The plan included also constructing a huge water channel along the route of Philadelphi: "The channel, which would take a year to construct, would eventually run the entire 12-kilometer length of the Philadelphi route, and could be completed after disengagement."[35] This "sterile zone" was apparently required because "the army fears that soldiers patrolling Philadelphi would be sitting ducks for Palestinians, who would be able to shoot at them unseen from within nearby buildings".[36]

Israel eventually discarded this idea. Instead, Sharon, with the aid of the US, managed to extract a commitment from Egypt that it would patrol the Philadelphi Route on Israel's behalf, and prevent smuggling along the length of the border. Israeli security sources voiced their belief that "Egypt will crack down on cross-border arms smuggling, both to placate Washington and because of worries over the growing ties between Islamic extremists in Egypt and Gaza".[37] (This is the type of cooperation that Israel expects of all its neighbours. Israel's tension with Syria during its occupation of Southern Lebanon was in part due to Israel's demand that Syria should take on the Hizbollah, in order to protect Israel's forces and its border.[38]) However, there is no reason to assume that the Egyptian army will be able to combat the tunnels any more efficiently than had Israel, so this may not be the last word on this matter.

Responding to yet another Israeli plan from the disengagement era – the construction of an underwater wall in the sea of Gaza – Saeb Erekat of the Palestinian negotiation team observed: "I hope the Israeli mentality of barriers will end . . . Now they have land barriers and tomorrow sea barriers and the day after sky barriers. What else? Will they put a barrier around each Palestinian house? This is the wrong policy. This is political blindness. The answer to all these woes of security is a meaningful peace process, building bridges with the Palestinians, and ending the occupation."[39] This is the one alternative that Israel under Sharon has never been willing to consider, despite having had plenty of opportunities to do so. Let us turn now to the next period in time that Sharon had a chance to pursue this avenue, had he wanted to.

4

Winter 2004–5:
The post-Arafat "Period of Calm"

ON 11 NOVEMBER 2004, Yasser Arafat, chairman of the Palestine Liberation Organization and elected president of the Palestinian Authority, died in a hospital in Paris at the age of seventy-five. Palestinian society geared itself up for new elections for the Palestinian Authority presidency (or chairmanship, in the terminology preferred by Israel).

From September 2000, the Israeli leadership, backed by the US administration, had singled Arafat out as the main obstacle to peace. Adopting this perspective, the media world believed that his departure would herald a new era. Both the Palestinian elections and the Iraqi elections that took place in January 2005 were hailed as great victories for democracy, with media elation obscuring the harsh reality: these were elections held in countries under occupation. On the day of the Palestinian elections, an enthusiastic CNN reporter spoke excitedly about future relations between the two "countries" (Israel and Palestine), as if the Palestinian state had already been founded on its liberated land.

The same post-Arafat euphoria was also dominant in the Israeli media, as Aluf Benn noted in December 2004: "The media atmosphere over the last few days has been reminiscent of the Oslo-era euphoria, or the early days of Ehud Barak's government . . . There is once again talk of cooperation, public embraces and peace conferences. International diplomats are once again viewing the Israeli–Palestinian conflict as an arena for diplomatic successes instead of a guaranteed recipe for frustration and failure."[1]

On 9 January 2005, Mahmoud Abbas was elected president, or chairman, of the Palestinian Authority. He took office almost a year after Sharon's unveiling of the Gaza disengagement plan as a first step towards relinquishing Israeli control of the occupied territories. Recall that Sharon had explained that his decision to implement his disengagement plan unilaterally was based on a lack of a suitable Palestinian partner for negotiations.[2] During the previous negotiating round of the Road Map, Abbas had served as prime minister under Arafat, who, Israel argued at the time, was secretly hindering any potential progress on the Road Map. With Abbas now emerging from Arafat's shadow, the way seemed open to a renewal of the peace process and the fulfilment of Sharon's declared wish to end the occupation – or at least, to resume implementation of the Road Map.

Yet the response of the Israeli press to Abbas's election as president, in the very first week after his victory, closely echoed that in the first period of the Road Map, in mid-2003. On the day of his election, Abbas called upon the various militant Palestinian organizations to resume the ceasefire. The same day, Hamas announced its openness to the idea. According to a report in the UK *Observer*, Hamas's announcement "follows a major escalation in the Hamas campaign of firing missiles at Israeli targets in and around the Gaza Strip . . . The escalation can be seen as a bargaining ploy to demonstrate to Israel and the expected winner of today's election, Mahmoud Abbas . . . the importance of a Hamas ceasefire."[3]

However, in a meeting with Jimmy Carter on the eve of the elections, Sharon had already clarified that "there will be no progress until . . . the terror organizations are eliminated".[4] In interviews with the international media, official Israeli spokesmen repeated Sharon's message: Abbas must dismantle the organizations entirely; simply achieving a ceasefire was unacceptable. In only his first week in power, Israeli security sources expressed "disappointment" with Abbas: " 'We became increasingly concerned by Abbas' apparent decision to use the same counter-terrorism measures he did last time [as Palestinian Authority prime minister], i.e., to persuade the terrorists and reach an agreement with them,' a senior source said."[5]

These, then, were precisely the same demands that Sharon put to Abbas in the previous round of the Road Map. As we have seen,[6] Israel demands the complete disarmament of the militant organizations prior to any further progress in the peace process – and before any Palestinian demands are met. Under conditions such as these, however, there is no reason to assume that the militant organizations will voluntarily disarm or dismantle themselves. Israel is therefore effectively demanding that Abbas's security forces engage in armed clashes with these organizations. It bears re-emphasizing that, even if Abbas had the power and the necessary resources to dismantle the militant factions by force, such confrontation might well mean a civil war in which Palestinian society would destroy itself.

The Palestinian spokespeople asked that, in return for a ceasefire, Israel make reciprocal commitments, such as bringing an end to targeted killings and house demolitions. In response, the Israeli army "renewed its incursions into Palestinian Authority territory, following a hiatus it had enforced in view of the elections in the territories. In operations to capture militants since the elections, two armed Hamas men were killed near Ramallah, and a Fatah man was killed in an incident in Tul Karm, after he shot a police officer."[7]

It is worth exploring what the Israeli army defined as "a hiatus it had enforced in view of the elections in the territories", one it found necessary to break, as soon as Abbas was elected, with these three new assassinations. What follows is a sample of events during the ten days in the run-up to the Palestinian elections, a period in which Israeli military action had supposedly been curbed. On 31 December 2003, it was reported that "Israel has been stepping up its military raids in the Gaza Strip with its troops killing 12 Palestinians in the past two days. The action comes as Palestinian presidential contenders campaign for the January 9 elections."[8]

On 30 December, Riziq Ziad Musleh, a seventeen-year-old Palestinian high school student, was shot dead as he was placing posters on a wall near his home in the Gaza Strip for Dr Mustafa Barghouti's presidential campaign. Barghouti's election headquarters reported that "without any warning or incident, he was shot . . . from the direction of the Rafah Yam Israeli settlement. An observation tower manned by Israeli soldiers is located in the settlement, about 500 yards from where Riziq was standing."[9] On 4 January, "seven Palestinians were killed . . . including six members of the same family, when an Israel Defense Forces tank shell hit an agricultural area in the northern Gaza Strip town of Beit Lahia. Eight others were reportedly wounded in the incident, two of them seriously . . . The IDF confirmed that troops fired a tank shell at the Palestinians, saying the target was a rocket-launching terror cell that had been seen near Nissanit. An initial investigation indicated that most of the Palestinians killed were members of the military wing of Hamas, the army said. The Palestinians said all of those killed were farmers working in their greenhouses and that the members of the rocket-launching cell had escaped uninjured."[10] The *Guardian* added that the dead (who the army claimed were members of the military wing of Hamas) were four children aged ten, twelve, thirteen and fourteen and three seventeen-year-olds.[11] Throughout this period, the Rafah terminal on the Egyptian border was closed, creating both a sense of isolation and economic suffocation.

Against this setting, on the night of 13 January 2005, four days after the elections, two Palestinians launched a suicide bombing at the Karni crossing between Israel and the Gaza Strip, which was manned at the time by Israeli civilian border authority personnel and a small Israeli army force. The explosion killed three Israelis and wounded five. The Palestinian interpretation of this attack was as a message from the organizations involved to the effect that "if Israeli attacks continue, the reaction to these attacks will continue".[12]

In a rare burst of independent thinking, a *Ha'aretz* editorial pleaded with the government to show restraint and give Abbas the time and support necessary to work on a ceasefire:

> If there is no sign that Abu Mazen is encouraging terror, if he means what he says, if he did not know about the attack planned a long time before it was carried out, it may be expected that the government of Israel will give him time and support so that he can work toward a total ceasefire. Demanding that he control Hamas and the other organizations one week after his election, even before being sworn in, by waging all-out war instead of reaching an agreement among the various Palestinian factions, abrogates from the outset Abu Mazen's chance of succeeding in his chosen path . . . Israel will gain nothing from a Palestinian civil war – and will certainly gain nothing from the failure of Abu Mazen, whom everyone believes harbors new hope for the entire region.[13]

But the Israeli government chose to respond differently – or rather, in precisely the same way that it had done during the Road Map period in mid-2003, when Abbas was prime minister. Here is how Amos Harel, the security analyst of *Ha'aretz*, described the Israeli reaction:

> Statements made by senior Israeli officials following the attack at the Karni crossing . . . sounded as if they had been taken from four years ago, during the days of Ehud Barak and Yasser Arafat: "This is the Palestinian Authority's test"; "The Palestinian security mechanisms are doing nothing"; "If they don't act, we'll do it for them"; "There's a limit to our patience."[14]

It is astonishing that Harel's analogy should lead the reader back to the far days of Barak and Arafat, rather than to the much more recent past of Abbas's previous attempts to restore calm when he was appointed prime minister during the Road Map period in 2003. Harel himself had reported precisely the same dissatisfaction of Israeli officials with Abbas at that time.[15] It is the media's responsibility to remind the readers of recent history in providing the context for events, but at the time, none of this happened in the Israeli media. As often before, there seemed to be absolute lack of collective memory. Rather than pointing out the repeated pattern of Israel's stalling Abbas, the picture that emerged in the press was once again that of a peace-seeking Israeli leadership that had attached great hopes to the change of leadership in the Palestinian side, and which had done everything in its power to help the development of Palestinian democracy – but which, four days after the elections, had sadly realized that there was after all no real Palestinian partner for peace. As Harel explained in the same report:

> In recent weeks, Jerusalem fostered many expectations of Mahmoud Abbas. Officials were impressed by his explicit statements denouncing terror, the orderly transfer of power after Arafat's death, the former chairman's quiet funeral, and Abbas' sweeping election victory. But the window of opportunity has not opened up by more than a narrow crack. Assuming Abbas plans to achieve a cease-fire with the Palestinian opposition groups, he wants to do it in his own way and time – through persuasive talks and quiet agreements, without aggressive steps. The trouble is that Israel does not have time to see if he succeeds.[16]

Just as in Abbas's previous period of office during the 2003 Road Map negotiations, Israel's leadership viewed a ceasefire as a threat. If Abbas were to restore calm and a ceasefire should prevail, Israel might again be expected to carry out some of its commitments. Sharon and the army seemed at the time determined to find ways to make this look impossible, by stalling any attempt for an enduring ceasefire, using the same methods as before.

Nevertheless, from the moment he assumed office, Abbas worked energetically to restore calm and renew the ceasefire.

On 17 January 2004, he issued orders for a special intervention force of between 500 and 700 officers of the Palestinian security services to deploy in the Gaza Strip, in the area from which rockets and mortars were being launched at Israeli targets.[17] Shortly after, the Israeli media reported that "in practice, all three organizations [Hamas, Islamic Jihad and Fatah] have already halted armed operations in Gaza, including Qassam launches at Sderot, in response to Abbas' decision to deploy PA security forces in northern Gaza last week. However, Hamas and Islamic Jihad officials said they will not formally agree to a ceasefire without an Israeli quid pro quo."[18] Palestinian security forces were also enforcing calm in the West Bank: "Zacharia Zubeidi, the Al-Aqsa Martyrs' Brigades leader in Jenin, announced that his group will halt attacks on Israel. Zubeidi's remarks followed comments by the PA's commander of Special Forces, Bashir Nafe, who said Palestinian security forces intend to disarm militant factions to prevent attacks on Israelis."[19] On 19 January, the Palestinian militant organizations announced their agreement in principle to a ceasefire, *Ha'aretz* reporting that "despite recent militant declarations by Fatah officials, sources in Gaza believe that most of the organization's armed factions in the Strip will accept the ceasefire in principle and that they and the security services will be able to enforce it if an Israeli commitment can be obtained to stop targeted killings and military activity in areas under Palestinian control".[20] Yet none of this was deemed sufficient to change Israel's constant "disappointment" at the Palestinians' lack of cooperation, let alone for Israel to accept a mutual cessation of military activities in the territories.

The prevailing perception, in both Israel and the West, is that Sharon has changed: Israel is, finally, led by a man of peace, with a respectable determination to make painful concessions. But on closer examination, this is far from being the case. In Israeli media reports of cabinet discussions, Sharon is often described as taking up the most militant and extreme positions, advocating eye-for-an-eye policies. It was not uncommon for military representatives to take a more balanced stand than Sharon, and to try to restrain him. Ze'ev Schiff described a leak from a cabinet meeting in mid-January 2005, in which it was debated how Israel should respond to a Palestinian rocket attack on the Israeli town Sderot, which left an Israeli teenage girl brain-dead:

> Prime Minister Ariel Sharon led the most extreme position in these discussions. He was evidently very agitated by events in Sderot. He demanded that the IDF deploy artillery to shell targets in the Gaza Strip, including in towns and villages, as long as Hamas continued to launch Qassam rockets or mortars at Israeli communities. He adopted a blatant eye-for-an-eye approach – to pay the Palestinians in kind, but with much more and much deadlier force . . . Facing off against him was Chief of Staff Moshe Ya'alon . . . Ya'alon said that Israel may eventually have no alternative but to mount a large-scale military operation in the Strip, but that first Mahmoud Abbas had to be given a chance to take action to put an end to the terror. A broad offensive before he kicked off his efforts would be a mistake. The world has to understand that Israel had no choice.[21]

Note that the debate between Sharon and Ya'alon is only one of timing. Sharon seemed to believe that the current situation would permit him to launch an offensive in the second week of Abbas's rule. Having consolidated his status as the darling of the peace camp in Israel, he would not have been totally mistaken in assuming that any actions he took would be interpreted as being part of the necessary preparation for disengagement. But Ya'alon, more sensitive to international opinion, suggested delaying any operation until ''the world understands that Israel had no choice''.

There were several other leaks of internal security debates, in which Sharon was always pushing the most extreme line, along with then chief of the Shin Bet security service, Avi Dichter. It is interesting that even Ya'alon emerges as slightly more moderate than Sharon. From the start of the Palestinian *intifada* Ya'alon, who was promoted to deputy chief of staff by the previous prime minister, Ehud Barak, had gained a reputation as the most devoted advocate of the destruction of the post-Oslo Palestinian institutions, the reinstitution of Israeli military rule, and the brutal oppression of the Palestinian people.[22] Nevertheless, as reported in *Ha'aretz*, ''off the record, Ya'alon complains that Sharon treats Chairman Abu Mazen like he treated prime minister Abu Mazen''.[23] Ya'alon's dispute with Sharon over this matter started eighteen months previously, in October 2003. Then, the *Washington Post* reported that ''Israel's senior military commander told columnists for three leading [Israeli] newspapers this week that Israel's military tactics against the Palestinian population were too repressive and were fomenting explosive levels of 'hatred and terrorism' that might become impossible to control . . . Ya'alon also said he believed the Israeli government contributed to the failure of Mahmoud Abbas as Palestinian prime minister because it was too ''stingy'' and was unwilling to make concessions to bolster his authority.'[24]

It seemed that perhaps for the first time in its history, Israel had a prime minister that pushed for military operations with even more alacrity than its army. The *Washington Post* continued to report that ''Ya'alon's remarks, echoed by equally vociferous criticism from other military officers interviewed [the same day], revealed a schism between military and political leaders over the government's handling of a conflict that many officers and soldiers say they believe is not winnable through military force, incites more terrorism than it prevents and mistreats innocent Palestinians''.[25] In June 2005, Ya'alon came to the end of his three-year term of office; although a one-year extension had been customary with Ya'alon's predecessors, Sharon refused to grant it.[26] He replaced Ya'alon with Dan Halutz, former chief of the Israeli air force, who in October 2000, at the outset of the Palestinian *intifada*, had recommended bringing ''the weight of the air force down on the Palestinians if the current unrest escalates,"[27] a philosophy he has since put into practice. On the night of 22 July 2002, Halutz authorized an assassination operation in which Israeli F-16 fighter jets dropped a one-ton bomb on a three-storey apartment building in Gaza, filled with sleeping people. Along with the targeted top Hamas militant Saleh Shehade, the assault left 14 other people, including children, dead and 150 injured.[28]

At the time of the mid-January cabinet debate on a response to the Sderot attack, the US administration had stressed to Israel that there should be no military operations in Gaza, or any escalation of tension that would undermine the just-elected Abbas.[29] The US tone had changed around the time of Abbas's election and, as we shall see, in contrast to the previous round of the Road Map, this was to remain a consistent policy through 2005.[30] The international climate was still buoyant following Abbas's election; none of the events described here had registered in the consciousness of the Western world and the air was full of renewed expectations for a big move towards peace. The script for giving the world what it wanted was ready and well rehearsed from the previous round of the Road Map – a big peace ceremony, such as the mid-2003 Aqaba summit before, that would prove that Israel was determined in its search for a lasting peaceful solution. So preparations for another such summit began.

In fact, the ground was not yet fully prepared for a big peace extravaganza. Abbas had not yet succeeded in securing the commitment of Hamas and Islamic Jihad to extend the ceasefire for a prolonged period. Given the recent experience of how Israel treated the ceasefire in the previous Road Map, the armed Islamist organizations insisted that some guarantees be provided that the same would not happen again. Specifically, they wanted a "guarantee that Israel will stop killing and arresting of militants and attacking Palestinian areas".[31] The groups also viewed this demand as a test of Abbas's leadership potential, believing that he should be able to attract international support for it, given the world's enthusiasm for the Palestinian democratic process. Obviously, Abbas could not solicit such guarantees from Sharon – who by that time had even refused to meet him. Nevertheless, the militant organizations declared they did not want to fail the newly elected Abbas. Meanwhile, discussions started on the possibility of Hamas entering the political system, and its participation in the parliamentary elections that were scheduled to take place several months later. The declared long-term aim was to turn the Palestinian *intifada* into a political, rather than an armed, struggle.

A compromise was reached on 23 January, after five days of negotiations with Abbas in Gaza. All Palestinian factions agreed on a lull of one month, during which they would "suspend attacks on Israel in order to give the new Palestinian leader, Mahmoud Abbas, time to secure international guarantees for a comprehensive ceasefire . . . Abbas' principal negotiator with Hamas, Ziad Abu-Amr . . . said the armed Islamist factions pledged to hold off from attacks while the Palestinian leader attempted to secure assurances of Israeli reciprocity, and negotiates final terms of a deal to bring the groups into the political process. 'There is a Palestinian tranquillisation. This is a Palestinian initiative intended to be a prelude to a ceasefire but there have to be conditions for a ceasefire', said Mr Abu-Amr. 'There has to be reciprocity [from Israel] and that means no attacks on Palestinians, no incursions or chasing militants.' "[32]

Reporting from Gaza on the Palestinian ceasefire agreement, Chris McGreal noted that "The [Israeli] military's continued detention of Palestinians, and more specifically their killing when they resisted arrest, was an important factor in the collapse of a 2003 ceasefire after 51 days."[33] The Palestinian demand that its suspension of attacks should be met by a reciprocal Israeli commitment to cease military incursions into Palestinian areas would normally be conceived as a defining condition for a ceasefire – what the term means. However, it was a condition that Israel refused to accept. In a meeting of the Israeli cabinet following the announcement of the Palestinian one-month lull agreement, Chief of Staff Ya'alon stated that "the military would continue operations against Palestinian militants in those areas where Palestinian security forces are not operating, which includes much of the West Bank".[34] As in 2003, Israel made it clear that it would not consider a truce with the armed Islamist factions. Instead, it allowed two options: either the Palestinian security forces move against the militant organizations, or Israel will continue to do so.

Neither the Palestinian demands nor Israel's rejection of them seemed to register in the consciousness of the West, which was so eager for a new peace process. The Palestinian one-month lull agreement was hailed as a big achievement for Abbas in the international media. The *New York Times* devoted an editorial to the issue:

> We hope that the Palestinian militant groups who say they are suspending attacks on Israel for a while actually do so . . . And we hope this puts the region back on the road to peace . . . Both sides, and particularly the Palestinians, are notorious for dashing those hopes . . . [But] Mr Abbas deserves credit as the only real Palestinian leader who candidly acknowledges what the world has always known. Palestinian violence against Israel is pointless, and has served only to bring forth overwhelmingly punishing responses.[35]

Typical of how the Western media has shaped the perception of events in Israel/Palestine, this piece nowhere makes any mention of any demands made to, or expectations from, Israel, nor is there a discussion of the Palestinian demand for reciprocity.

In the broader context of the proposed ceasefire, the Palestinians wanted Israel to take steps towards the implementation of the Road Map. It is worth recalling that, according to the first stage of the Road Map, on the declaration of a ceasefire Israeli forces should pull back to the positions they held in September 2000, before the Palestinian uprising. At the same time Israel is required to freeze settlement expansion and dismantle all settlement outposts erected since March 2001 (when Sharon entered office). [36]

Israel responded to these demands with precisely the same interpretation it had offered to these requirements in the previous round: it transferred authority to the Palestinians in five West Bank towns, without moving its forces back to their September 2000 positions, and promised to lift some roadblocks and ease restrictions where calm prevails, rather than dismantling all roadblocks erected since that time. The settlement issue was not addressed at all. (On the ground, according to the Israeli Central Bureau of Statistics, settlement population rose in 2005 by 4.3 per cent. [37])

In accordance with the Road Map, the Palestinians also suggested resuming negotiations regarding its final goals – the end of occupation, and the establishment of a Palestinian state. But "Palestinian hopes that a ceasefire would lead to an immediate revival of political negotiations . . . were dampened when the US secretary of state, Condoleezza Rice [who visited the area for two days], made it clear that Washington would not press Mr Sharon to begin talks now . . . and insisted that Washington intends to give Mr Sharon a relatively free hand while he completes his "disengagement plan" to withdraw Jewish settlers from the Gaza Strip.' [38]

As the summit approached, the Israeli government agreed to release 900 (out of an estimated 7,500) Palestinian prisoners and "to suspend the assassination of men wanted by Israel [but rather to] set up a joint committee with Palestinians to decide how to deal with them". [39] On the eve of the summit, Sharon even announced a willingness to declare that Israel would cease military activities against all Palestinians, which provided an optimistic setting for the event.

The summit took place on 8 February 2005 in the Egyptian Red Sea resort of Sharm el-Sheikh, "which often served as the setting for peace summits that were followed by more violence". [40] Along with Sharon and Abbas, the participants this time were Egyptian President Hosni Mubarak and Jordan's King Abdullah II. At the level of declarations, all looked extremely promising, as the sides announced an agreement of full cessation of violence. Abbas announced that "We have agreed with Prime Minister Ariel Sharon to cease all acts of violence against the Israelis and the Palestinians wherever they are." Sharon too took a solemn commitment: "Today," he said, "in my meeting with Chairman Abbas, we agreed that all Palestinians will stop all acts of violence against all Israelis everywhere, and, at the same time, Israel will cease all its military activity against all Palestinians everywhere." Then the two leaders stated their vision of the future. "Abbas added that peace means the establishment of 'a democratic Palestinian state alongside Israel . . . A new opportunity for peace is born today in the city of peace,' he said, referring to the nickname of Sharm el-Sheikh earned through past peace summits. 'Let's pledge to protect it.' " Sharon revived his declared commitment to the Road Map: "Our disengagement plan can pave the way to the start of the implementation of the Road Map to which we are committed, and which we want to complete . . . We hope that from today there will be a new period of calm and hope."[41] Sharon could not resist mentioning also his precondition for any progress: "We must all make a commitment not to agree for a temporary solution . . . [but] to dismantle the terrorist infrastructure, to disarm and subdue it once and for all."[42] Nevertheless, at the level of words, the ceremony certainly fulfilled expectations that a new era of calm was about to begin.

News of the Sharm el-Sheikh "breakthrough" was received enthusiastically. UN Secretary-General Kofi Annan said that he was "relieved and thankful" that Israeli and Palestinian leaders "have stepped back from the abyss, and renewed their commitment to resolve their differences by peaceful means".[43] As with the Aqaba summit, the event received extensive Western media coverage, with front pages and headlines proclaiming a new dawn in the Middle East.[44] More sober voices, like that of the

UK *Guardian*, did show some recollection of how the previous ceasefire ended, observing that "ceasefires have been declared before," but nevertheless suggested that "major changes in the region – chiefly the death of Palestinian leader, Yasser Arafat, in November and Sharon's Gaza pullout plan – have generated hopes that this one will stick."[45]

In Israel, the level of optimism was even higher than in 2003. Then, there was still a substantial amount of frustration over how Sharon handled the first chance of a ceasefire, noticeable in a burst of criticism from the Israeli media after some of the Israeli assassinations. Sharon's subsequent announcement of his disengagement plan, however, had had the effect of elevating him above any criticism or suspicion. As Matan Vilnai, one of the contestants for the Labor party leadership, exclaimed: "Only Sharon can bring peace!" In this heady atmosphere of optimism, who would pay attention to what actually happened on the ground?

It didn't take long for Sharon to manifest how seriously he was committed to his Sharm el-Sheikh declaration that "Israel will cease all its military activity against all Palestinians everywhere". The day after the summit, "the first conflict-related fatality since Israel and the Palestinians declared a truce" was a twenty-year-old Palestinian in Gaza, shot dead from an Israeli army post near the settlement of Atzmona.[46] The next day, another Palestinian was shot and killed as he was driving through the neighbourhood of Wadi al-Haramiya near the West Bank city of Ramallah. The Israeli army claimed that he refused to stop at a roadblock.[47] It was, however, unlikely that these two killings were part of a planned escalation of military activities; rather, they just formed part of the routine of the occupation, where no day passes without the occasional and arbitrary killing of a Palestinian. The army continued its daily habits as if it had heard nothing of the momentous declarations of the previous day.

With the exception of *Al Jazeera*, these two routine shootings never made it to the international media. What attracted rather more attention was the first Palestinian violation of the ceasefire, which followed the day after on 11 February when, in response to the two killings, Hamas fired mortars and Qassam rockets at an Israeli settlement in Gaza. MIFTAH – the Palestinian Initiative for the Promotion of Global Dialogue and Democracy – produced a report on the media coverage of this mortar attack.[48] It is painfully useful to read it, precisely because what it describes is not exceptional: time and again, when Palestinian violence is reported, the background of how and why it started is consistently ignored:

> According to mainstream Israeli and US media organizations, Palestinians broke the ceasefire only two days after the historic Israeli–Palestinian ceasefire agreement at Sharm El-Sheikh. It is true. Palestinians fired several rounds of mortars and home-made rockets, weapons that have killed people in the past, at illegal Jewish settlements in Gaza on 11 February. Luckily, no one was hurt in the attacks. However, these media are either marginalizing or not reporting at all some very relevant facts, in particular that Israeli troops killed two unarmed Palestinians in separate incidents prior to the attacks, and that the rocket and mortar attacks were carried out explicitly as a response to the killings . . . Israel should therefore be held responsible for endangering the calm in the region . . . Yet the Israeli and American publics are hardly likely to think so, simply because they do not know . . . The liberal Israeli daily *Ha'aretz*, often celebrated for its unbiased approach, points an unambiguous finger of blame at the Palestinian organization that claimed responsibility for the mortar and rocket attacks: 'Hamas Rockets Deal a Blow to Sharm Optimism' (*Ha'aretz* staff, *Ha'aretz*, 11 February) . . . The Atlanta-based CNN . . . (cnn.com, 10 February, US EST), referred to Palestinian attacks on 'Israeli communities in Gaza', but with not one word spilled on the prehistory of those attacks . . .
>
> The media pressures contributed to the search for accountability among Palestinians for the Palestinian attacks. That is

good media work. But should accountability not be demanded for the preceding deadly attacks? Not according to the Israeli and US media whose absolute silence on the matters speaks volumes . . .[49]

As we shall see in the next chapter, throughout the "period of calm," Sharon and the security forces pursued precisely the same policy they employed during the previous Palestinian ceasefire in mid-2003, continuing to discredit Abbas. As Amos Harel reported, "the insulting epithets absorbed by Palestinian Authority chairman Mahmoud Abbas are practically on a par with the attitude to which his predecessor, Yasser Arafat, was accustomed. Abu Mazen may have come to terms with descriptions like 'a chick that hasn't yet grown feathers' when he was prime minister, but this week, they were already talking about him in the Knesset's Foreign Affairs and Defense Committee as 'an impotent man in need of Viagra.' "[50] Just as in the previous round of the Road Map, Sharon and members of his administration tried to convince the Bush administration that Abbas was a failure, and that Israel could not be committed to a ceasefire as long as Abbas did not "crack down on the terror organization". However, the second-term Bush administration apparently stood firm:

"American officials have made it clear to Israel that the administration is sticking to its support for Abbas even though it is concerned about his apparent weakness. The Americans have made clear to Israel that it must fulfill its commitments made at the Sharm el-Sheikh summit — continuing to hand over West Bank towns to the PA, releasing security prisoners and removing checkpoints that restrict Palestinian freedom of movement in the territories."[51]

Under these circumstances, Sharon could not overtly break the ceasefire as he had done in 2003, and was forced to preserve at least an appearance of cooperating with the Palestinian declaration of calm. Of the commitments made in the negotiations preceding the Sharm el-Sheikh summit, fulfilment of which the US insisted upon, Israel carried out the transference of the police missions in some West Bank cities to the Palestinian Authority, and (as mentioned above) the release of 900 Palestinian prisoners, out of around 7,500 Palestinian prisoners held by Israel, many of them for many years. The release of prisoners has been of focal importance for Palestinian society, and a recurring demand in all negotiations since Oslo. But the actual release carried out by Israel left the Palestinians with a deep sense of disappointment. Many of those released had been held for criminal activity and for working illegally in Israel, or were reaching the end of their term. Of the political prisoners, Israel agreed only to release prisoners that did not belong to opposition Palestinian parties. Amira Hass described the reaction in Palestinian society: "Doubts regarding their future were particularly heavy among the more veteran prisoners and their families. They found it hard to believe that they had been left out not due to apathy toward their cause and therefore a lack of effort, but due to an asymmetrical balance of power in which the Palestinian side is too weak to effect changes in the Israeli position, too weak to prevent the inclusion of Palestinians caught in Israel without permits and criminal prisoners in the Israeli 'gestures' . . ." The insistence on releasing only Fatah members "who supported Abu Mazen from inside the prisons (meaning they did not support the opposition) . . . contributes to the atmosphere of mistrust and the assumption that the Palestinians themselves are the ones who asked and are asking the Israeli representatives not to release opposition members (mainly from Hamas and Islamic Jihad, but also from the Popular and Democratic Fronts for the Liberation of Palestine – the PFLP and the DFLP). For Abu Mazen to succeed in persuading Hamas and Islamic Jihad to agree to a ceasefire, he cannot afford the suspicion that he prefers to leave members of the Islamic opposition in Israeli prisons."[52]

These exhaust the measures taken by Israel to cooperate with the Palestinian period of calm. Although by definition "ceasefire" means the mutual cessation of all military activities, no trace of Sharon's Sharm el-Sheikh commitment that Israel would cease military activity could in practice be found over the coming months. Under the heading "Sharon's Sharm statement not yet implemented by army," *Ha'aretz* reported shortly after the summit that according to security sources "the Israel Defense Forces are continuing at this stage to operate according to instructions issued by Chief of Staff Moshe Ya'alon two weeks ago [i.e before the summit]." At that time, Ya'alon gave orders to limit operations in the West Bank "to actions required by an urgent need to prevent planned terror attacks . . . The sources said that until such time as the Palestinian Authority takes over security responsibility for towns in the West Bank, the IDF will have to act in cases of need."[53] In other words, behind the solemn declarations, the Israeli army continued military activities against Palestinians, describing them as necessary in the war on terror. In this, there was no change whatsoever in Israel's military operations, which have always been presented as fulfilling a pressing security need.

Initially, Israel did reduce the number of its overt "targeted killings," although it fell short of stopping them altogether. What did dramatically decrease was media coverage of the assassinations that did take place (at that period targeting mainly members of the Al-Aqsa Brigades, a branch of Mahmoud Abbas's Fatah party). These killings were reported only in small corners of the Israeli media. Often, they did not make it at all into the Israeli press and were covered only by Palestinian sources. For example, the online *Palestinian Monitor* reported that on 15 February 2005 the Israeli army assassinated two members of the Al-Aqsa Brigades near the West Bank town of Nablus. "Assam Hamza Mansour, 27, from Balata refugee camp and Mahyoub Halkini, 24, from Kufar Qalil were killed near Kufar Qalil village in an empty home they used as a place of refuge."[54] A small item in *Ha'aretz* reported that on 14 April Ibrahim Hashash, "a member of Fatah's military wing was killed in Nablus in an exchange of fire with a Border Police undercover unit . . . The IDF defined Hashash as 'a ticking bomb', who was continuing to prepare terror attacks, despite the ceasefire." It was further reported that "the Israel Defense Forces is preparing for a possible retaliatory strike from the organization".[55]

In other instances, Israel denied involvement in assassinations, which it would describe jokingly as "work accidents" – a militant blowing himself up accidentally, while preparing explosives. (This explanation had been often used by Israeli military sources in the past.[56]) On 29 May, two "work accidents" happened to take place in two different towns in the Gaza Strip, *Ha'aretz* reporting that "two Palestinians were killed and two others were wounded yesterday afternoon in an explosion in a house in Gaza. The blast apparently occurred when a bomb they were preparing exploded prematurely. The four were members of the military wing of Palestinian Authority Chairman Mahmoud Abbas' ruling Fatah party. Also yesterday, Hamas activist Tahsin Kelah was killed in a large explosion in Khan Yunis, in the Gaza Strip. The circumstances surrounding the blast are unclear, although it was apparently caused when a mortar shell or rocket-propelled grenade Kelah was trying to shoot misfired."[57] No Israeli newspaper reported a Palestinian version of the events, or raised any questions about the text that "military sources" prepared for the papers to print. Qualifying the text with the word "apparently" is the furthest *Ha'aretz* would go to demonstrate a degree of media independence.

Neither did Israel halt its arrest operations in the territories, contrary to its declared intention at Sharm el-Sheikh. According to Israeli security sources, 400 Palestinians were arrested in such operations in a two-month period between the Sharm summit in February and the end of April. It is interesting to observe how the sources described this to *Ha'aretz*: "The senior sources added that since the Sharm summit the IDF has substantially reduced its offensive activity in the West Bank, 'in an attempt to give Abu Mazen a chance,' and based on the commitment given to him by

PM Ariel Sharon." Now come the details of these noble measures of restraint and cooperation on Israel's part:

> During this time, the IDF carried out 400 arrests, a decrease of 40% compared to the previous period, most of them of terror activists that were about to carry out attacks in the short term and were defined as 'ticking bombs'. Sources in IDF rejected the Palestinian claim that the IDF activities are hindering the ceasefire and clarified that "we will be happy to stop these activities as soon as the Palestinians will take action instead of us."[58]

Recall that by the time of the Sharm el-Sheikh summit, all that Abbas could bring to the table as a basis for a ceasefire deal was a one-month period of calm declared by all Palestinian factions on 23 January, in order to enable him to solicit Israeli reciprocity. On Friday night, 25 February, came the first Palestinian terror attack since the Sharm summit, when a suicide bombing in a Tel Aviv bar killed five people and wounded fifty others. The attack was carried out by an Islamic Jihad cell in the Tulkarm region of the West Bank. "Speaking from an undisclosed location in Lebanon, an Islamic Jihad official, who insisted on being identified only by his nickname of Abu Tareq, told the Associated Press that the attack was in retaliation for Israel's violation of the Israeli–Palestinian truce. 'The calm period with the [Palestinian] Authority was an agreement for a month, and that has ended,' he said. 'Israel has not abided by the pacification period. This is the main reason that led to this operation'."[59]

The Palestinian Authority reacted swiftly. Abbas convened a meeting of the heads of the PA security forces in his home over the weekend and demanded "results and not efforts".[60] The security forces arrested six Islamic Jihad militants in Tulkarm who were suspected of involvement in the bombing.[61] At the same time, Abbas resisted Sharon's repeated demand that "there will be no progress . . . until the Palestinians carry out a determined campaign to destroy the terrorist groups and their infrastructure".[62] Abbas insisted that "inter-Palestinian dialogue is the only way to reach a national consensus on how to protect national interests and repeatedly rejected Israeli dictates to crack down on Palestinian factions as a recipe for infighting and civil war."[63] He intensified the negotiations with the Palestinian factions on extending the period of calm, and on reaching a more long-lasting agreement.

On 17 March, following several days of internal talks in Cairo, the various Palestinian organizations reached an agreement to continue the lull, with the understanding that it should last at least until the end of 2005. The organizations present included Fatah, represented by PA President Mahmoud Abbas, Hamas, represented by the head of its political bureau, Khaled Meshal, Islamic Jihad and several smaller groups. They signed a six-point document stating that "the participants agree on a plan for 2005 that focuses on continuing the current state of reciprocal Palestinian–Israeli calm and ending all forms of aggression, anywhere . . ."[64] The militant organizations did not agree to term the new period a *hudna* (truce), as they had done in the previous round of the Road Map, but insisted on the Arabic term *tahadyie,* meaning lull or calm. It was obvious by then that in reality, the "reciprocal Palestinian–Israeli calm" was a one-sided cessation of aggression, and that Israel's "reciprocity" would continue to exist in declaration only. Nevertheless, Abbas expressed hopes that by the end of 2005, he would be able to turn the *tahadyie* agreement into a real ceasefire. The document, however, also stated that "continued settlement, construction of the [wall] and the Judaization of East Jerusalem are issues liable to explode the calm."[65]

This agreement tied in with the participants' emphasis on the need to complete the process of democratization in Palestinian society. The document "recognized 'the need to continue reforms [of the PA] in every area' and expresses 'support for the Palestinian democratic process,' including both local elections and new elections for the Palestinian Legislative Council . . . The participants also agreed to set up a 'new PLO' [Palestinian Liberation Organization] by the end of the year, which would, for the first time, include the Islamic organizations (Hamas and Islamic Jihad)'' [66] – a significant step, given that the then PLO included only the secular factions. [67]

It is worth noting the general context in which this agreement was made. As far as Israeli society was concerned, there was at the time only one topic on the agenda – the disengagement plan, which had dominated the media and political life for about eighteen months, accompanied by stories about the sorrows and struggles of those to be evacuated. For the Palestinians, the prospect of the Gaza evacuations was heavily overshadowed by what Israel was doing at the same time in the West Bank, where the annexing of Palestinian land and the massive expansion of settlements constituted the harsh reality of everyday life. As Danny Rubinstein wrote at the time, ''as opposed to the sentiments in Israel (among supporters of the plan) that the withdrawal from Gaza is an important step toward the Palestinians and in the direction of resolving the conflict, many among the political leadership in the West Bank and Gaza Strip believe that the pullout only intensifies the conflict. To blame are the numerous reports on the expansion of the settlements in the West Bank and East Jerusalem. While discussions go ahead on the dismantling of less than 2,000 Jewish homes in the Gaza settlements, reports in the West Bank speak of preparations for the construction of 6,400 new housing units. In other words, Israel is planning to build in the West Bank more than three times the amount of homes it will be dismantling in Gaza.''[68] Nevertheless, against this setting of anger and frustration, the Palestinians resolved to work on turning their *intifada* into a political struggle.

Following this Palestinian declaration of an extended period of calm, nothing changed on the ground in the next four months.

Israel continued its military business as usual. According to a report of the Palestinian Ministry of Interior, in the period between 1 March and 30 June 2005, 46 Palestinians were killed and 462 injured. Additionally, the report said, 1,249 Palestinians were arrested in Israeli army raids during this period.[69] On the Palestinian side, the calm was largely maintained, with the exception of mortar attacks launched occasionally from Gaza in retaliation for Israeli violations, but at a rate incomparable to that before the period of calm.[70]

I have focused here on Israel's military operations against Palestinian militants, because the essence of a ceasefire is holding fire against enemy militants. As we have seen, Israel has refused to reciprocate ever since the Palestinian militant organizations started offering ceasefires in 2003. But the promise that Sharon made to the cameras in Sharm el-Sheikh was far more than just a ceasefire with the militants. "Israel will cease all its military activity against all Palestinians everywhere," he said. This must surely also mean ceasing military activity against Palestinian civilians. But nothing of the sort happened. Through this whole "period of calm," the Israel army continued uninterrupted its brutal routine of occupation.

Leaving aside "targeted" killings, the arbitrary killings of Palestinians has become part of the norm, background noise that is barely noticed by the Israeli or Western media — certainly not something that might affect Sharon's image as a "man of peace". One could attempt to classify these killings, find reasons, perhaps some underlying system as to why today this Palestinian man or woman was killed, and yesterday another Palestinian child. But these attempts are ultimately futile because, peace process or not, Israeli soldiers kill arbitrarily because they are part of a system which permits such things to happen. Rather than enumerating the killings of civilians that took place in the post-Arafat "period of calm," let me quote excerpts of what the *Guardian*'s Chris McGreal documented in this period:

It was the shooting of Asma Mughayar that swept away any lingering doubts I had about how it is the Israeli army kills so many Palestinian children and civilians.

Asma, 16, and her younger brother, Ahmad, were collecting laundry from the roof of their home in the south of the Gaza Strip in May [2004] when they were felled by an Israeli army sniper. Neither child was armed or threatening the soldier, who fired unseen through a hole punched in the wall of a neighbouring block of flats.

The army said the two were blown up by a Palestinian bomb planted to kill soldiers. The corpses offered a different account. In Rafah's morgue, Asma lay with a single bullet hole through her temple; her 13–year-old brother had a lone shot to his forehead. There were no other injuries, certainly none consistent with a blast.

Confronted with this, the army changed its account and claimed the pair were killed by a Palestinian, though there was persuasive evidence pointing to the Israeli sniper's nest. What the military did not do was ask its soldiers why they gave a false account of the deaths or speak to the children's parents or any other witnesses.

When reporters pressed the issue, the army promised a full investigation, but a few weeks later it was quietly dropped. This has become the norm in a military that appears to value protecting itself from accountability more than living up to its claim to be the "most moral army in the world" . . .

According to the Israeli human rights group B'Tselem, the army has killed 1,722 Palestinian civilians – more than one-third of them minors – as well as 1,519 combatants, since the intifada began nearly five years ago . . . The army has investigated just 90 Palestinian deaths, usually under outside pressure. Seven soldiers have been convicted: three for manslaughter, none for murder . . .

In southern Gaza, the killings take place in a climate that amounts to a form of terror against the population. Random fire into Rafah and Khan Yunis has claimed hundreds of lives, including five children shot as they sat at their school desks. Many others have died when the snipers must have known who was in their sights – children playing football, sitting outside home, walking back from school. Almost always "investigations" amount to asking the soldier who pulled the trigger what happened – often they claim there was a gun battle when there was none – and presenting it as fact.

The military police launched an investigation into the death of Iman al-Hams last October [2004] only after soldiers went public about the circumstances in which their commander emptied his gun into the 12-year-old. He was recorded telling his men that the girl should be killed even if she were three.[71]

Colonel Pinhas Zuaretz was commander in southern Gaza two years ago when I asked him about the scale of the killing. The colonel, who rewrote the rules of engagement to permit soldiers to shoot children as young as 14, acknowledged that official versions of several killings were wrong, but justified the tactics as the price of the struggle for survival against a second Holocaust.

Perhaps that view was shared by the soldier who shot dead three 15–year-old boys, Hassan Abu Zeid, Ashraf Mousa and Khaled Ghanem, as they approached the fortified border between Gaza and Egypt in April [2005]. The military said the teenagers were weapons smugglers and therefore "terrorists", and that the soldier shot them in the legs and only killed them when they failed to stop.

The account was a fabrication. The teenagers were in a "forbidden zone" but kicking a ball. Their corpses showed no evidence of wounds to disable them, only single high-calibre shots to the head or back. The army quietly admitted as much – but there would be no investigation.[72]

5

Summer 2005: The Gaza Pullout: The Role of International Pressure

1. What Did Sharon Have in Mind?

A S WE SAW IN CHAPTER 2, Sharon's disengagement plan was cooked up as a response to international pressure, as well as the expectations of Israeli voters. But the question remains as to whether Sharon was genuinely determined to implement it. As I wrote when the plan was introduced in 2004: "the catch is that in order to achieve Sharon's declared goals [of reducing international and internal pressure on Israel], one does not need to dismantle a single settlement. It is sufficient to declare intentions, and start a new process of negotiations. This is precisely what all Israeli governments have done successfully since 1993, and what Sharon has done for the last three years. All that is needed is to throw a pacifier at the majority and to convince them that this time Sharon really means it. This way, the majority will continue to sit silently another year or two, and let Sharon apply the Gaza model also in the West Bank."[1]

But if the disengagement plan were to prove yet another Israeli fraud, it would be of a different magnitude than previous plans, in which only vague, undefined commitments to the evacuation of settlements had been made; never before had there been a concrete date and – apparently – concrete preparations for evacuation, involving the entire political and military establishments. Although the political right, and particularly the settlers' leadership, had always furiously opposed even the most nebulous plans, never before had they been subjected to actual uncertainty about their future. If Sharon was indeed hoping to find a last-minute way of evading implementation of the plan, he kept such thoughts to himself, like in the most inconceivable conspiracy plots; so it is, in fact, hard to believe. Nevertheless, the possibility that Sharon was never fully committed to the plan's fulfilment cannot be dismissed; as we shall see, Sharon has a long history of not telling the truth. Although Sharon's real intentions will probably never come to light, there is a sequence of puzzling events regarding the eighteen-month "preparation period" between the plan's announcement in February 2004, and August 2005, when it was implemented.

The first of these puzzles concerns the question of compensation and relocation plans for the evacuees. After the Israeli cabinet approved the disengagement plan in June 2004, many of the Gaza settlers began inquiring how and when they might be compensated. Behind the noisy protests of their leaders, many settlers were exhausted by a life of constant fear and tension; they were relieved to be able finally to leave, and awaited the compensation that would enable them to rebuild their life elsewhere. Any serious plan to evacuate them would presumably start by compensating first those who expressed a willingness to leave of their own free will, leaving only the ideological minority to be forcibly evacuated. Indeed, for a five-month period after the cabinet's June 2004 ratification of the disengagement plan, both the settlers and the Israeli public believed that such compensation would be made at any moment – yet this did not happen. Special committees were established, and worked with much publicity on every detail of the compensation plan. However, they also explained that no actual compensation could be issued before the passing of a compensation law in the Israeli parliament – the Knesset. This law was passed on 4 November 2004 to a great media fanfare – but the media's small print explained that the law had only passed a preliminary first hearing. In principle, the second and third hearing could take place within a few weeks, but it was decided that the law's next stage would take place no earlier than February 2005.[2] The settlers willing to be evacuated hired lawyers, put direct pressure on the special parliamentary committee preparing the law's final draft, and managed eventually to push the law through parliament by mid-February 2005.

At this point, there appeared to be no barrier to the immediate compensation of settlers wanting to leave. In fact, nothing happened. This was not because the settlers were not ready and willing to leave. Shortly after the compensation law was passed, Yonatan Bassi, head of the Disengagement Administration, revealed that by that time "some 800 of the 1,700 families living in Gush Katif and northern Samaria have already expressed willingness in principle to leave their homes under the disengagement plan and negotiate over financial compensation . . . Of the remaining 900 families, he believed . . . [only] 300 families, the hard core of settlers opposed to the evacuation, would refuse to leave of their own accord."[3] Yet none of the 800 families who were willing to leave before the disengagement received even a portion of the compensation due them. A month and a half after the law was passed, "Sela, the government agency handling compensation, social assistance and resettlement – says they do not have the money yet . . . there is no committee to allocate the funds yet."[4]

By March 2005, it had become clear that no concrete plans had been put in place to prepare for the evacuation. The Israeli media widely documented the growing frustration of the Gaza Strip settlers, who felt that the government was leaving them in the dark concerning the disengagement. Itzick Ilia, the deputy mayor of the regional council of the Gaza Strip settlements, who claimed to represent between 70 and 80 per cent of the settlers who were willing to leave, reported a meeting where "people poured out their problems . . . People cried and shouted. No one talks to them."[5] As I observed at the time, the issue of the evacuees "is a real problem. The Gaza Strip settlers went there at the behest of the Israeli government. They must be compensated for this dreadful idiocy, to allow them to rebuild their lives. A government that really wanted to evacuate them would have already given them compensation, so they could leave before the evacuation. In the evacuation of Yamit, in 1982 [as part of the peace agreement with Egypt], the overwhelming majority of the residents were compensated and left before the evacuation. Those who were present in the confrontation on the scene were settler activists from the outside, with whom it is easier to deal than with families actually living there.''[6] But Sharon, who oversaw the Yamit evacuation, did not let the settlers leave this time. Lily Galili of *Ha'aretz* summed up the state of affairs four months before the planned evacuation: ''An estimated 600 new residents have moved into Gush Katif to reinforce the settlers in recent weeks, and none of the veteran residents has yet been able to move out. Contrary to the declared policy of encouraging early voluntary evacuation, the government is imprisoning the residents who want to leave in the region it has decided to evacuate.''[7]

Another related issue was the relocation of those evacuees who wanted to move en bloc, in order to preserve their communities. When the disengagement plan was unveiled in February 2004, National Security Advisor Major General Giora Eiland, who was appointed head of the disengagement steering committee, prepared with his team a detailed and comprehensive plan for a staged relocation. The first stage, to start immediately after the plan's announcement, involved the building of temporary caravan housing to absorb the evacuees while their permanent communities were being planned and built within the Green Line, Israel's pre-1967 border. The much-publicized assumption in Israel was that special large caravans (''caravillas'') were being manufactured for this purpose; these are relatively expensive, and take a long time to assemble in the required quantity. But in April 2005, it transpired that this was not being done: *Yediot Aharonot* reported that ''the Settlement

Department of the Jewish Agency, responsible for providing the 'caravillas' has so far received no order from the government".[8]

As the evacuation date drew near, it became evident that no infrastructure had been set up – even for temporary accommodation for the evacuees – and that there were in fact no real relocation plans in place. Rather, new ideas for their eventual relocation were floated every few weeks, and committees formed to check their feasibility. As *Ha'aretz* commentator Uzi Benziman wrote, "it is hard to find any person with authority in the Israeli government who knows for sure where the disengagement initiative is going. This historic move appears increasingly like a chain of improvisations rather than a calculated, well-considered outline that is being carried out judiciously. In contrast to the planning that the National Security Council invested into resettling the evacuees in existing communities within the Green Line, the prime minister suddenly drops an alternative proposal: to move them en bloc to the Nitzanim region."[9]

In June, as questions mounted over the significance of this lack of preparation, it was reported that "Prime Minister Ariel Sharon's bureau has grown increasingly concerned in recent days over the difficulty of conveying to the public that preparations for implementing the disengagement are progressing, and that all the settlers to be evacuated from the Gaza Strip and northern Samaria will be provided with suitable housing and schooling."[10] Sharon's response was to categorically deny the lack of preparation: "In an effort to prove that preparations were advancing apace, Sharon decided to open to the media the weekly meeting of the ministerial committee for disengagement affairs, which met at his Jerusalem bureau yesterday. This was an unusual step. The press . . . were allowed to remain and hear the surveys by ministers and officials."[11] Though Sharon hoped to show by this how advanced the preparations were, the meeting provided an opportunity to confirm what was already widely known: that two months before the planned evacuation, committees were still discussing the preparations, and still no settlers were able to leave the Gaza Strip. While the construction of temporary caravan accommodation was accelerated at the time, there was no way the required amount could be completed by the specified disengagement date.

And so, by the time the evacuation took place, the Gaza settlers had still not received compensation, and the majority was placed in hotel rooms and rented apartments. On the eve of the evacuation, *Yediot Aharonot* confirmed that almost no steps had been taken to prepare for the absorption of the evacuees in Israel. This, the newspaper revealed, was not just lax administration: rather, it was Sharon himself who had stalled the preparations. According to the article, from the very beginning, back in 2004, "the Prime Minister rebuffed the recommendation of Eiland [head of the disengagement steering committee] and decided that the government will not build temporary housing".[12] Thus, while the relevant evacuation bodies like the disengagement committee were doing necessary and serious work, Sharon was busy stalling any concrete implementation of their plans.

There may be various ways to explain Sharon's strange conduct, but the most natural one would be that, without sharing his thoughts with the public or even the government, he hoped to find a way to cancel the whole disengagement plan – or at least postpone it indefinitely. As Amir Oren concluded when the evacuation date was moved from 25 July to 15 August: "behind the sudden wrapping in the *tallit*[13] . . . there lurks a stubborn suspicion that the government of Ariel Sharon . . . is maneuvering to turn the evacuation into a horizon – always there, approached but never quite reached. The longer the execution of the evacuation is delayed, the intensity of the vow in its name will increase. It won't be canceled, just its timing will go through occasional updating, from time to time, as required by developments on the ground . . . Sharon cannot cancel the evacuation, lest he ignite George Bush's rage. But nor can he actually go through with it. That's the perfect situation as far as he is concerned: an eternal limbo, an evacuation that neither lives nor dies.''[14]

Another curious issue that received almost no attention was that in practice there was no formal approval of the evacuation of the Gaza settlements by the Israeli government until the very last minute. On 6 June 2004, four months after the disengagement plan was announced, it was the subject of a stormy debate in the Israeli cabinet, following which Israeli and international media headlines announced a historical resolution. *Ha'aretz*'s front-page ceremonial headlines declared ''Disengagement on its way''. But the body of the report read somewhat differently:

> At the end of a dramatic cabinet meeting yesterday, the government passed Ariel Sharon's revised disengagement plan, by a vote of 14–7, but the decision does not allow for the dismantling of settlements and the prime minister will have to go back to the cabinet when he actually wants to begin the evacuation process . . . The decision on the evacuation of settlements will be brought to the government at the end of a preparation period . . . [that] would end next March 1 [2005].[15]

In the same issue, *Ha'aretz* reported that ''there was no approval of actual evacuations . . . A second government discussion would be held in this regard, 'taking into account the circumstances at the time'.''[16] The only thing the Israeli government approved, then, was to have a discussion about the idea of dismantling Gaza settlements eight months later.[17] The cabinet also decided in its 6 June meeting that building and development in the Gaza settlements would continue in the meantime: ''The approved plan ensures 'support for the needs of daily life' in settlements slated for evacuation. Bans on construction permits and leasing of lands were also removed from the prime minister's proposal.''[18] And indeed, new building permits in the Gaza settlements were later granted by a special committee appointed by the government in the same "dra-matic" meeting on 6 June.[19]

Four months after the June cabinet meeting, on 26 October 2004, the Knesset also approved the disengagement plan, following another heated debate. The headlines were again hyperbolic, some comparing Sharon to Churchill. The fact that the Knesset only voted to approve the cabinet's previous resolution, which did not include any concrete decision to dismantle the settlements, was noted in the Israeli media, but mention of it was buried deep inside the euphoric reports:

> Knesset members voting tonight on the disengagement plan have received a copy of the "amended disengagement law" the cabinet passed on June 6, plus appendices containing the principles of the plan and its implementation . . . According to the compromise negotiated at the time . . . the cabinet decision 'contains nothing to evacuate settlements.' To remove any doubt in this regard, the cabinet decision also states that 'after the conclusion of preparatory work, the cabinet will reconvene to separately debate and decide whether or not to evacuate settlements, which settlements, and at what speed, in consideration of circumstances at that time'.[20]

So the Knesset had not in fact passed any resolution to dismantle settlements, but only expressed its approval that the cabinet should return to discussion of this option in the future.

As the scheduled date for the cabinet's final decision on whether to evacuate the settlements approached, the Labor party had joined the government, citing its support of the evacuation plan as its rationale for siding with Sharon's coalition. Sharon therefore had an overwhelming cabinet majority for the disengagement; there could be no possible obstacle to the evacuation's approval in a formal, committed resolution. The special cabinet meeting took place amid much publicity, on 20 February 2005. The headlines again announced that the final decision on evacuation had taken place. Yet again, however, they did not reflect the actual wording of the cabinet's resolution, which was run by *Ha'aretz* as a "preview" on the day of the government's decision: "The decision on evacuation will state that, before the actual withdrawal from the settlements – which have been divided for this purpose into four groups – the cabinet will reconvene to 'discuss, examine and decide' whether at the time of implementation there are circumstances that 'could affect the evacuation'."[21] The actual text of the resolution appeared the next day in *Ha'aretz*'s online Hebrew edition, with precisely this content, repeated four times for each group of settlements. In other words, Sharon managed to pass a resolution that still left open the possibility that there might be "circumstances that can affect the evacuation".

However, the actual content of the cabinet's decision went completely unnoted – because Sharon, a master of mass manipulation, took care to hide it. To enhance the effect of a "historical" decision having been taken, at the end of the cabinet meeting Sharon and Defense Minister Shaul Mofaz signed a televised "evacuation order". In the blaze of publicity, who would notice that this order would take effect only after the approval of actual evacuation – which itself had not yet taken place? The fact remains that, six months before the planned evacuation, Sharon was still leaving scope for it not to happen at all.

At the same "historic" cabinet meeting, the Sharon–Labor government also voted to approve the continuation of the West Bank wall's construction, extending it to Ma'ale Adumim, east of Jerusalem. Ma'ale Adumim lies deep in the West Bank, reaching close to the Jordan Valley. The decision to include it on the Israeli side of the wall meant approving its future annexation to Israel. But this did not deter the Israeli media, which competed to find the right superlatives for Sharon's visionary and sweeping concessions. Some compared Sharon to de Gaulle, others to Gorbachev. Here is, for example, Aluf Benn's psalm: "Ariel Sharon's government made history yesterday with its decision on the evacuation of the settlements from the Gaza Strip and northern West Bank . . . The fence route approved by the cabinet marks the change in Israel's war goals vis-a-vis the Palestinians – from one of guarding every centimeter until the enemy gives in, to a rearguard battle to save the blocs of settlements, to annex Ma'ale Adumim, Ariel and Efrat."[22]

Compared to the efficiency with which Sharon executed his West Bank "security fence" project, and his expansion of settlements during the eighteen months since the announcement of his February 2004 disengagement plan, the preparations for the Gaza settlement evacuation were highly incompetent. During the whole period, and particularly as the planned date for evacuation drew near, Sharon and the army's chief of staff, Dan Halutz, repeatedly declared that "there would be no disengagement under fire". But at the same time, as we have seen, Sharon and the army did nothing to encourage calm on the Palestinian side.[23] As we shall see, towards the summer of 2005, the Israeli army was even attempting to provoke Palestinian aggression, and brought a halt to cooperation with the Palestinian Authority on the evacuation's coordination. It is hard to avoid the conclusion that Sharon entertained the possibility that at the last minute the evacuation would be cancelled or indefinitely "postponed".

2. The US Changes its Tune

If Sharon hoped he could eventually succeed in reversing the disengagement process, he certainly had some basis for that hope, based on his past experience with the White House. In the previous round of talks, when confronted with the Bush administration's Road Map, he committed himself to a ceasefire, during which Israel was to freeze settlement construction, remove outposts, and revert to the status quo of pre-September 2000. As we have seen in Chapter 1, none of this was carried out. Sharon and the army claimed that Mahmoud Abbas, who had been prime minister in April 2003, was not trustworthy and had failed to rein in Hamas. The army continued its assassination policy and succeeded in bringing the occupied territories to boiling point, followed by the inevitable Palestinian terror attacks that shattered the ceasefire.

Throughout all this, as we have seen, the first-term Bush administration stood by Sharon's side and dutifully echoed all his complaints against Mahmoud Abbas, even expressing support of Israel's liquidation policy, in violation of the ceasefire, which it referred to as "Israel's right to defend itself". The US looked the other way even when Sharon avoided fulfilling the most straightforward commitment of the Road Map: dismantling the illegal outposts that were erected in the West Bank after September 2000. It was obvious that the collapse of the ceasefire would deal a fatal blow to Mahmoud Abbas's new cabinet.[24] But Sharon had no interest in seeing the cabinet survive. He feared that a process of stabilization and democratization in Palestinian society could increase pressure on Israel to fulfil its Road Map commitments.

With the death of Arafat in November 2004 and Palestinian society gearing up for election, this threat, from Sharon's perspective, was increasing. For three years, he had been able to rely on the argument established during Prime Minister Ehud Barak's administration: Israel was ready to make big concessions, but could not find a suitable Palestinian "partner for peace". The only reason why Israel needs to maintain its occupation of the Palestinian territories, so this story goes, is to defend its citizens against Palestinian terror. A democratic Palestinian society that fights terror and declares its will to live as an independent state side by side with Israel, would therefore undermine this argument for occupation, and would require evacuating the territories, and dismantling the West Bank settlements and wall. Sharon did his best to avoid this scenario. As we have seen, from the moment that Abbas was elected president in January 2005, Sharon used the same strategy as he did in the previous round of negotiations, with Israeli sources expressing deep dissatisfaction with Abbas's attempts to broker a ceasefire rather than tackling the militant organizations head-on. As he had done before, Sharon made substantial efforts to convey to the US the message that, despite Israel's profound commitment to Palestinian democratization and a process of calm, the process was not working and should therefore be brought to a halt.

Sharon's attempts to discredit Abbas reached a peak during his White House visit in mid-April 2005. As reported in *Ha'aretz*, "the main question discussed during the visit was what to do with the head of the Palestinian Authority, Mahmoud Abbas'.[25] Sharon's visit was carefully prepared. In Chapter 4, I quoted Chris McGreal's report of the shooting of three fifteen-year-old boys near the Philadelphi Route on Gaza's Egyptian border. From the perspective of the Israeli policymakers, this shooting was perhaps less arbitrary than it seemed. The boys were shot on 9 April, just as Sharon was making his way to the meeting with Bush. As might be expected, the unprovoked killings of the boys managed to shatter the calm, and various Palestinian factions retaliated with heavy mortar and rocket fire towards the Gaza settlement of Gush Katif.

The timing of the Palestinian shelling was perfect for Sharon's message to Bush. The media in both Israel and the US devoted considerable space to analysis of this new wave of Palestinian aggression, in violation of the ceasefire that Israel had been trying so hard to maintain. In Israel, Likud Knesset Member Yuval Steinitz, chair of the Knesset Foreign Affairs and Defense Committee, "demanded immediate Israeli military actions in the Gaza Strip, specifically calling for Operation Defensive Shield II there, 'to put an end to the fake cease-fire' ".[26] Sharon meanwhile could appear as a "moderate" voice: "The Israeli response to the heaviest bombardment by Palestinians on the settlements since the end of January is . . . a combination of gritting teeth and stepping up the complaints about Palestinian Authority President Mahmoud Abbas.'[27] As Defense Minister Shaul Mofaz was calling Abbas "to impress upon him the need to crack down on the armed groups in Gaza," it was reported that "Prime Minister Ariel Sharon will be emphasizing to U.S. President George W. Bush and other administration officials this week that Palestinian leader Mahmoud Abbas' control over the Palestinian Authority's territories is collapsing."[28]

Indeed, Sharon did his best to deliver this message in his meeting with Bush, as Aluf Benn of *Ha'aretz* reported:

> Sharon brought harsh messages from home, describing the Palestinian leader as worthless, a disappointment, a man with good intentions whose actions are strengthening the terrorist organizations. His security services are rotten, Arafatian and dysfunctional . . . The impression received from the briefings of Sharon and his men was that once again there is nobody to talk to. That Arafat's successor is having difficulty functioning. That the thing we feared most has happened: Sharon warned Abbas at the Sharm el-Sheikh summit that the attempt to embrace the terrorist organizations would turn out to be a mistake, and he ignored the warning.[29]

But what Sharon failed to predict (as would anyone else at the time) was that the second Bush administration, the most hawkish and neoconservative administration the US has ever had, may suddenly change direction. In reality, the newly elected administration insisted firmly that, this time, Abbas must be given a chance. As Benn continues, Sharon's well-rehearsed strategy of discrediting all Palestinian leaders failed to work on this occasion:

> Bush refuses to give up on Abu Mazen, his Great White Hope for the establishment of an independent and democratic Palestine. He made it clear to Sharon that Israel must do

everything possible to help him, so it won't look as if Israel has once again caused his downfall. On the Israeli side they are saying that the Americans have changed their attitude since the failed attempt to appoint Abbas as the Palestinian prime minister in 2003 . . . This time they understand that he has severe internal difficulties, that Palestinian politics are falling apart, that the security heads don't obey him. But they expect to hear from the Israelis what they will do to rescue him.[30]

Sharon made further attempts to change the White House's stance. On the eve of Abbas's visit to Washington, on 25 May, Sharon's advisors Dov Weisglass and Shalom Turjiman, together with Israeli ambassador Danny Ayalon, held a meeting with Condoleezza Rice on this topic. Again, however, the meeting did not yield the results they had hoped for. *Ha'aretz* reported that "the Israeli message to the Americans as delivered by Weisglass, Turjiman and Ayalon in their meeting with Rice, is that Abbas is weak and unable to act against the terrorist organizations, which have turned into a 'parallel authority' in the territories. Rice made clear at the meeting that the US would stick to its support for Abbas, asked Israel to continue humanitarian gestures toward the Palestinians and emphasized the need for . . . Israel to fulfill its commitments made at Sharm el Sheikh."[31] It was further reported that "the Bush administration will not be demanding that the Palestinian Authority disarm the armed groups in the territories, including Hamas, at least until after the Palestinian elections later this year," despite the fact that "for months, Israel has been saying that there can be no diplomatic progress until the Palestinians 'dismantle the terrorist infrastructure'".[32] Compared to the Bush administration's first-term stance, this represented a significant change in policy.

Another bone of contention between Israel and the second-term Bush administration revolved around the Palestinian legislative elections. This disagreement surfaced around the time of the

February 2005 Sharm el-Sheikh summit and reached its peak after the Gaza pullout, as the elections drew near. As we saw in Chapter 4, Hamas declared its intention to participate in the elections and to shift its focus from armed to political resistance. One would think that this should be viewed as an encouraging and positive development after years of bloodshed. But Sharon and his administration viewed this instead as a massive threat: right from the start, they called for the elections to be cancelled should Hamas participate. The elections were first scheduled for 17 July 2005, but in May Abbas announced that they would be postponed to a later date, which was eventually set as 25 January 2006. As "a senior source in the Prime Minister's Bureau" explained, "Abbas" postponement of the elections . . . was related, among other things, to Israel's reservations about the participation of 'a racist party that calls for the annihilation of the Jews'."[33] Subsequently, the Israeli political system massed its forces behind Sharon to convince both Europe and the US that the January elections should not take place because of Hamas' planned participation. Justice Minister Tzipi Livni told UK Foreign Secretary Jack Straw that "banning Hamas is the act of a 'defensive democracy',"[34] while the then finance minister, Ehud Olmert, exclaimed that "Israel opposes the participation of any terrorist organisations such as Hamas in the Palestinian election".[35] By October 2005, it was reported that "the fight against Hamas" participation in the elections now tops Israel's agenda in its international relations. The Foreign Ministry has reportedly instructed all its representatives abroad to make it clear to foreign governments that Jerusalem is opposed to Hamas' playing a part in the Palestinian political process. In recent talks with foreign statesmen, both Prime Minister Ariel Sharon and Foreign Minister Silvan Shalom have said that Israel will . . . obstruct the ballot if the movement plays a part in the election.'[36]

Why were Sharon and his administration so determined to cancel the elections? One explanation is that Israel was worried about Hamas gaining political power in the coming elections, thereby shifting Palestinian society to a more extreme position.

(At the time no one predicted Hamas's victory, which was not even foreseen in the Palestinian polls and analysis.) However, if this was a concern at the time, there was an obvious solution: strengthen Abbas, so that he could offer genuine evidence of progress to his people, who were growing increasingly disappointed with the lack of results gained by his diplomacy. Palestinian society has been traditionally largely secular. It was only despair of the secular leadership that could lead a majority towards Hamas. But, as we have seen, instead of strengthening the secular leadership, Sharon did everything to weaken Abbas, hinting even that it may be time to replace him.

I would contend that the real motive behind Sharon's campaign against Hamas's participation in the elections was that he was in fact trying to stall the whole electoral process. In Sharon's eyes, his biggest "achievement" was that from 2002 onwards he had succeeded in completely destroying the Palestinian social and political infrastructure that had gradually developed over the years since the 1993 Oslo Accords. Though Palestinian society was far from democratic during these years, there was at least a functioning system of local governance, with many thriving semi-independent institutions. All this was erased in the massive military "Operation Defensive Shield" in April 2002, which completed the process of re-establishing direct military rule in the West Bank.[37] Now, a new process of democratization and elections was threatening to undo this major "achievement". Not only would the Palestinian political system revive, but this time it would also have the legitimacy of real elections, with a leadership recognized internationally as being representative of the Palestinian people. Sharon did everything he could to prevent this scenario, constantly insisting that Abbas should disarm Hamas before the elections. His "senior government sources" hastened to explain that this effectively meant that "Abbas would have to call off the elections to prevent a head-on clash with Hamas".[38] If Abbas did not do so, Sharon threatened, he would have to disrupt the elections.[39]

While the Europeans hesitated to throw their weight behind the Palestinians, the US administration, which had generally adopted the most extreme positions against Muslim organizations that it views as supporting terror, insisted on the elections taking place as scheduled – with Hamas's participation. In Israel, it was reported that "senior U.S. officials have told their Israeli counterparts that opposition to the Palestinian elections is flawed both in principle and for practical reasons. The U.S. administration does not want the elections disrupted, noting such a move could be damaging, and lead to a further rise in Hamas" strength."[40] The US objected to Sharon's demand that Hamas be dismantled before the elections, and insisted that Sharon back Abbas: "Contrary to the Israeli stance, the U.S. administration has accepted the position of Palestinian Authority Chairman Mahmoud Abbas (Abu Mazen) that the right time to confront Hamas and its disarmament is after the Palestinian elections in January [2006]. The U.S. believes Abu Mazen should first be allowed to deal with the chaos in the PA and the Fatah before the elections and not begin a forceful confrontation with Hamas now. Washington believes it is of paramount importance that Abu Mazen be in a strong position before the elections, and to this end is putting pressure on Israel to make concrete concessions to the Palestinian population to assist him."[41]

Israel continued a cat-and-mouse game with the US administration on this issue right up until election day. In November 2005, there was reportedly a change in Israel's stance, which apparently yielded to US pressure: "Defense Minister Shaul Mofaz tells U.S. Secretary of State Condoleezza Rice Israel would not interfere with Palestinian elections even if Hamas participates, backing off earlier threats, made by Prime Minister Ariel Sharon."[42] Nevertheless, until his last day in office, Sharon continued his efforts to cancel the elections. In December 2005, Israel declared it would not allow elections in East Jerusalem, which led Abbas to announce that he would re-examine whether the elections could take place at all. Yet the US remained steadfast on this issue, the White House announcing on 3 January that "U.S. President George W. Bush 'wants Palestinian elections to go forward as scheduled'," and that Israel should not bar Palestinians from voting in East Jerusalem. The White House stressed that "people must have access to the ballot . . . Arrangements have been made in the past to ensure that those persons can vote, and we believe some arrangements should be possible at this time."[43] Subsequently, the US administration continued to exert solid pressure on Sharon's successors to allow elections in East Jerusalem, and facilitate the Palestinian elections.

There was, then, a visible change of tune in the second-term Bush administration. What had brought this about?

At the time of the US elections in November 2004, and increasingly throughout 2005, it became evident that the military "victory" in Iraq had been anything but, with Sunni armed resistance growing faster than predicted. At home, support for Bush had diminished to under 40 per cent, while his international standing was also sinking fast. In the fall of 2004, an internal report by the Pentagon-appointed Defense Science Board stated that in "the war of ideas or the struggle for hearts and minds, American efforts have not only failed, they may also have achieved the opposite of what they intended. American direct intervention in the Muslim world has paradoxically elevated the stature of, and support for, radical Islamists, while diminishing support for the United States to single digits in some Arab societies". Furthermore, it continued, "the war has increased mistrust of America in Europe . . . [it] weakened support for the war on terrorism and undermined US credibility worldwide".[44] This report was soon to be confirmed by an extensive worldwide BBC poll that found that "58 percent of those surveyed across 21 countries thought the re-election of George W. Bush had made the world less safe". Among the traditional European allies of the US, the results were 77 per cent in Germany, 75 per cent in France and 64 per cent in Britain.[45]

Along with Iraq, at the heart of this global discontent lay the question of Palestine: in the eyes of the world, the situations in both countries have become inextricably linked, and after each world terrorist attack, one heard the paired words, Iraq and Palestine. Referring to repeated statements from the White House that those who oppose the US in the Middle East "hate our freedoms," the Pentagon report says: "Muslims do not 'hate our freedoms', but rather, they hate our policies. The overwhelming majority voice their objections to what they see as one-sided support in favor of Israel and against Palestinian rights."[46] This sentiment, it turns out, is not only dominant in the Muslim world. In a poll conducted by the European Commission in October 2003, Israel came top of a list of countries considered a "threat to world peace" by citizens of the European Union. Israel is considered a threat by 59 per cent of those polled. The United States, Iran, and North Korea, come only second on this list, each considered a threat by 53 per cent of the EU population. (In the Netherlands, one of Israel's most devoted allies in Europe, the results were around 70 per cent.)[47]

The Pentagon report did not recommend any change of policy facing this failure in the "struggle over hearts and minds", but rather the allocation of greater resources to "strategic communication" and "psychological operations" to boost the US image.[48] However, it is not obvious that "psychological operations" alone can change the views of the silent majorities, which is hardly heard anyway in mainstream media. This is particularly dubious in the case of European public opinion on Israel. There is hardly any other country in the world so efficient in the allocation of efforts and budget to propaganda as Israel. An organized network of devoted pro-Israel lobbyists, as active in Europe as in the US, bombard the media with protest and threats whenever a critical word on Israel is mentioned, persecute individuals who dare expose their opinion on the brutality of the occupiers, or take them to court. (A French court has found the editor-in-chief of *Le Monde* and the authors of an opinion piece in the paper guilty of "racial defamation" against Israel and the Jewish people.[49]) This pressure has proved successful in silencing European intellectuals, leaders and media. One can find much more open criticism of US policies in the European media than that of Israel, and hardly any information on the daily horrors of Israel's oppression of the Palestinians. Still, with all this successful propaganda effort, the majority of people in Europe view Israel as the country most threatening to world peace, and in other – smaller-range – surveys, "British, Italian, French and German respondents said they sympathized more with the Palestinians than Israelis".[50] It is not obvious for how long the US's European allies can continue to go against the sentiments of their people.

Bush certainly had no intentions of changing his global policy. In January 2005 Seymour Hersh reported that since the November 2004 US election "the President and his national security advisors have consolidated control over the military and intelligence communities" strategic analyses and covert operations to a degree unmatched since the rise of the post-Second World War national-security state'. "Iraq is just one campaign," a "former high-level intelligence official" told Hersh, "Next, we're going to have the Iranian campaign. We've declared war and the bad guys, wherever they are, are the enemy. This is the last hurrah – we've got four years, and want to come out of this saying we won the war on terrorism."[51]

But what Bush could afford to do to ease world pressure (conveyed to him repeatedly by British Prime Minister Tony Blair) was to improve the US image on the Israel/Palestine question. No longer running for election, one factor lost its relevance: Bush no longer needed to be cautious about the vote of the Jewish and religious right whose leaders had sided vocally with Sharon. Bush declared that he would put more emphasis on diplomatic efforts, to be led by the new secretary of state, Condoleezza Rice. During her previous involvement in the Middle East as national security advisor in the first Bush administration, Rice relied heavily on a group of advisers led by Elliot Abrams, whose strong pro-Israel tendencies we have already examined. In the second Bush administration, Abrams did not lose his influence on Israeli affairs – he was promoted to deputy national security advisor, but he was no longer such a dominant figure in Rice's team. In her new position, Rice appointed as her own assistant David Welch, a former US ambassador to Egypt. A special security envoy was also appointed: Lieutenant General William Ward, former commander of the Nato stabilization force in Bosnia and Herzegovina. Later, Rice's team was reinforced by the Quartet's economic envoy, James Wolfensohn, formerly president of the World Bank. Overall, this new team was not directly dominated by pro-Israel neoconserva tives, as the previous team had been during Bush's first term, and it showed much greater involvement in monitoring the Israel/Palestine situation. Personally, I was unimpressed when these changes took place, and remained sceptical about the prospects of any US pressure on Israel, but it did become gradually clear that the US stance had temporarily altered somewhat; later, as we shall see, this resulted in concrete pressure on Sharon to implement the disengagement plan.

During Bush's first term, there was general agreement in Israel that there had never been a US president friendlier towards Israel than George W. Bush. Presumably no one in Israel thought that a love of Jews on the part of the evangelical Bush was behind this support. But there was a feeling that Israel's superior army and air force was a huge asset in the Middle East arena of Bush's global "war on terror". With the euphoria of the power that was felt in Israel at the time, it seemed as if Afghanistan and Iraq were already "in our hands," and that Israel and the US would then proceed together towards Iran and maybe even Syria. There was, for example, ample talk in the Israeli media about plans for an Israeli attack on Iran and, more than once, international media reported "leaks" regarding concrete preparations.[52] In early 2005, Israel security circles still viewed themselves as active partners to the US, not only in a future war on Iran, but also in shaping US policy on that front. As Amir Oren reported in February 2005:

Two or three Israelis who are close to the defense establishment waited tensely last week for U.S. President George Bush's State of the Union address. What they were most interested in hearing about was the state of Iran in the eyes of the administration. Ahead of the speech, Iran experts in Israel persuaded Bush's aides – notably Elliot Abrams . . . who has been promoted to deputy national security adviser – to include in the president's remarks a call to the Iranian nation to rise up against the rule of the ayatollahs. The text was more moderate than that, but there was no mistaking its import: Bush invited the opponents of Ali Khamenei, the supreme religious leader and successor to Ayatollah Khomeini, to topple the regime and thus spare Iran an American operation against its nuclear facilities.

If [Bush's message] trickles down – and experts in Tel Aviv are willing to bet that within a year or two, the ferment in Iran will reach the boiling point – it will represent the success of the interim channel recommended by Abrams' Israeli interlocutors . . . a popular, quasi-Ukrainian movement that will spring up in Tehran, in Kom and in Isfahan and will win over the army and the Revolutionary Guards until it vanquishes Khamenei. A development of this kind would confront Bush with tough decisions, should Khamenei try to suppress the uprising with violence and should the insurgents cry out to Washington for help . . . Bush's readiness to risk this shows that the most consistent thrust of his foreign policy is toward bringing about internal upheavals in target countries. This can be seen in the invasion of Afghanistan to liberate that country from the Taliban . . . in the assault on Saddam Hussein and his regime [and] in the activity against Khamenei[.][53]

Iran was also on the agenda in Sharon's visit to the US in April 2005: "The Iranian issue was the main point of Monday's discussion during the lunch Bush served at his ranch to Sharon and the Israeli officials who accompanied him. The premier's military secretary, Maj[or] Gen[eral] Yoav Gallant, delivered a presentation with an analysis of the latest satellite imagery taken above Iran's nuclear development facilities, explaining how those facilities have expanded since 2002."[54] It was frequently reported in the Israeli media that Israeli officials constantly attempt to convince the US administration that the nuclear danger posed by Iran is far more immediate than the US estimates: "When will Iran reach the point of no return in its effort to acquire nuclear weapons? Israeli and American statesmen and intelligence officials provide contradictory answers to the question, with the Israelis saying it is a matter of a few months, while the Americans say it is a matter of a few years."[55]

But on this front, too, things were not going precisely as Israel would have wanted. After the war with Iraq, Iran was ready for any terms of surrender; by now, however, it was drawing fresh encouragement from its ties with the pro-Iranian Shia militias in Iraq on which the US was becoming increasingly dependent. At the same time, oil agreements with China gave a boost to the Iranian economy. Suddenly the possibility of an attack on Iran didn't seem as certain. As David Hirst observed, "to America's growing exasperation, Iran has two 'colonial' situations to exploit at its expense: the old one in Palestine, and the new, better one in Iraq; and it makes it clear that, if it is targeted by Bush-era pre-emptive force, it will exploit them to the hilt."[56] It appeared that developing the "Iranian campaign" would have to take longer than originally thought, and would require a slow and patient soliciting of European and other support, for which addressing the "Palestinian problem" was essential. For the time being at least, Bush had no choice but to pursue the diplomatic route through the United Nations on the issue of Iran's disarmament, a situation that Israel had to accept. In the months to come, Bush would be described in Israeli circles as one of the most difficult presidents with whom Israel has ever had to deal.[57]

The agenda of the new Condoleezza Rice team was restricted. It focused on two goals. The first, which Rice viewed as the most important, was to make sure that Sharon would indeed pull out of Gaza by the fixed deadline of the summer 2005. Next, during the interim period leading up to the evacuation, Rice insisted on keeping Abbas afloat, allowing the Palestinian election – including Hamas's participation – to go ahead, and forbidding any substantial Israeli military operations inside the territories. The US emphasis on the Gaza disengagement as "the only game in town" had a heavy cost for the West Bank Palestinians. Throughout this period Sharon, given a "relatively free hand" by the US, continued undisturbed his massive expansion of the settlements, the dispossession of Palestinians along the route of the wall and construction of the road system that split up the West Bank into cantons.[58] Nevertheless, enforcing even these restricted aims was no small task, given Sharon's history.

Israel had long been accustomed to pulling the wool over the eyes of its giant American protector,[59] but the mastermind of Israeli deception was Sharon, who at the time of the Lebanon war succeeded in concealing his plan even from Israel's then prime minister, Menachem Begin. As Robert Fisk observed, "Sharon's ability to scorn the Americans was always humiliating for Washington". Here is one of the incidents Fisk cites: "Before the massacres of 1982 [in the Palestinian refugee camps Sabra and Shatila in Lebanon], Philip Habib was President Reagan's special representative, his envoy to Beirut increasingly horrified by the ferocity of Sharon's assault on the city. Not long before he died, I asked Habib why he didn't stop the bloodshed. 'I could see it,' he said. 'I told the Israelis they were destroying the city, that they were firing non-stop. They just said they weren't. They said they weren't doing that. I called Sharon on the phone. He said it wasn't true. That damned man said to me on the phone that what I saw happening wasn't happening. So I held the telephone out of the window so he could hear the explosions. Then he said to me: "What kind of conversation is this where you hold a telephone out of a window?'"[60]

Returning to more recent history, one of the sole points that the US administration seemed to insist on already during Bush's first term was the dismantling of the settlement outposts that had been constructed since Sharon took power in March 2001. This demand was first made at the end of 2002[61] and reiterated in the Road Map, which as we have seen required the immediate dismantling of these outposts.[62] This is an easy task given that most of them simply consist of a caravan or two and a few settlers, protected by an army post.[63] Sharon promised the US that he would adhere to this commitment, something he reconfirmed in June 2003, following the Aqaba summit. But for Sharon, these outposts were part of his long-standing strategy of expanding existing settlements by first securing the hills around them. The outposts have been useful for him in bypassing whatever limited restrictions Israeli law has put on the theft of Palestinian land. Usually, the lands appropriated should become first "state land," a process involving some compensation to the previous owners. But in a report commissioned by Sharon himself (to show he was acting on the matter) and released in March 2005, Attorney Talia Sasson found out that "many of the outposts built in the territories since March 2001 were established on lands that are not state-owned: 15 are on private Palestinian land, and 46 on lands of unknown ownership."[64]

So Sharon reneged on his commitments. Every few months, when the Bush administration pressed him on them, he would enact a ritual covered by international media, in which a few of these outposts were presumably evacuated by the army, only for them to be reconstructed the following week. For Sharon, promises and commitments were just necessary means to play for time. By August 2004, *Ha'aretz* reported that a senior American source described the feeling in the administration as 'frustration and bitterness' from Sharon's failure to evacuate the illegal outposts or freeze the construction in the settlements, as he had promised . . . Administration sources say that for 18 months Sharon's promises are not being kept and this is harming his credibility and status in Washington.[65]

The source even added that "when President Bush is elected for a second term he will no longer treat Sharon as he did the first term if the promises are not kept".[66] Sharon responded with a new promise, delivered through Elliot Abrams, saying: "I am steadfast in my promise on the issue of the outposts . . . It's true that the pace of evacuation until now is not alright, but I hope that we will move the issue forward quickly."[67] Despite these renewed commitments, Sharon continued to ignore warnings from the US, not only permitting the outposts to stay, but allowing their growth and expansion. This is how the situation remained until Sharon's departure from politics in January 2006.[68]

It was not only Sharon that viewed public commitments as nothing more than a means to gain time. Over the years, the military system has acquired enormous power in Israel, and has reached considerable levels of sophistication in dealing directly with both US security and political echelons, feeding them with fabricated security information, and evading commitments under the pretext of "security needs".[69] As Middle East Security Coordinator General Ward would put it later, it was necessary that "the Israeli leadership, including the military" internalize what the US expects this time.[70] To ensure that Sharon and the army carried out the commitments on which the Bush administration had chosen to focus – specifically, the Gaza pullout – some measures of coercion were needed, beyond simply repeating the White House's expectations. Procedures that might result in open conflict with Israel, such as freezing US aid to Israel, would be hard to pass in Congress, and would be inconsistent with the overall US Middle East policy, in which Israel remains a reliable and necessary ally. Instead, massive pressure was applied by the US behind the scenes, combined with public praise that consolidated Sharon's image as a brave leader of peace, courageously seeing through his tough resolutions.

3. Sanctions Work: The Gaza Pullout

Many in the world believe that the only way to force Israel to end the occupation is to bring sanctions against it, as done in other cases of states seen as threatening world peace. The US would of course never allow this, and even the idea of imposing military sanctions on Israel is perceived as nothing more than a radical fantasy of campus movements in the US, calling on their universities to divest from companies doing military business with Israel. But something that has attracted very little attention is that in order to bring about the Gaza pullout, the US did in fact impose drastic military sanctions on Israel. This has gone unnoticed because the sanctions were apparently unrelated to the issue of Israel's maintenance of its commitments on the Palestinian front.

From early 2005, Israel found itself entangled in two serious conflicts with the US administration, which on the face of it seemed to have nothing to do with each other, or with the issue of the disengagement. Both were already beginning to surface before the US elections in August 2004, when the first leaks regarding Bush's administration dissatisfaction with Sharon were disclosed. The well-briefed *Ha'aretz* analyst Ze'ev Schiff attributed the initiative for at least one of these conflicts to the CIA, explaining that

> the timing of the affair's exposure is connected with the U.S. election campaign and the struggle against the group of neoconservatives in the administration, who are accused of leading President Bush to war with Iraq . . . Israel has noticed that relations between the CIA and the Mossad

had begun to cool . . . Israeli sources knowledgeable about the CIA say that unlike other American intelligence organizations, the CIA has political differences of opinion with Israel about the Arab–Israeli conflict. The CIA sees Israel as disruptive in American efforts to improve its relations with the Arabs.[71]

Nevertheless, both issues were further pursued by the second Bush administration and developed into open conflict as the disengagement date grew nearer, in mid-2005.

The first crisis started in August 2004 when a Pentagon analyst and two officials of the American Israel Public Affairs Committee (AIPAC) were investigated and later indicted on charges of transferring classified information to an Israeli representative. The FBI announced that a top Pentagon analyst, Larry Franklin, who had access to all the executive branch deliberations on Iran, was under investigation for handing over highly confidential documents to AIPAC officers, who in turn gave them to the Israeli embassy. Franklin was indicted in June 2005, and the two AIPAC officials – its policy director, Steven Rosen, and Iran specialist Keith Weissman – followed suit on 4 August 2005. *Ha'aretz* reported that "FBI investigators are interested in questioning more than one embassy worker (Naor Gilon, whose name was already mentioned in the early stages of the probe), and that they also apparently wish to present ambassador Danny Ayalon with questions."[72]

In an attempt to detach itself from the investigation, AIPAC had already fired the two suspected officials in April 2005.[73] Nevertheless, if the two are convicted, it could have serious ramifications for AIPAC, possibly forcing it to register as a foreign-agent organization, thereby losing its tax-exempt status. The indictments themselves were a serious blow to the pro-Israel lobby. As the New York Jewish paper *Forward* reported, "some observers in the Jewish community argue that the indictments are the culmination of a long-running effort by some elements in the

FBI and CIA to clip the influence of Israel and its allies in Washington . . . [They] believe that the indictment against Rosen, Weissman and their associate, Franklin, is a test case in the effort by these factions to rein in the pro-Israel lobby.''[74] In June 2005 Ze'ev Schiff wrote that "the affair is far from the climax," arguing that "It is clear that the FBI is aiming to create conflict between Steve Rosen and the organization in which he has worked for some 23 years. Perhaps it hopes that Rosen, in his anger, will point to others, so that the FBI will be able to widen its investigations. The FBI has made an effort to talk with wealthy Jews as well, apparently in order to deter them from supporting Rosen financially [in his trial expenses].''[75]

Be that as it may, it was clear that in the meantime, AIPAC and the pro-Israel lobby would have to keep quiet, regardless of what the Bush administration demanded of Israel. And indeed, this is precisely what happened. For example, one of the many disagreements Israel had with the Rice team on the eve of the Gaza disengagement in August 2005 revolved around the supplying of ammunition to the Palestinian Authority forces, something the US demanded should be allowed. *Forward* described the reaction of the US Israeli lobby as follows:

> While Israelis have spoken out forcefully on the arming of the Palestinians, American Jewish groups have remained notice-ably silent on the issue in the American political arena . . . Officials at the American Israel Public Affairs Committee, the Washington-based lobbying organization, said there was a hesitance to enter the arena because the dispute involved a matter of Israeli national security, to be dealt with by the Israeli government. That has not barred all criticism. At a meeting Tuesday with Jewish communal leaders in New York, the chairman of the Republican National Committee, Ken Mehlman, was 'strongly questioned' on recent admin-istration policies by the president of the Zionist Organization of America, Morton Klein. 'Bush is one of the most difficult

presidents Israel has ever had to deal with', Klein said, explaining his exchange with Mehlman. Most of the other leaders in attendance asked only polite questions, however, disregarding the recent tensions between Israel and the United States.[76]

It transpired that the powerful pro-Israel lobby could be silenced easily, if the White House so desired.

The second conflict with the White House erupted over an Israeli arms deal with China. This was not the first time that the US and Israel had been at loggerheads over this issue. In 2000, US pressure scuttled Israeli plans to sell Phalcon early-warning spy planes to China, a deal valued at more than $1 billion. But at that time, the conflict was over as soon as Israel agreed to cancel the deal. This time, the disputed matter, which surfaced in the summer of 2004, seemed smaller, but the tension continued long after Israel backed away. The Israeli version of events was that Israel intended to provide China with ''spare parts for a fleet of Harpy armed drone aircraft it sold to China [earlier] with U.S. approval. U.S. defense officials objected on the grounds that the spare parts constituted a significant upgrade of the anti-radar aircraft, possibly including the addition of sensors that could even detect radar sites that are turned off.''[77] Nevertheless, the Bush administration chose to turn this apparently minor issue into an unprecedented and enduring crisis. Israel agreed to cancel the deal, at a cost of hundreds of millions of dollars in compensation for breach of contract. But the US administration did not stop there. Rather, it posed a set of further demands, requiring revisions to the entire system of the Israeli government's supervision procedures of the government, personnel changes, and other requirements that Israel viewed as humiliating.[78]

While these demands were under discussion, the US imposed severe military sanctions on Israel. The sanctions were surveyed in June 2005 by Ze'ev Schiff of *Ha'aretz*, who disclosed that they had been enforced several months earlier:

The sanctions against Israel were approved by the highest-ranking American officials. Secretary of Defense Donald H. Rumsfeld and Secretary of State Condoleezza Rice approved them about seven months ago, and they were imposed with the knowledge of Steve Hadley, national security adviser to President George W Bush.

The sanctions have been imposed on Israel's entire security industry, not merely on plants that made deals with China. One company that could be damaged, although it did not make arms deals with China, is Elbit. Elbit is contending with other companies in the U.S. to sell equipment for the advanced F-22 Raptor aircraft . . . The U.S. has halted cooperation on a large advanced simulation system for the IDF's ground forces, dealing with the future battlefield, and stopped the information exchange on Hunter 2, the assault UAV Israel is developing with an American company . . .

The crisis has disrupted the contacts of senior Defense Ministry officials with their counterparts in the American Defense Ministry, who are not responding to telephone calls from Israel . . . Following the crisis, one can sense the repulsion toward Israel among lower- and middle-ranking officials in Washington. More and more of them are saying that it is not worth doing business with Israel.[79]

Schiff and others revealed later that the sanctions also dealt "a major blow to the Israel Air Force, since its access to the Pentagon's [F-35] Joint Strike Fighter program [JSF] has now been restricted. Israel, together with a number of Western countries that are to purchase the new jet fighter, had been invited to present its own technological and operational requirements before manufacturing of the plane begins in the next decade."[80]

It turns out, then, that imposing military sanctions on Israel is possible if the White House wishes to do so.

The US's tactics in handling this crisis can best be described as dragging. It demanded that the new monitoring procedures should be drawn up in a memorandum of understanding between Israel and the United States; only on conclusion of such a document would sanctions be lifted. But as late as June 2005 it was reported that "a draft of the memorandum is currently being prepared [by the U.S. administration] and has yet to be submitted to Israel, despite repeated requests . . ."[81] The same month, in a visit to the US, Israel's defense minister, Shaul Mofaz, pleaded with the administration to resolve the affair before the implementation of the disengagement,[82] but the preparation of the memorandum continued to drag on for two more months. On 16 August, as the evacuation of the Gaza settlements started, the memorandum was finally signed by the US Department of Defense and the Israeli Defense Ministry.[83] But the sanctions were not lifted. The signed memorandum determined that "the sanctions against Israel will be lifted gradually, and that their complete removal depends exclusively on a U.S. decision".[84] Over the next three months, the US gradually renewed the activities of a series of committees on security and strategic cooperation, which had ceased to convene during the crisis period, but the thing that mattered most to Israel – the ban on its participation in the JSF (F-35) programme – remained in effect.[85] Its lifting was announced only in November 2005,[86] on the eve of the Gaza crossing agreement.

Against this backdrop of crisis, the declared date of the disengagement was approaching. The evacuation date was postponed, as we saw, from July to August 2005. Then in mid-July the area was suddenly on the verge of a new conflagration. Till then, the calm had been largely maintained under the circumstances we examined in Chapter 4, and Hamas strictly refrained from terror attacks.[87] From April onwards, however, Israel started provoking Hamas in Gaza, first with the killing of the three boys on 9 April, to which Hamas and other militant groups responded with mortar and rocket fire.[88] Next the Israeli army restarted its direct targeting of Hamas militants in Gaza, disguised as "work accidents".[89] When Hamas responded with mortars, the army replied with the killing of a Hamas militant with helicopter gunships.[90] During the 2003 ceasefire in 2003, Hamas's Gaza leadership made the fatal mistake of not controlling its cells in the West Bank, which, following Israeli provocation in Gaza, launched a terror attack from the West Bank.[91] This time, Hamas strictly adhered to its no-terror vow, although it did respond with – often symbolic, but sometimes heavier – mortar attacks. In Hamas's eyes, this was their response to Israeli aggression, but their response was nevertheless a violation of the Palestinian declared period of calm. Abbas and the Palestinian security sources intervened each time a burst of this sort happened and usually managed to restore the calm within a day or two after it erupted.[92]

However, Islamic Jihad in the West Bank did not adhere to the no-terror vow. On 12 July 2005 it launched another terror attack on a shopping mall in the Mediterranean town of Netanya. Israel immediately declared a renewal of its policy of targeted assassination, and retaliated heavily in the West Bank. At the same time, it also declared a – completely unrelated – all-out war against Hamas in Gaza. The supposed motive for this declaration was that on 14 July, a Hamas cell in the Gaza Strip launched four rockets in the direction of Netiv Ha'asara, a residence in the Israeli Negev, in response to Israel's retaliation in the West Bank. Though the Palestinian rockets did not usually cause casualties, on this occasion one of them hit and killed an Israeli woman sitting on the porch of her home. From the fuller background as given by *Ha'aretz* it transpired that Israel had been looking "for quite a while" for a trigger to its next escalation:

> Senior diplomatic and defense officials have been trying to define for quite a while a threshold for Palestinian terror that once crossed would obligate Israel to resume offensive

operations in Palestinian Authority territories prior to the disengagement . . . It seems that this week the threshold has been crossed, and the militant group that tipped the balance was the Hamas more than the Islamic Jihad, which has already in the past shaken off any responsibility toward the cease fire agreement and launched the suicide bombing in Netanya . . .[93]

On 15 July, the Israeli army killed seven Hamas militants in separate air attacks in the West Bank and in the Gaza Strip "as it renewed its policy of pinpoint targeting of militants".[94] The same day, "Defense Minister Shaul Mofaz . . . ordered the IDF to prepare for a large-scale ground offensive in the Gaza Strip but told commanders to wait for the diplomatic level to determine when the operation would get underway."[95]

As soon as Israel renewed its offensive against Hamas, the Palestinian Authority declared a state of emergency in Gaza, with the aim of preventing potential Hamas retaliation that would cause the situation to deteriorate further. Mahmoud Abbas headed immediately to Gaza, and his security forces clashed with Hamas in an attempt to restore the calm.[96] Nevertheless, by mid-July, Israel had massed thousands of troops along the border with Gaza in preparation for a big military operation. The *Guardian* reported that "in Gaza, residents were preparing for Israeli military action, speculating that it might begin when Condoleezza Rice, the US secretary of state, leaves after a short visit this week. Israel stopped all movement between the north, centre and south of Gaza and prevented men between the ages of 18 and 35 from crossing the border into Egypt."[97]

The speed at which the crisis escalated, and the way Israel's reaction developed into a massive mobilization of soldiers could not be spontaneous. In fact, since Sharon had announced the disengagement plan in February 2004, there had been talk about the need for a big offensive operation in Gaza prior to the evacuation, on the scale of "Operation Defensive Shield" in the West Bank and Jenin in April 2002. As the evacuation date approached, there were numerous reports in Israeli media on military preparations for a massive operation in Gaza that was referred to as "Iron Fist". In early May 2005, Alex Fishman reported that

in the Southern command and the Gaza battalion, preparations for the 'Iron Fist' series of operations has entered high gear . . . The orders for opening fire during these operations are very similar to those that prevailed during the 'Defensive Shield' [operation] in the West Bank. This means, very few restrictions. It will not be just one operation, but a series of wide range hits.[98]

Why was this operation needed? Fishman explains that it was necessary in order to "paralyze any possible disturbance by the Palestinians during the disengagement". This explanation – that such an operation was needed in order to ensure that the disengagement would not take place under fire – was repeatedly issued by security sources to the media, which recycled it faithfully. Yet if this really was the goal, there were more obvious ways to obtain it – such as coordinating the pullout with the Palestinian security forces, who were not only willing, but even begging, to be involved. (That they were capable of doing so was eventually proven in the actual evacuation, which took place with absolutely no Palestinian "disturbance".) Indeed, Fishman himself reports in the same breath that such cooperation was perfectly possible:

The contacts that developed between the Israeli and the Palestinian security forces in February–March left the impression that things could be done differently. Then, there was a daily dialogue between the officers [on both sides] . . . The Palestinians prevented 14 Qassam launches, carried out 21 joint operations to prevent attacks, exposed 18 tunnels and neutralized 11 booby traps. There was a feeling that the cooperation is developing and tightening.[99]

Why, then, did this dialogue with the Palestinian security forces stop all of a sudden, with the army preparing instead for the Gaza "Defensive Shield"? Fishman continues to explain:

> [I]n the last weeks [of April], Israel, on its own initiative, reduced the level of coordination. This was based on its understanding that the heads of the [Palestinian] security forces, including those who were just recently appointed, are very restricted. They don't have any backing from the Palestinian Authority. They talk, but they cannot do much. So all this intimate coordination only creates frustration.[100]

In other words, although the Palestinian security forces were active and successful in preventing attacks on Israel, the Israeli army decided that this was just "frustrating" and nothing but a big operation would serve its security needs. (Note that this was already decided two months before the Hamas shelling of 14 July, which was the apparent trigger for Israeli military mobilization.)

A glimpse of the deeper motivation behind the Israeli army's planned operation can be found in Amir Oren's report from March 2004, just after the announcement of the disengagement plan, where he states that "[chief of staff] Ya'alon, [defense minister] Mofaz, Prime Minister Ariel Sharon and the head of the Shin Bet security service, Avi Dichter . . . are agreed on one common denominator: If the Gaza Strip is to be evacuated of Israelis, that is best done after it has been freed (relatively and temporarily) of the terrorist networks, and Hamas especially."[101] Why they all wanted the operation is a different question. Ya'alon, the most philosophical of the Israeli generals, gave his rationale in a conference on low-intensity warfare, shortly after the assassination of Sheik Ahmed Yassin. One can observe in his words the frustration of the head of a sophisticated military machine that cannot be put to full use. As Oren recounted, Ya'alon "argues that in the confrontation between the army and terrorism, which operates from within a civilian environment, terrorism has the advantage, because the army can use only a small part of its strength against it". To offset this advantage, "when needed, and especially after serious terrorist attacks", the army must change its strategy "for an allotted period, from a low-intensity confrontation . . . into a high-intensity confrontation". Only in these allotted periods "in which the army utilizes its capabilities with tremendous strength, which are of no value most of the time, is it able to realize its military superiority . . . The most cogent Israeli example, Ya'alon says, is Operation Defensive Shield."[102] Oren adds that "the implication of this conception is that before the withdrawal, the Israel Defense Forces should enter in large numbers, lure Hamas, Islamic Jihad and the other organizations into a clash with the IDF, kill them in their masses, and only then pull out".[103]

April 2002's Operation Defensive Shield was indeed a salient example of Ya'alon's vision of "high intensity war".[104] – something which Gaza was spared at the time. On 8 May 2002, following an awaited trigger of a Palestinian terror attack, the army was "hard at work, issuing emergency call-up orders (tzav 8) to reservists," in preparation for such an operation in Gaza. It was however cancelled, partly as a result of reservists' objections, who argued that such an operation does not have wide public support in Israel.[105] Sharon was in the US at the time; in his absence then Defense Minister Benjamin Ben Eliezer (of the Labor party), who objected to the operation, managed to stall it.[106] Since then, the army has been waiting for its chance for a "high intensity" operation in Gaza. As we saw in Chapter 3, a series of brutal local operations were carried out in Gaza in 2004, but they were brought to a halt with the US's policy change and the enforced period of calm following Arafat's departure and the Sharm el-Sheikh summit in February 2005.

But why would Sharon have wanted such an operation, having just announced the Gaza evacuation? Given the political atmosphere in Israel during the summer of 2005, with the excitement of the disengagement, and the peace camp united in worshiping Sharon as a man of peace, it might have been possible for him to convince the Israelis that another big blood-bath was needed for the disengagement's sake – and this time the reservists might well have acquiesced. But what would it be needed for? Sharon and the army viewed 2002's Operation Defensive Shield as a big success: it weakened the militant organizations and eroded Palestinian civil society; it also destroyed whatever was still left of the Palestinian institutions that were built during the Oslo period, and returned the West Bank to direct Israeli military control. However, its "success" lay in the fact that it not only destroyed the semi-autonomy achieved by the Palestinians after Oslo, but also enabled the army direct control over each "territorial cell" in the West Bank. None of these "achievements" would have been maintained had the Israeli army not remained in the areas it devastated. As Ya'alon's military philosophy makes clear, "high intensity" operations can be meaningful only if their effects are constantly maintained with "low intensity" warfare. This means that the army has to be constantly present in the "cells" to destroy any new attempts at organizing resistance, to arrest or assassinate suspects and to control the movements of Palestinians. The success of "low intensity" warfare rests on a network of informants and collaborators that direct the army towards the suspects. (The Israeli security forces, pride themselves on having established such networks in the territories and are offering their experience in this area to the US.) However, for such a network to function it is essential that the informants have direct access to their operatives, which is only possible if these operatives are in the Palestinian territories.

All this would not be possible if the Israeli army were to leave Gaza following a "high intensity" operation. Even if Hamas and all the Palestinian infrastructure were to be destroyed, as happened in the West Bank in 2002, it would take only a short while for them to reorganize and rebuild. Ya'alon, who understood this well, was against the unilateral evacuation of Gaza from the outset. It is not clear, therefore, what the purpose of such an operation could be if Sharon really intended to evacuate Gaza. It is possible that Sharon and the army just wanted to disseminate maximum destruction and leave the Palestinians in Gaza substantially weakened before the army withdrew to its external system of control. But it is also possible that Sharon believed that under cover of conflict, he could evade the evacuation, or at least postpone it for the time being, following his mantra that there would be no disengagement under fire. If that's what he hoped for, it is certainly possible that he would not share it even with the army. It would not have been the first time that Sharon would entertain the idea that one can plan military moves without sharing their purpose with the political or even the military system – after all, he had done it before in Lebanon.

We will never know for sure what Sharon intended, because the US steamroller intervened to prevent this scenario. Rice's Jerusalem visit of 21 July 2005 had not in fact been scheduled. As Israel was massing forces at the Gaza border, Rice cut short a visit in Africa and rushed to Jerusalem "in order to prevent a crisis that would threaten disengagement".[107] The US state department explained that Rice would demand "maximum effort . . . to keep Israel's planned pullout from Gaza on track despite fresh violence".[108] On her way Rice, who sent her team ahead of her, "warned Israel and the Palestinians the deadline for the disengagement was looming and they needed to hammer out how to implement the mid-August pullout".[109] Behind a public show of cordiality, her hardline visit spelled out that the US would not countenance any military operation, or any delay of the evacuation. The *New York Times* later disclosed (in a story covering the fuller spectrum of US–Israeli tensions) some remarks made by Middle East Security Coordinator General William Ward, one of Rice's team:

> General Ward, a careful man, confirmed that two weeks ago, American pressure helped stay the Israeli military when it was poised to go into Gaza . . . He predicted that there could be similar pressure should the need arise. "That scenario is a scenario that none of us would like to see," he said. "There is a deep realization on the part of the Israeli leadership, including the military, about the consequences of that type of scenario."[110]

The report added that Israeli officials, "who agreed to speak only on background, acknowledge the new pressure from Washington . . . Ms. Rice in particular has been forceful and even abrupt in her dealings with senior Israeli officials, including the foreign and defense ministers, Silvan Shalom and Shaul Mofaz. On her recent trip here, she ran the meetings with them in their offices, taking control of the agenda and even announcing when they would end . . ."[111]

With the US military sanctions in the background, Sharon and the army had no choice but to obey. The army called off the operation, and three weeks later, the Gaza pullout took place promptly and smoothly. The drama of sanctions and pressure was kept fully behind the screens. In public, throughout the whole period, the Bush administration praised Sharon for his leadership and courage in implementing the disengagement plan. They trapped him in his words, and then gave him the sole credit for the pullout – but it was US pressure that really achieved it. When the US really does exert pressure, no Israeli leader is able to defy its injunctions.

As we shall see in the next chapter, US pressure on Israel ended at this point. The Gaza Strip remained under Israeli occupation in a new form, and in the coming months, Israel was once again given a free hand. Nevertheless, I maintain that

Sharon left the scene defeated. In the long run, as we have seen, dismantling the Gaza settlements was a blow to the Israeli military vision of occupation.

Although the daily reality of the Palestinians in Gaza has not changed for the better after the pullout, from the Palestinian perspective the evacuation of the Gaza settlements can be viewed as a victory, albeit small. These settlementss, together with their security belts and Israeli-only roads, occupied about a third of the strip's land, land that has now returned to its rightful owners. We should never forget that the Palestinian struggle is not only for liberation and statehood, but for the regaining of their lands in the occupied territories – land that Israel has been expropriating since 1967. As long as the Palestinians manage to hold on to their land, under even the worst conditions, they will also eventually gain their liberation. Without their land, what is at stake is not just their liberation, but their survival. Hence, regaining this land is a step forward.

At the same time, the story of the Gaza evacuation shows that international pressure can lead Israel to concessions. The reason the US exerted pressure on Israel, for the first time in recent history, was because at that moment in time it was no longer possible to ignore world discontent over its policy of blind support of Israel – the US had to yield to international public opinion. This also shows the limits of power and propaganda. Despite the silencing of criticism of Israeli policies in Western political discourse, the fight for justice for the Palestinian people has penetrated global consciousness. This fight has been spread in the West by persistent indivduals – a few courageous journalists who insist on covering the truth, despite the pressure of an acquiescent media and pro-Israel lobbies, solidarity movements that send their people to the occupied territories and take part in vigils at home, professors who sign boycott and divestment petitions, subjecting themselves to daily harassment. Often this fight for justice seems futile; nevertheless, it has had an effect on public opinion, which in turn can force governments to act.

6

Winter 2005–6: A Return to the "Long War"

1. Gaza after the Pullout

I N THE DOMINANT WESTERN CONSCIOUSNESS, the Gaza pullout story ends with the evacuation of the settlements. The Western world saw the pictures of Israeli settlers leaving the Strip and of Palestinian joy in the first days after the disengagement. It could then move on to other matters, assured of the end of the Israeli occupation of Gaza, soon to be followed by Israeli disengagement from the West Bank. From that time on, there was very little coverage of the realities of the situation in Gaza, let alone noting of the fact that all Israel had done was to replace one form of occupation with another.

One question that did attract some international attention was the extent to which the Gaza Strip would be allowed access to the outside world, on the one hand, and to the West Bank on the other. The Rafah crossing on the Egyptian border is presently the only exit from the Strip to a country other than Israel. Amira Hass has explained its importance for the Gaza Palestinians: "In the 1990s, Israel gradually cut the Strip off from the West Bank, prohibiting Gazans from leaving via the Allenby Bridge [to Jordan]. At the same time, Palestinians were almost completely forbidden from leaving via Ben-Gurion Airport [in Tel Aviv]. Rafah remained Gaza's only connection with the outside world. In 1999, more than half a million people passed through the crossing. [Since 2000], Israel's restrictions on Palestinians' movement" and its closure of the terminal for weeks on end reduced the number of people passing through to about 133,000 in 2004".[1]

As we saw in Chapter 2, the disengagement plan stipulated from the outset that Israel would continue to maintain full external military" control of the Strip after the pullout. As far as the international Rafah crossing was concerned, the plan specified that "existing arrangements will remain in force".[2] The "existing arrangements," established since the Oslo Agreements, placed the crossing under the control of Israeli security and customs, ostensibly in cooperation with Palestinian Authority officers. After the pullout, however, the Israeli army no longer maintained a presence inside Gaza, and therefore could not retain control over Gaza's border with Egypt and the Rafah crossing. In response to Israel's security concerns, the European Union offered to monitor the traffic; Israel refused, demanding instead that the Rafah crossing point be closed altogether. On 8 August 2005, the Israeli security cabinet decided to replace the Rafah checkpoint with a new terminal at Kerem Shalom on the Israeli–Egyptian border, close to the Gaza Strip. This would mean that all traffic to and from the Strip would go through Israel, under its direct control. Thus, the Gaza Strip would be denied any independent connection with the outside world.[3]

As always, Israel justified its demand for full direct control of the crossing by citing security concerns: the fear that through it, weapons and terrorists could enter Gaza, bypassing Egyptian, PA and EU supervision. But in practice, as we saw in Chapter 3, maintenance of the crossing points has been Israel's major means of controlling Gaza's population and economy, enabling it to block Palestinian exports and imports. Over the years, Israel has destroyed any chance for Palestinian economic independence in Gaza, reducing its population to one of the poorest in the world, with hardly any means of self-sustainability. In Israel's eyes, keeping Gaza in these conditions of poverty and despair is necessary to prevent political development and struggle. The inevitable social collapse of the Strip, Israel believes, would force the Palestinians to accept the prison conditions that Israel has set for their future after the disengagement.

On this issue, however, the US again exerted some pressure. The tension surrounding Condoleezza Rice's July 2005 visit to Israel was in part due to "pressure from Washington to resolve questions of Palestinian life in Gaza: access, assets, security, travel and the import and export of goods and people,"[4] and specifically to enable the smooth operation of the Rafah crossing. On this front, an influential figure was outgoing World Bank President James D. Wolfensohn, who in April 2005 had been appointed as the Quartet's envoy for the supervision of the economic and civilian aspects of Israel's impending withdrawal from the Gaza Strip, and who received full backing from Rice. Wolfensohn's role was described, inter alia, as "to revive the economy in Gaza,"[5] and he constantly warned that without a solution to the economics and crossings issues, the Strip would turn into a big prison. Wolfensohn often expressed frustration over Israel's stalling on a solution to the problem of the crossings. In a mid-October 2005 letter to United Nations Secretary-General Kofi Annan and the foreign ministries of the Quartet, Wolfensohn wrote that "The Government of Israel, with its important security concerns, is loath to relinquish control, almost acting as though there has been no withdrawal, delaying making difficult decisions and preferring to take difficult matters back into slow-moving subcommittees."[6]

Israel dragged out the issue for three months after the pullout, during which time the crossings were essentially closed. During this time, however, US military sanctions against Israel were still enforced. Eventually, Condoleezza Rice intervened directly, and Israel was forced to address the issue. In early November 2005, the Israeli cabinet approved the plan for European Union officials to monitor people entering Gaza from Egypt through the Rafah border crossing; it was noted that this was "the first time Israel will allow the EU to play a major role in Israeli–Palestinian relations".[7]

Nevertheless, Israeli concessions were minimal. The crossings agreement ("Movement and Access from Gaza") signed on 15 November specified that the Rafah crossing would be used for the passage of people in and out of Gaza – but that goods, vehicles and trucks to and from Egypt would have to pass through the Israeli crossing at Kerem Shalom, under full Israeli supervision. As far as people traffic is concerned, entry to the Strip would be permitted only to those holding Palestinian ID. Any foreign nationals would only be allowed to enter "by exception in agreed categories with prior notification to the GoI [Government of Israel] . . . The PA [Palestinian Authority] will notify the GoI 48 hours in advance of the crossing of a person in the excepted categories – diplomats, foreign investors, foreign representatives of recognized international organizations and humanitarian cases. The GoI will respond within 24 hours with any objections . . ." Although there would be no direct Israeli presence in the Rafah crossing, it was agreed that "cameras will be installed to monitor the search process," so that Israel would be able to monitor all movement from its inspection point a few kilometres away.[8] Effectively, therefore, entry to the Gaza Strip would continue to remain under Israeli control. During the years of the Palestinian *intifada*, Israel had placed severe restrictions on international volunteers and NGOs wishing to visit Gaza to provide solidarity and aid; now, after the disengagement, it would have precisely the same means of preventing their entrance.

The signing of the crossings agreement on 15 November 2005 received considerable international attention. Rice again over-stretched her visit and held an all-night negotiating session to enforce an agreement. The agreement reached at the end of this session was depicted in the Western media as the climax of US pressure on Israel to improve Palestinian life in the Gaza Strip. From this perspective, the agreement brought the Israeli pullout to a successful conclusion. In reality, however, it marked the end of US pressure on Israel. US military sanctions had been lifted shortly before the signing of the agreement, in the same week that the Israeli cabinet agreed to EU inspection of the Rafah crossing. On 4 November 2005, following a meeting of Israeli Defense Minister Shaul Mofaz and US Secretary of Defense Donald Rumsfeld, US sources announced that "Israel has been reinstated to the group of countries taking part in the program to develop the next-generation combat plane, the F-35 Joint Strike Fighter."[9]

The impact of the lifting of sanctions could already be discerned during the "dramatic night" of the crossings negotiation. According to Palestinian sources, Rice and her team promptly agreed to the many changes demanded by Israel to the original document prepared by Wolfensohn; the sources add that at critical moments Wolfensohn was sidelined from the negotiations.[10] But the effects of the relaxation of US pressure became fully evident a few weeks later, in the other central focus of the crossings negotiations: the link between the Gaza Strip and the West Bank.

The Gaza Strip depends economically on its contact with the West Bank, which involves trucks and goods passing through the Erez and Karni crossings on the Gaza–Israel border, and making their way to the West Bank through Israel. According to the World Bank's representative in the occupied territories, Nigel Roberts, "before the Intifada broke out . . . some 225 trucks a day passed through these crossings, compared to only 35 a day in the six months prior to the disengagement. Since the disengagement, however, the situation has deteriorated even further, and over the last two months, only about a dozen trucks per day have been allowed into Israel."[11] In addition to permitting goods through the crossings, the Palestinians and Wolfensohn's team demanded that Israel allow unfettered passage of people between the West Bank and the Gaza Strip, which had been blocked since the outbreak of the *intifada*. Prior to Rice's visit, it was reported that she would demand that "Jerusalem immediately remove all obstacles to the passage of cargo between Israel and Gaza through the Erez and Karni checkpoints. Rice and Wolfensohn plan to demand that Israel not close the checkpoints in response to terror attacks or general warnings about planned attacks, but only do so when there are specific warnings about a planned attack involving a particular checkpoint."[12]

The 15 November agreement did indeed specify that "Israel will allow the passage of convoys to facilitate the movements of goods and persons". Specifically, it determines that Israel will establish bus convoys for the passage of people by 15 December, and truck convoys for goods by 15 January 2006.[13] However, as we have seen, official commitments signed by Israel were often dead letters without some form of serious external pressure on Israel to implement them. Sharon, in what was to be his last month of office, commenced his habitual game of cat-and-mouse. First, the Israeli cabinet announced a freeze on the convoys; then, as the date specified in the agreement for establishing the convoys approached, under what was described as international pressure, it promised on 14 December to start them a few days later than the specified date,[14] only to announce the following day that they would not allow the convoys, citing as reasons the security situation and the launching of Qassam rockets from Gaza. Here is how the *New York Times* summed up the situation at the end of December 2005:

> With much fanfare, after an unscheduled all-night negotiating session, Secretary of State Condoleezza Rice announced Nov. 15 that she had reached an agreement with Israel and the Palestinians on . . . establishing a bus convoy for Palestinians to travel between Gaza and the West Bank starting Dec. 15. But the deadline for the bus convoy has come and gone. And despite open American disappointment, Israel says it has no intention of continuing discussions on the convoy so long as Palestinians continue to fire homemade rockets out of Gaza . . .[15]

Saeb Erekat, the Palestinian negotiator, said he was disgusted with the situation. "There's no security issue for Israel," he said. "They will have names submitted in advance, they screen the passengers, no one leaves the buses and they're escorted by Israel to Tarqumiya [in the south of the West Bank]. So why hasn't it started? . . . And how should the Palestinians expect to make any agreement if someone so high[-up] as Rice arranges something of so little risk to Israel and nothing happens?"[16]

Relieved from the pressure of sanctions, Israel could stand on its dignity as a sovereign state to explain why it would not comply with its commitments. An Israeli security official told *Yediot Aharonot*: "No country in the world would allow interference in its sovereignty to the extent that the American representatives are asking of us."[17] The tone of Israeli security officials had changed substantially since the previous clash with Washington in July. The road was clear for a return to business as usual.

The US reaction, this time, has indeed been mild. The assistant secretary of state, David Welch, in a donor conference for the Palestinian Authority in London, "expressed public annoyance on Dec. 14, saying, 'We fully expect Israel and the Palestinians to implement all aspects of the movement agreement on schedule' ".[18] But "in Washington, a State Department official said that Ms. Rice would not have a comment, but said, 'Obviously [Israel] hasn't met the timeline, but there have been security incidents that have affected implementation.' "[19] Not much was left by then from Rice's earlier demand "that Israel not close the checkpoints in response to terror attacks".

The West Bank, then, remained inaccessible to Gaza Palestinians. In Amira Hass's words, "since Israel forbids Gazans to enter the West Bank via the Allenby Bridge at the Jordanian border, the opening of the Rafah crossing point perhaps makes it possible for them to reach Australia, but not Hebron, Ramallah or Nablus".[20] When the second deadline of 15 January 2006, which was supposed to mark the commencement of goods convoys, passed, it was not even commented upon. In the coming months, the issue disappeared completely from the international agenda. The situation in Gaza remained as Mahmoud Abbas described it shortly after the Israeli pullout: "The Strip is one large prison, and the army"'s departure does not change this situation.'[21]

From the US perspective, its goal of appeasing international pressure had been achieved with the evacuation of the settlements.[22] Western leaders and media were euphoric over the new developments in the Middle East. Sharon was widely hailed for the successful implementation of his visionary disengagement plan, and it was evident that international pressure over the peace process had been lifted from Israel: "The U.S. administration has made it clear . . . to its friends in Europe and the Arab world that Israel has fulfilled its part of the process, and now it is time to leave Israel alone and expect the Palestinians to do their part."[23] And this message was reiterated time and again by European leaders and media. As long as international calm is maintained, Palestinian suffering plays no role in US calculations.

In this new dispensation, Sharon and the army were given a free hand to handle the Gaza prison in any way they saw fit. In September 2005, shortly after the withdrawal, in response to Palestinian mortars, an Israeli aircraft attacked a school building in a crowded Gaza City neighbourhood, a building that the army said was being used by a Hamas-linked foundation to raise money for terrorist attacks. The blast collapsed part of the school, and caused damage to at least five nearby homes. Fifteen people, including women and children, were injured.[24] This attack was to establish the pattern for Israel's handling of the Strip following the disengagement. At the same time, assassinations returned to the level that they had been at before the Sharm el-Sheikh summit in February 2005, and were carried out against all militant organizations, including Fatah and Hamas.

As Sharon and the army knew well in advance, control of the Gaza prison from the outside would be harder and less efficient than before. We saw in Chapter 3 that there is one problem Israel has no solution to, even if the world lets it keep Gaza sealed, impoverished and despairing: the imprisoned Palestinian can launch homemade rockets into neighbouring Israeli areas severely disturbing the life of the occupiers. The evacuation of the settlements created a particular problem in the north of the Gaza Strip. Previously, the settlement block in this area formed a "security zone" between the Strip and Israel. With the evacuation of the settlements, the Palestinians would be closer to the Israeli border. A major concern of the Israeli army long before the evacuation was that this would enable Palestinian mortars and rockets, whose range is about 9 km, to reach deeper into Israel. In January 2005, the National Security Forum presented a report stating that "the withdrawal of the Israel Defense Forces from the Gaza Strip . . . will bring numerous large population centers and communities [in Israel] within the range of Qassam rockets and mortar shells," with the greatest danger anticipated to be in Israel's Ashkelon region, home to many strategic facilities.[25]

The military's strategy for tackling this problem was revealed shortly after the evacuation of the settlements. On 24 September 2005, the security cabinet approved Defense Minister Shaul Mofaz's proposal that "the IDF be instructed to create buffer zones within the Gaza Strip in areas near the border, in order to move the rocket launchers away from Israeli communities".[26] What this means is that Palestinians would not be permitted to settle in, or even enter the "buffer zones," the areas that encompassed the evacuated settlements in the north of the Gaza Strip; anybody doing so would risk coming under Israeli fire. Military sources told *Ha'aretz* that the buffer zone would include not only the open areas left after the evacuation of the settlements, but also two Palestinian towns nearby: "If necessary," the sources said, "we will create ghost neighbourhoods, we will use artillery to prevent the rocket launchers from entering even at the price of removing civilians from their homes."[27] Since this announcement, these two towns have been steadily bombarded, with the army gradually increasing the intensity of fire.[28]

The Israeli army's operations were aimed not only at the militants, but at the population as a whole, using sophisticated methods of collective punishment. In September 2005, air-force jets started flying over Gaza at low altitude, breaking the sound barrier in order to create sonic booms. At the end of that month, Dr Eyad El-Sarraj wrote:

> During the last few days, Gaza was awakened from its dreams of liberation with horrible explosions which have shattered

our skies, shaken our buildings, broken our windows, and thrown the place into panic.

We have been bombed since Friday 23 September, day and night. Usually between 2:00–4:00am, between 6:30–8:00 in the morning during the time children go to school, and in the afternoon or early evening . . . Gaza is in a state of panic, children are restless, crying, frightened and many are wetting their beds. Some children are afraid to leave home and refuse to go to school. Many are dazed, pale, insomniac and have a poor appetite. Some pregnant women reported colics and some were admitted to hospital with precipitated labour. Many people complain of ear pressure. All are stunned.

Israel's new method of creating intentional sonic booms in our skies was never used before the disengagement, so as not to alarm or hurt the Israeli settlers and their children. Israel is inducing learned helplessness to the Palestinians in Gaza with the aim of making the whole population captive to fear and paralysis.[29]

In early November 2005, the *Guardian*'s Chris McGreal reported that "Over the past week, Israeli jets created 28 sonic booms by flying at high speed and low altitude over the Gaza Strip, sometimes as little as an hour apart through the night . . . Palestinians liken the sound to an earthquake or huge bomb. They describe the effect as being hit by a wall of air that is painful on the ears, sometimes causing nosebleeds and 'leaving you shaking inside'." He adds that "the Palestinian health ministry says the sonic booms have led to miscarriages and heart problems. The United Nations has demanded an end to the tactic, saying it causes panic attacks in children. The shockwaves have also damaged buildings by cracking walls and smashing thousands of windows."[30] But the Israeli army views this diabolic invention as an educational act, in its view displaying the humanitarian face of the Israeli army and society: "A senior Israeli army intelligence source, who the military would not permit to be named, said the tactic is intended to break civilian support for armed Palestinian groups. 'We are trying to send a message in a way that doesn''t harm people. We want to encourage the Palestinian public to do something about the terror situation,' he said. 'What are the alternatives? We are not like the terrorists who shoot civilians. We are cautious. We make sure nobody is really hurt.' '[31]

The Israeli security system has never lacked creativity in its committed search for such "educational" methods. In his last two weeks in office, Sharon added another milestone to his "legacy", when he came up with a proposal to shut off Gaza's electricity supply (which remains fully controlled by Israel) in retaliation for Palestinian rocket attacks. In late December 2005 *Ha'aretz* reported that "Prime Minister Ariel Sharon was 'wavering' over the idea during a meeting on Wednesday, but senior IDF officials strongly opposed it, arguing that it constituted collective punishment and would be hard to justify. Attorney General Menachem Mazuz also opposes the idea. As a result, it has been rejected for now, but will be discussed again if the escalation continues, the officials said."[32]

Yet from the very first month after the pullout, the US and Europe turned a blind eye to Israel's methods of collective punishment. The US returned to its stance of the Road Map era, providing total endorsement of Israel's actions against the supposedly "liberated" Gaza. "We understand the situation in which Israel finds itself," State Department spokesman Sean McCormack said in September 2005. "And we fully understand Israel's right to defend itself."[33] "We all know that the terrorists are trying to provoke Israel . . . at a very sensitive time, and we understand exactly what the government's position is," added the newly appointed US ambassador to Israel, Richard Jones.[34] The EU followed suit in placing the blame for Israel's actions squarely on the Palestinians. In late September the EU presidency – at that point held by the UK – issued a statement calling on the Palestinian Authority to reign in militants in Gaza: "The Presidency recognises Israel's right to act in self-defence . . ."[35] This tacit approval of Israeli violence continued in the coming months.

So, although forced to evacuate the Gaza settlements, Sharon had managed to maintain Israeli control of the Strip. On 4 January 2006, Sharon exited the political arena following a stroke. He left behind a well-defined legacy, followed faithfully by his successor Ehud Olmert and the Israeli army. By this legacy, Israel can continue to imprison the Palestinians, to bombard them from the air, deprive them of the means of sustenance, steal their land in the West Bank – and still be hailed as the peacemaker in the Israel–Palestine conflict.

With the Bush administration's determination to move its planned Iranian campaign into high gear, Israel's stock was rising again; Israeli officials could not conceal their pride over the country's role in aggressive US diplomacy. When in early February 2006 the United Nations' International Atomic Energy Agency referred Iran to the Security Council, Olmert, in broadcast remarks at the start of the weekly cabinet meeting, said that "Israel had played an important role" in what he described as "an intensive and stormy diplomatic effort". He went on to predict that "Iran will pay a "heavy price".[36] Olmert later thanked Bush for what he termed "the closest thing to an announcement of a military alliance with Israel".[37]

2. The Palestinian Elections

The one point the US administration did continue to insist upon after the disengagement from Gaza was that Israel should allow the upcoming Palestinian elections, scheduled for 25 January 2006, to proceed as planned. Sharon did his best to stall the elections, citing Hamas's participation as a reason to cancel them. On 21 December 2005, following earlier threats, Israel announced that it would not permit elections to take place in East Jerusalem.[38] Israeli spokesmen did not conceal their hope that Abbas would cancel the elections following this act. This time, however, the US stood firm, a White House official stating that Bush "wants Palestinian elections to go forward as scheduled". Insisting that

Israel should not bar Palestinians from voting in East Jerusalem, he said: "We believe that people must have access to the ballot . . . Arrangements have been made in the past to ensure that those persons can vote, and we believe some arrangements should be possible at this time." '[39] Acting Prime Minister Ehud Olmert, who replaced Sharon on 4 January, kept up his objections to elections in East Jerusalem, but eventually conceded ground in a phone call with Condoleezza Rice on 10 January. "Thus ended Israel's failed attempt to protest Hamas' participation in the elections,'" summed up *Ha'aretz* analyst Aluf Benn. "It began with threats by Prime Minister Ariel Sharon to obstruct voting in the West Bank and refrain from coordinating with the Palestinian Authority, continued with threats not to open polling stations in Jerusalem, and ended in consent, at American behest."[40]

The 25 January elections, which saw a turnout of almost 78 per cent, produced a massive shock: Hamas won the elections with 74 seats in the 132-seat legislative body. Mahmoud Abbas's Fatah party came a distant second with 45 seats, while Palestinian secular and democratic forces, who had formed four separate lists, achieved a combined result of 9 seats.

At first, US reaction to Hamas's win was quite calm: " 'Democracy can open people's eyes to reality', an upbeat President Bush said at a press conference [on 26 January] regarding Hamas' election victory. 'I like the competition of ideas,' Bush said, praising the power of democracy and the significant voter turnout."[41] The *Ha'aretz* commentator reporting this from Washington explained that "he is right to a certain extent. If his goal is to make the region more democratic, he has no choice but to accept the result, gloomy as it may be."[42] This first reaction would seem to be the natural one. Hamas has been on the US terror list, yet this was already known when the US insisted that Hamas be allowed to participate in the elections. Anybody interested in a cessation of bloodshed would undoubtedly welcome the commitment that Hamas had undertaken in early 2005, when it decided to abandon the armed struggle and join the democratic process instead. There did not seem to be a reason, therefore, for any change of attitude when Hamas won.

The first reactions of the Middle East Quartet (United States, Russian Federation, the European Union and the United Nations) were also moderate. The Quartet reportedly saw its mission as "encouraging Mahmoud Abbas to choose an acceptable prime minister and form a cabinet with which they can negotiate. [It] did not say at any stage [it] would sever ties with the Palestinian Authority." It was evident that certain members of the Quartet did not rule out recognizing the new Hamas government, and a meeting was scheduled "to air out the differences between those who want to legitimize anyone willing to talk, and those who want a slower, more selective process of choosing the Palestinian partner".[43]

Prior to the elections, Israel's security sources did not seem to be unduly concerned that Hamas's growing power might pose an immediate security threat, expecting Hamas's year-long hiatus in attacks to hold. "Senior IDF officers" told *Ha'aretz* that, "assuming Hamas does well at the polls, it is likely to maintain the calm it agreed to about a year ago . . . 'Since the understanding it reached with the Palestinian Authority at the end of January 2005, Hamas has generally avoided perpetrating attacks.'"[44]

The Israeli public also received the results with relative calm. In a poll taken on election day, 48 per cent of Israelis favoured negotiating with a Hamas-led Palestinian government.[45] A few days later, polls still indicated that "about half the public thinks Hamas will now moderate its involvement in terror attacks, and close to half say it is now the Palestinian people's legitimate representative in every way and that negotiations should be conducted even with a Palestinian government that it forms".[46]

In contrast to – and regardless of – public opinion, Israel's official reaction was one of hysterical fury. By the weekend after the elections, Israeli officials were working to "drum up international support for a boycott of Hamas and to set conditions for talking to a Palestinian government led by or including the organization".[47] Very soon after, the US and Europe fell into line with Israel. To understand better the official Israeli reaction, it is worth exploring the context and the implications of Hamas's victory.

The reason why the election results came as such a surprise is that Palestinian society is largely secular. Although the religious parties have gained ground in the Palestinian territories, especially during the recent wave of Israeli oppression, they still do not by any means represent the majority view. According to the Palestinian organization BADIL,[48] Hamas normally enjoys the stable support of around a third of the Palestinian population in the occupied territories; nobody, "neither Palestinian voters, pollsters, local and international analysts, nor Israeli intelligence or even Hamas itself, had expected these election results". BADIL's report echoes many in the Palestinian society in arguing that a major factor behind Hamas's win was "a general public fatigue and disgust of the Fatah-led Palestinian political leadership which – as the Palestinian Authority – has ruled Palestinian political life since the 1993 Oslo Accords. The vote for Hamas is a vote for change . . . Hamas has a proven record, as elected head of municipalities and local councils, of being a more credible, impartial and committed civil servant than the old guard of notable and Fatah-affiliated communal leadership."[49]

To understand this Palestinian statement, one would have to go into the history and the role of the PA during the Oslo years, which I discuss, partially, in *Israel/Palestine*[50]. The tragedy of the Palestinian people is that by the time of the Oslo Accords in 1993, they were, for the first time in their history, close to the prospect of liberation. The six years of the first Palestinian *intifada* (1987–93) convinced the majority of Israelis that maintaining the occupation is unfeasible. Combined with the victory of the reconciliation line in Palestinian society, following the meeting of the Palestine National Council in 1988, many people felt for the first time that a two-state solution might be realistic. At the time, a local Palestinian negotiations body was formed, headed by Haidar Abd-el Shafi from Gaza, and it was gradually gaining more respect in the occupied territories than

Arafat's anachronistic administration in exile. (At that time, Yasser Arafat's status was deteriorating in the occupied territories, as well as in the refugee camps in Lebanon and in Jordan. There was much protest regarding the corruption of his aides in Tunis, his undemocratic rule, and his sole control over the organization's finances.) But, as we saw in Chapter 3, Israel preferred to close a deal with Arafat, who in secret negotiations in Oslo agreed to conditions rejected by the local delegation.

Israel under Yitzhak Rabin used Arafat's weakness to solidify the occupation in a new form. As we saw in Chapter 3, rather than working towards the eventual withdrawal from the occupied territories within five years, as determined in the Oslo Agreements, Rabin turned to implement the Alon plan, which robs the Palestinian of forty per cent of their land. As David Hirst wrote in the *Guardian*, when Arafat returned to the occupied territories in 1994, "he came as collaborator as much as liberator. For the Israelis, security – theirs, not the Palestinians" – was the be-all and end-all of Oslo'. Along the road, "he acquiesced in accumulating concessions that only widened the gulf between what he was actually achieving and what he assured his people he would achieve, by this method, in the end".[51]

The first Palestinian *intifada* (1987–93) was largely a grassroots struggle, organized and directed locally by popular committees in towns and villages. But with the return of Arafat and his organizations from exile, they destroyed this grassroots layer and introduced a tight system of control, enforced by security services that worked in collaboration with Israel. Over the years since 1993, this system of centralized control and collaboration with the Israeli occupiers resulted in degrees of corruption typical of banana republics.[52]

In return for recognizing the PLO and Arafat, Israel expected the Fatah-led PA to contain the frustration of their people and guarantee the safety of the settlers, as Israel continued to build new settlements and appropriate more Palestinian land. The PA followed suit. An Amnesty International report of 2000 charges that "in the six years since its establishment, the Palestinian Authority (PA) has detained dozens of human rights defenders, journalists, religious figures, writers, government officials, trade unionists and academics solely for exercising their legitimate rights to freedom of expression."[53] Commenting on this report, Ramzy Baroud explains that the question of how to address these human right violations, well known to Palestinians even without the Amnesty report, "has presented a peril to Palestinian intellectuals within Palestine as well as abroad, who have feared that by speaking out against the PA's practices, they indirectly feed into the frequently repeated statement, suggesting that Israel is 'the only real democracy in the Middle East' ".[54] They knew that, given the international atmosphere prevailing then and now, no one would pay attention to the fact that in its offence on human rights, the PA is simply carrying out Israel's orders.

Much attention has been paid already in the Western media to the corruption of the PA and its lack of democracy, as a major cause of the vote shift. But the crucial aspect, that received little attention, is its failure in the Palestinian struggle against the occupation. As BADIL states this, "the Palestinian Authority has become both a prisoner and indispensable partner in endless diplomacy whose purpose is to cover up the fact that nothing is done to bring about a just and lasting peace, and it has failed to take action against those from its own ranks, who publicly undermine the national consensus and struggle for freedom from occupation."[55] With the beginning of the current wave of Israeli oppression in 2000, there was no longer much that the PA could do. Israel was determined to re-establish the Israeli military rule in the occupied territories, and proceeded to accomplish this with brutal force. This could not be stopped by any diplomatic means. Still, where the PA failed was in organizing, or even just supporting, a popular struggle, of the sort that proved successful in the first Palestinian *intifada*.

While the political branches of the Fatah-led PA may have been just passive in the Palestinian struggle for freedom, some of its security forces have been active collaborators with the Israeli occupation, most notably the Preventive Security apparatus, headed by Mohammed Dahlan in the Gaza Strip and Jibril Rajoub in the West Bank. These forces, trained by the CIA,[56] have worked during all years of the Oslo Agreements in tight collaboration with the Israeli security forces, including collaborations in assassinations of Hamas militants. I discuss some of the history of these collaborations in *Israel/Palestine*, with a detailed example of the operations of Rajoub's apparatus.[57] Ample information was published in the Israeli media regarding this cooperation, and Israeli ''security sources'' were at the time full of praise for the achievements of the Palestinian security forces. Dr Boaz Ganor, a security expert from the Interdisciplinary Center in Herzliyah, explained the security concept that underlied the Oslo Agreements: ''At the basis of the conception was the idea of reliance upon the Palestinian intelligence capabilities, especially since in 1993 they were vastly superior to our [intelligence capabilities] as occupiers. This is a system that lives within its people, is familiar with it, and receives cooperation from it.''[58]

If the Palestinian public was fed up with the ''old generation'' of the Fatah and the PA, its ''young generation'' that emerged as a political power towards the Palestinian elections would seem even scarier. The new Fatah faction that was formed in December 2005 is headed by Dahlan and Rajoub, who for many Palestinians are the symbols of the collaboration with Israel. They received their early training in long years of serving in Israeli jails, prior to 1993, where Israel's sophisticated methods of building cooperative new leaders could be put into use. They proved their usefulness to the Israeli occupation during the Oslo years. On the eve of and at the beginning of the 2000 escalation, they were mentioned in the Israeli media as potential candidates favoured by the Israeli security system to replace Arafat. In their new political career on the eve of the elections, they were joined by the jailed Marwan Barghouti, who, prior to his arrest in April 2002, was also mentioned by the same security circles as a favoured potential next leader of the

Palestinian people. While many view him as a national hero – a Mandela in the making – others wonder why he is the only Palestinian who has received the special treatment of being tried by a civilian (rather than a military) court, and who is allowed so much public exposure, including openly running matters of Palestinian politics, while in jail.

In voting for Hamas, Palestinians were opting for a party which had no history of collaboration with the occupiers, and which they believed would not be coerced into such collaboration in the future. But from the perspective of the Israeli army, Hamas's victory entails the complete loss of the network of control it has constructed in the territories since 1993. When it accepted the US demand to allow Hamas's participation in the Palestinian election, Israel – like the US – assumed that although Hamas would be in some measure legitimized, this would only entail a small change in the PA, which would essentially remain controlled by the same apparatuses as before. However, if Palestinians are permitted to implement their own democratic decisions, their security services will come under the jurisdiction of the new government, and can no longer be manipulated by Israel; the days of Israel's appointment or training of Palestinian leaders will be over. As Alex Fishman noted following the election, "defense officials see the results as returning the region to the days before the 1993 Oslo Accords".[59]

With the realization that its apparatuses in the occupied territories were on the verge of collapse, Israel managed within days to mobilize both the US administration and Europe. Overnight, the West forgot its noble words about democracy and threatened to impose an economic stranglehold on the Palestinians for having made the wrong choice at the ballot box. Robert Fisk summed up the situation well:

And now, horror of horrors, the Palestinians have elected the wrong party to power. They were supposed to have given their support to the friendly, pro-Western, corrupt, absolutely pro-American Fatah, which had promised to 'control' them, rather than to Hamas, which said they would represent them. And, bingo, they have chosen the wrong party again . . . God damn that democracy. What are we to do with people who don't vote the way they should?

Way back in the 1930s, the British would lock up the Egyptians who turned against the government of King Farouk. Thus they began to set the structure of anti-democratic governance that was to follow. The French imprisoned the Lebanese government which demanded the same. Then the French left Lebanon. But we have always expected the Arab governments to do what they were told.[60]

After a short period of deliberation, Hamas appointed Ismail Haniyeh[61] as Palestinian Authority prime minister, and Dr Abed al-Aziz Duaik as head of the new Palestinian Legislative Council; Abbas was to remain president of the PA. Both appointees come from the moderate wing of Hamas, and *Ha'aretz* explained that the decision to appoint them "is seen as capitulation to international pressure on the movement".[62] Haniyeh and Duaik announced that "once the new government was formed, Hamas would formulate its own peace plan, with a long-term truce with Israel at its center".[63]

But the fact that Hamas had already renounced terror for a full year before the election, and was offering a long-term truce, was not good enough for Israel and the West. They came up with three conditions that could spare the Palestinian people from Western punishment, which have been since repeated like a mantra: Hamas must recognize Israel, it must recognize existing agreements with Israel, and it must renounce violence. Ismail Haniyeh answered these demands in a phone interview with the *Washington Post* from his home in a Gaza refugee camp:

We are surprised that such conditions are imposed on us. Why don't they direct such conditions and questions to Israel? Has

Israel respected agreements? Israel has bypassed practically all agreements. We say: Let Israel recognize the legitimate rights of the Palestinians first and then we will have a position regarding this. Which Israel should we recognize? The Israel of 1917; the Israel of 1936; the Israel of 1948; the Israel of 1956; or the Israel of 1967? Which borders and which Israel? Israel has to recognize first the Palestinian state and its borders and then we will know what we are talking about.[64]

But Haniyeh's responses appear to fall on deaf ears. It is clear from the way the interview continues that no answer can apparently satisfy dominant Western opinion:

Washington Post: Do you accept the Oslo agreement signed by Yasser Arafat?

Ismail Haniyeh: Israel has completely stopped committing itself to Oslo.

Washington Post: I am not asking about Israel. Are you, as the new Palestinian prime minister, committed to Oslo?

Ismail Haniyeh: Oslo stated that a Palestinian state would be established by 1999. Where is this Palestinian state? Has Oslo given the right to Israel to reoccupy the West Bank, to build the wall and expand the settlements, and to Judaize Jerusalem and make it totally Jewish? Has Israel been given the right to disrupt the work on the port and airport in Gaza? Has Oslo given them the right to besiege Gaza and to stop all tax refunds from the Palestinian Authority?

Washington Post: So you will not abide by past agreements made by the Palestinians and Israel?

Ismail Haniyeh: I have not said that. I have said that Israel . . .

Washington Post: But you are not the prime minister of Israel. Will you abide by past agreements made by the Palestinian governments and Israel?

Ismail Haniyeh: We will review all agreements and abide by those that are in the interest of the Palestinian people.[65]

In its concerted campaign to prevent international recognition of the new Hamas administration, and to impose tough sanctions on the Palestinians, Israel has been exploiting the Islamophobic atmosphere that resurfaced in the US at the beginning of 2006. Israeli security officials flooded the West with reports on the dangers of Hamas's future ties with Iran and Syria, painting a disturbing picture of a global fundamentalist Islamic threat. The conditions were ripe for such propaganda. On 3 February, the Pentagon released its 2006 Quadrennial Defense Review (QDR), where it lays out its vision for what it describes as a "long war". It states that "this war requires the U.S. military to adopt unconventional and indirect approaches. Currently, Iraq and Afghanistan are crucial battlegrounds, but the struggle extends far beyond their borders. With its allies and partners, the United States must be prepared to wage this war in many locations simultaneously and for some years to come."[66] The report lays out "a new 20-year defense strategy that envisions U.S. troops deployed, often clandestinely, in dozens of countries at once to fight terrorism and other nontraditional threats".[67] In its opening paragraph, one can find the themes that Israel was striving to apply also towards Hamas:

> The enemies in this war are not traditional conventional military forces but rather dispersed, global terrorist networks that exploit Islam to advance radical political aims. These enemies have the avowed aim of acquiring and using nuclear and biological weapons to murder hundreds of thousands of Americans and others around the world. They use terror, propaganda and indiscriminate violence in an attempt to subjugate the Muslim world under a radical theocratic tyranny while seeking to perpetuate conflict with the United States and its allies and partners.[68]

With the drums of the long war banging, Israel's line on Hamas appears to have been well received. The US administration urged European and Arab countries to freeze direct aid to the Palestinian Authority, and on 15 February, the US Congress started moves in the same direction. *Ha'aretz* reported joyfully that these moves were unsurprising "considering that most opinion polls show that not since the first Gulf War in 1991 has sympathy for Israel among Americans been as high as it is now . . . The PA, on the other hand, is seen in a positive light by 11 percent of Americans, while 78 percent see it negatively."[69]

This renewed wave of Islamophobia has also bolstered AIPAC's newfound self-confidence. Only a few months previously, its leaders had kept silent as the US exerted pressure on Israel, but its annual policy conference in March 2006 was held in an atmosphere of neocon celebration. The Jewish newspaper *Forward* described the event as follows:

> Even as President Bush's popularity dropped to record lows, his administration was embraced warmly this week by the thousands of delegates at the most influential annual gathering of American Jewish activists . . . Several of the most hardline administration officials, including Vice President Dick Cheney and Ambassador to the United Nations John Bolton, drew a resounding response . . . Cheney's personal approval ratings have dropped to below 20%. But the vice president was received enthusiastically at the Aipac conference, drawing 48 rounds of applause from the 4,500 assembled delegates – including eight standing ovations . . . Cheney – a bugaboo of the left for his role in the Iraq War – spoke for more than 35 minutes, [stressing] the need to stand firm against Islamic extremists, including the newly formed Hamas government in the Palestinian territories, and Iran, whose president has vowed to "wipe Israel off the map".[70]

Forward added that AIPAC "appears to be out of step with the American Jewish community on Iraq. Like many other American Jewish organizations, it supported the Iraq war. But 70% of American Jews oppose the Iraq war, according to a poll commissioned by the American Jewish Committee at the end of 2005."[71]

Regardless of the opinions of the Jewish community they are supposed to represent, the leaders of the pro-Israel lobby are optimistic that, paradoxically, the drop in Bush's approval ratings in American public opinion will force him to adopt the hard line advocated by AIPAC and Israel. Morton Klein, national president of the Zionist Organization of America, said that "President Bush and his advisers believe that if he would relent in this crucial fight against Islamic terrorism, his poll numbers would fall even further . . . Not only would it be wrong for America, it would hurt him politically. The American people want this evil to be crushed."[72]

In this atmosphere, Israel had carte blanche to do what it wanted. On 26 February, after a period of hesitation to assess the response of the international community, it announced that it would withhold Palestinian tax and customs revenues that Israel collects from Palestinian importers. As Amira Hass explains, this is an outrageous, illegal act: "[T]o judge by the actions of the Israeli Cabinet, the money belongs to Israel . . . But it's not supposed to work this way. According to the Oslo accords (and by any standards of common sense and basic justice), the revenues should serve the people who ultimately buy the goods. These tax receipts are not donations of goodwill from Israel; they are not charity. This is not like, say, Dutch foreign aid money, which is given freely by the Dutch people and can be withheld if the Dutch choose to stop giving it. These are tax revenues that are due to the people in the territories where the goods are headed, and the Israelis have no right to hold them up. Since 1994, these revenues, transferred each month from the Israeli Ministry of Finance, have made up a critical portion of the Palestinian Authority budget. When Israel briefly stopped transferring the revenues in 2001, pressure from the EU and other countries – including the U.S. – forced Israel to reverse its decision. Unfortunately, after the Hamas victory, such pressure seems unlikely." [73]

Israel does not conceal its hope that economic strangulation of the Palestinian territories will eventually lead to the collapse of the new Palestinian government. As Dov Weisglass, now Olmert's policy adviser, explained, Israel intends to "put the

Palestinians on a diet . . . The Palestinians will get a lot thinner, but won't die."[74] As part of this "diet," the whole Gaza Strip has been starved as a collective punishment for its "wrong vote". In the first sixty days since the Palestinian elections, the Karni crossing was fully closed by Israel for forty-six days.[75] Karni is the major pipeline for food and industry supplies to the Gaza Strip. As a result of its closure local markets have run out milk, flour, sugar, dairy produce and fruits. The Palestinian PCHR reported that "most bakeries have stopped working due to the lack of flour. Hundreds of Palestinians have been seen standing in long queues in front of some bakeries, which have continued to work but with minimum capacity, to buy bread for their families. This scene is unprecedented in the Gaza Strip."[76]

Until the collapse of the newly elected Palestinian government happens, Israel is determined to disable it from functioning. Israel has refused to let Prime Minister Haniyeh and the other newly elected officials travel from Gaza to the West Bank. When the new Palestinian cabinet was sworn in, on 29 March 2006, the ceremony took place simultaneously in Gaza and Ramallah by video conference. Israel made it perfectly clear that the fourteen ministers from the West Bank and ten from the Gaza Strip will not be permitted to attend cabinet meetings together, because they will not be allowed to travel from one region to the other.[77] Moreover, Israeli officials clarify that even this sort of functioning may not last for long: former Shin Bet chief Avi Dichter, who was singled out by Sharon as his top confidant, and who is the minister of internal secrurity in Olmert's government, announced that "Hamas top man Haniyeh is a legitimate assassination target."[78]

Against this setting, as US and European backing for Israel grows even stronger following the Palestinian elections, Sharon's successors can continue to further undisturbed his ambitious project of land grab in the West Bank.

7

A System of Prisons:
The Plans Behind the West Bank Wall

DURING THE TIME GAINED THROUGH the disengagement plan, Sharon worked on realizing his long-standing vision of Israel's control of the West Bank with frightening efficiency. Let us turn now to what this vision is.

The question that had preoccupied the Israeli political and military elites since the seizure of the Palestinian territories in 1967 was how to retain as much of the occupied land as possible – with as few of its Palestinian inhabitants as possible.[1] The Israeli Labor party's Alon plan, realized in the Oslo Agreements, involved retaining about 40 per cent of the West Bank, but allowing the Palestinians autonomy in the other 60 per cent. However, Barak and Sharon's aim was to undo the Oslo Agreement. From mid-2002 onwards, the entire West Bank and Gaza once again came under direct Israeli military occupation. The current Israeli leadership, which has no intention of ever giving up these territories, needed to devise a long-term method of control over millions of occupied people. The solution that has been developed under Sharon is a complex system of prisons, in which the Palestinians are being pushed into locked and sealed enclaves, fully controlled from the outside by the Israeli army, which also enters them at will. As far as I am aware, this imprisonment of a whole people is an unprecedented model of occupation – and it is being executed with frightening speed and efficiency.

Sharon's project has been to implement throughout the West Bank the model of control perfected in the Gaza Strip. Compared to Gaza, the West Bank population enjoyed relative

**Carte du statut final de la Cisjordanie
présentée par Israël en mai 2000**

Zones autonomes palestiniennes

Zones devant passer un jour
sous souveraineté palestinienne

Zones de sécurité sous contrôle israélien
«temporaire»

Zone sous souveraineté israélienne

Colonies
israéliennes
devant être
annexées
par Israël

△

Colonies
israéliennes
à l'intérieur
des zones
«palestiniennes».

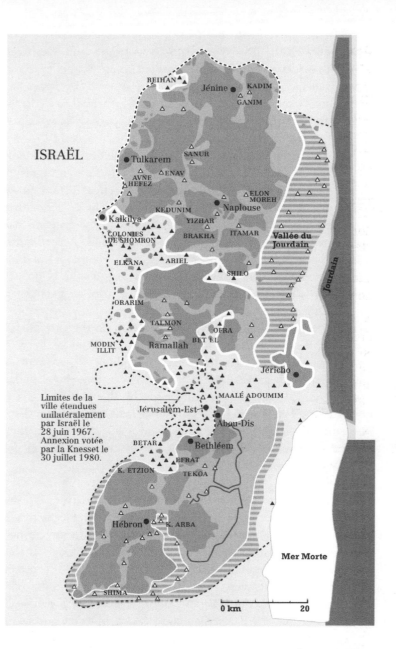

ISRAËL

REIHAN
Jénine
KADIM
GANIM

Tulkarem
SANUR
AVNE
HEFEZ
ENAV

ELON
MOREH
KEDUNIM
Naplouse
Kalkilya
YIZHAR
COLONIES
DE SHOMRON
BRAKHA
ITAMAR
Vallée du
Jourdain

ELKANA
ARIEL

SHILO

ORARIM

TALMON
OFRA
MODIN
ILLIT
Ramallah
BET EL

Jéricho

MAALÉ ADOUMIM

Limites de la
ville étendues
unilatéralement
par Israël le
28 juin 1967.
Annexion votée
par la Knesset le
30 juillet 1980.

Jérusalem-Est
Abou-Dis

BETAR
Bethléem
EFRAT
K. ETZION
TEKOA

Mer Morte

Hébron
K. ARBA

SHIMA

0 km   20

Jourdain

A System of Prisons: 159

freedom of movement, both internally and externally, until September 2000. The West Bank is a bigger and wealthier region than Gaza, and until recently turning it into a prison seemed an inconceivable idea. But since May 2002, Israel has been constructing a wall in the West Bank, referred to by Israel as a "separation fence", or "security barrier", which if completed would make this system of control a reality.

At a meeting of 23 June 2002 in which the first blueprints of the wall's route were approved, the then foreign minister Shimon Peres protested that "the plan in effect meant Israel was annexing some 22 percent of the West Bank".[2] Since that time, the segment of the wall already under construction has been extended much further into Palestinian land. According to a November 2003 UN report, the section completed at that point – which at that point did not yet include the region of Jerusalem – had already annexed 14.5 per cent of Palestinian land.[3] If the extended plans approved by Sharon's subsequent government are executed – including a wall on the east side of the West Bank, separating it from the Jordan river – the wall system would enclose on the Israeli side about 40 per cent of Palestinian land in the West Bank. Along the route under construction, Israel is uprooting tens of thousands of trees, dispossessing Palestinian farmers of their land, and pushing them into small enclaves between fences and walls; eventually, they will be surrounded on all sides, as is currently the case in the Gaza Strip.

Israel presents the wall as vital for its security – a necessary barrier to Palestinian terror that would protect the lives of Israeli citizens. Compared to preventing the deaths of innocent Israeli civilians, runs the Israeli line, the regrettable inconvenience caused to the Palestinians is secondary. In reality, though, it was not security considerations that determined the present route of the wall. If the goal were really to prevent terrorist infiltration into Israel, the wall could just as easily have been built on Israel's 1967 border, leaving Palestinian lands intact. In Israel's declared plans for the final agreement, the big settlement blocks in the centre of the West Bank are to be annexed to Israel. However, even if it had been based on these plans, the wall would have followed a different route. The route planned by Colonel Shaul Arieli, head of the Barak government's "Peace Administration," also deviated from the 1967 border and incorporated the large settlement blocs into Israeli territory. But the 300 square kilometres of West Bank territory annexed in this plan is less than a third of the land enclosed by the present route. Arieli's plan would have cut off 56,000 Palestinians from contiguous connection within the West Bank; the current route will leave 400,000 stranded.[4]

Sharon and the Israeli army designed the wall's route with a view to annexing as much West Bank land as possible. Yet it wasn't only territorial greed that drove Israel to send its bulldozers into the Palestinian lands of the northern West Bank, where the wall has now been completed. These lands are on the western part of the Mountain Groundwater Basin – the large reservoir in the West Bank whose waters flow underground to central Israel. Of the 600 million cubic metres of water that the Mountain reservoir provides annually, Israel takes about 500 million.[5] Control over water resources has always been a primary motivation for Israel's occupation of Palestine. The Labor governments of the 1970s first approved settlements in areas that they defined as "critical locations" for drilling, in a plan misleadingly entitled "Preservation of the Sources of the Yarkon [River]".[6] All these settlements (such as Elkana, six kilometres from the 1967 "Green Line" border) now sit on the Israeli side of the wall.

To get a better grasp of the motives behind the wall project, it is worth examining the map in figure 2. This is the only formal map that Israel has ever presented as its proposal for the final agreement. It was put forward by Prime Minister Ehud Barak in the Taba-Eilat negotiations in May 2000, two months before the Camp David summit, and was originally published in the Israeli newspaper *Yediot Aharonot*, on 19 May of that year.[7] According to this map, the darker areas would come under "Palestinian sovereignty," and together comprise 60 per cent of the West Bank. The rest of the territory will remain Israeli, the white areas to be annexed immediately, and the striped areas to be held "temporarily". "Sovereign" Palestinian land is divided into four isolated enclaves, with no territorial continuity. (The two northern enclaves are separated by a narrow strip of Israeli settlements; in other versions of the plan, these two would constitute one unit.) In practice, the wall project aims at the realization of this map. At present, the wall follows the line separating the dark (Palestinian) areas from the white areas that border Israel, on the western side of the West Bank. Work on the eastern wall that will separate the West Bank from the Jordan River has not started yet, but Israel has been taking systematic steps to isolate these areas from the rest of the West Bank.[8]

In a detailed account of the development of the Wall plans, Meron Rappaport points out that they are partially based on an older plan of the right-wing academic Arnon Sofer, a geography professor at Haifa University and the prophet of "the Arab demographic danger". Sofer has advocated for years that Israel should set its permanent borders unilaterally – "otherwise the Arabs will inundate us and there will be no Jewish entity here anymore". As a geographer, he prepared maps that detail where this border should be and how it should be enforced: "The West Bank," Sofer explained, "must be split into three parts, three cantons, basically three sausages. One sausage from Jenin to Ramallah, a second sausage from Bethlehem to Hebron and a third tiny sausage around the city of Jericho. An electric fence must be put up around these three Palestinian sausages, which extend on less than half the West Bank, and finish the business."[9] According to Sofer, on 6 February 2001, just after Sharon was elected prime minister, Sharon's aides approached him requesting the maps. Rappaport explains further:

When Sofer sees the map of the separation fence going up, he smiles to himself. "This is exactly my map," he says, "it"'s as if an exact copy is being put up.' [But] Sofer takes too much credit for himself. This map is not something new for Sharon. "I haven't sat with the prime minister recently," says Ron Nahman, the mayor of [the West Bank settlement of] Ariel, 'but the map of the fence . . . is the same map I saw during every visit Arik [Sharon] made here since 1978. He told me he has been thinking about it since 1973.'

There are some who call this plan of Sharon's "the bantustan plan" (according to *Ha'aretz*, Sharon used this term when talking to the former prime minister of Italy four years ago), there are those who call it the canton plan. But it is clear that this plan is now taking on concrete and barbed wire. Only now it is called the seamline [separation] plan.[10]

When work started on the construction of the wall, Israel argued that it would be a temporary security barrier, and that its route would not represent any permanent borderline. But on 2 January 2006, shortly before Sharon left office, the Israeli paper *Ma'ariv* disclosed the plan he intended to present for the West Bank. The plan rests on US eventual acknowledgement that the Road Map was stalemated – and that in fact it has always been a non-starter, given that there has never been a genuine Palestinian "partner for peace". This was still before the Palestinian elections that brought Hamas to power, but as we have seen throughout this book, from Israel's perspective no Palestinian leadership was ever found an appropriate partner. The argument Sharon's plan was based on was that the Road Map failed because the PA under Abbas failed to fulfil its obligations to combat the terror network. In the absence of a suitable partner, Israel should set its borders unilaterally – that is to say, decide for itself how much of the Palestinian land it needs to take, and disengage from the rest. According to this plan, as soon as they are agreed that the Road Map is dead, Israel and the US will start "secret and intensive negotiations" leading to a "signed agreement with Washington that determines the final eastern border of Israel". The American–Israeli agreement will include "fast completion of the fence [wall] . . . that would become a real border fence".[11]

Although Sharon has left the political scene, this solution remains Israel's official plan. On the eve of the Israeli elections of 28 March 2006, Olmert publicly unveiled the new disengagement plan that he as Prime Minister would strive to implement. The plan was given a new name: *consolidation,* or *convergence,* but other than that, it simply reiterates Sharon's plan, emphasizing that Israel's new border would correspond to the route of the wall, which would be completed before the disengagement starts. "I believe that in four years' time," Olmert declared, "Israel will be disengaged from the vast majority of the Palestinian population, within new borders, with the route of the fence – which until now has been a security fence – adjusted to the new line of the permanent borders."[12] Olmert believes that circumstances are currently favourable for enforcing this solution on the Palestinians, because following Hamas's victory in the Palestinian elections it should become even more evident to the world that there is no Palestinian partner for peace negotiations: "There is now a 'window of opportunity' for reaching an international agreement on setting the border, in the wake of Hamas' rise to power and . . . support following the Gaza pullout," he said.[13] To bring the plan to fruition, the wall would have to move even further east than its present route, and Olmert is explicit in outlining his views on its final location, at which point it would serve as Israel's permanent border with the Palestinians: "He wants to make sure Israel holds on to [the settlements of] Ariel, Ma'aleh Adumim, the Jerusalem envelope and Gush Etzion," as well as establishing Israeli control in the Jordan Valley.[14] A glance at where these points are located in the map in Figure 2 reveals that Olmert, like Sharon and Barak before him, is indeed striving to impose the reality represented by this map on the Palestinians and officially annex the white areas to Israel.

Olmert's consolidation plan, which has later become the official plan of Olmert's new government, was received by the Israeli media with the same enthusiasm as all previous Israeli "peace plans". As it also mentioned the possibility of future evacuation of settlements east of the new border, Olmert and his party, Kadima, were hailed as the new left, or the "peace camp" of Israel. Labor's leader Amir Peretz even announced his support of the plan already before the election. No one in the mainstream Israeli media or politics has bothered to examine the maps and note that this plan deprives the Palestinians officially of over 40 per cent of the West Bank's land.

As we have seen, this 40–60 per cent division of the West Bank also formed the basis of the Alon plan, which was adopted by the Labor party in the 1980s and which formed the underlying concept of the Oslo Agreements. The Palestinians and the Israeli peace camp have always opposed the Alon plan; nevertheless, there are substantial differences between that concept and its current implementation by Sharon and his successors. In the Alon plan, the Palestinians would have autonomy over the 60 per cent of territory which remained to them, possibly in some kind of confederation with Jordan. They would have complete control over their internal affairs and economy, and would be allowed to maintain some form of civil society and development. For this to be possible, it is crucial that this portion of the West Bank come under autonomous Palestinian control – something very far from the present reality.

To gain some understanding of the kind of life Palestinians can expect inside their 60 per cent of land under Sharon's plans, it is worth examining the current situation inside the darker areas denoted in Figure 2. In these regions, there are still around forty isolated Israeli settlements (represented here by white triangles), connected by security roads and military zones. The lighter gray areas inside the dark areas in the map are, thus, lands presently controlled by Israel. Contrary to prevailing assumptions, in the plan put forward by Barak at Camp David in July 2000, none of these settlements would be dismantled.[15] This means that in practice Barak's offer was to preserve the situation in the Palestinian enclaves precisely as it was under Israeli occupation. Obviously, Sharon was no different. There is no evidence in Sharon's plans, repeated verbatim by Olmert, that Israel has any real intention of willingly dismantling even the settlements that are inside the so-called "Palestinian areas". Sharon had declared that settlements such as Kiryat Arba (near the West Bank city of Hebron) and even the settlements in Hebron itself, as well as others like Beit El and Ofra to the east of Ramallah, will remain Israeli in the future, even though they are not part of the big settlement blocks that Israel formally intends to annex. In his first interview as Sharon's replacement, Olmert remained vague on this issue: "We are moving toward separation from the Palestinians, toward setting Israel's permanent border," Olmert said. However, "he declined to offer any further details, and in particular failed to mention settlements such as Hebron, Beit El and Ofra, which Prime Minister Ariel Sharon had viewed as part of the settlement blocs that Israel would retain."[16] In the official plan that Olmert later made public, he maintains this vagueness with regard to which settlements will be evacuated. But in any case, the timeframe that he sets for this potential evacuation is four years, which in practice means that there is no commitment to evacuate anything before the end of his first term in office.

If this map is fully implemented, and the four Palestinian enclaves are surrounded by a wall, the situation in the West Bank will be precisely as it was in Gaza prior to the summer 2005 evacuation: a system of prisons, studded with Israeli settlements, isolated from the world, and controlled both from the outside and from the inside by the Israeli army.

No present Israeli leader would ever dismantle settlements of his own free will. However, Sharon, Olmert and the army may have taken into account the possibility that Israel might eventually be forced to evacuate some of the settlements inside the

Palestinian enclaves, in the same way that it was compelled to evacuate the Gaza settlements. Should this scenario arise, they plan to keep the enclaves under full Israeli control from the outside, as has happened in Gaza since the evacuation. Olmert was explicit on this in the public announcement of his plan. The arrangements after the disengagement will "provide the Israel Defense Forces with freedom of action in the West Bank, similar to the post-disengagement situation in the Gaza Strip".[17]

But even without taking into account Israel's future plans, currently the most horrifying aspect of the wall project is what is happening to the lands around Palestinian villages and towns, which are designated to be eventually annexed by Israel. The aim of the wall is to include the land inside Israel's border, but not the villages and towns themselves. To achieve this, the present line of the wall is not straight, but winds around areas of human habitation, creating in many cases a loop that encircles a town, leaving only one exit connecting it to the West Bank. (For a segment of the constructed wall see Figure 3 in Chapter 8, p. 175.) In this way, the wall separates towns and villages from the agricultural lands on which Palestinians depend for their existence and livelihood. In many places the wall is built right around dwellings, leaving the fields on the Israeli side. The Wall also permanently separates the villages from each other, turning them into isolated enclaves. A trip to a neighbouring village or town – for work or study, a hospital visit, or to visit friends and family – must be done along bypass roads controlled by the Israeli army and its checkpoints. In some cases, the villages will not have any connecting exit to the West Bank, but will remain fully on the Israeli side of the wall, surrounded by their own system of fences and walls separating them from their fields and from the rest of the West Bank – and turning them into actual prisons.

This is no less than a massive project of land grab on Israel's part. At the level of declaration and diplomacy, Israel says that the farmers in the enclaves will be allowed access to their fields through special gates; in practice, the gates are often closed, or permits are not granted. In many areas where the wall is completed already, farmers can no longer access their land. Under Ottoman law, which still applies in the West Bank, land not cultivated for three years can be legally confiscated. The biggest fear of the Palestinian farmers unable to access their land is that, even if Israel does not get international permission to annex these areas, it will apply this law to appropriate their lands. In fact, even without recourse to this law, Israel can decide at any moment to declare these lands to be state lands (lands belonging to the state of Israel). In January 2005 *Ha'aretz* reported a decision by the Israeli cabinet of July 2004 to apply the "Absentee Property Law" to lands in the Jerusalem area. This legislation was passed in 1950 in order to expropriate the land of Palestinians who fled their homes when Israel was founded in 1948. According to the law, absentee assets are transferred to the authority of the Israeli Custodian of Absentee Property, without the owners being eligible for any compensation. Since the Jerusalem area has been formally annexed to Israel, the law can technically be applied. What this means is that Palestinians separated from their lands and properties by the wall would count as absentees, and their property would be expropriated by Israel. *Ha'aretz* reported that Palestinian landholders from Bethlehem and Beit Jala in the Jerusalem region requested permission to continue working their fields, which are within Jerusalem's municipal jurisdiction. "The state's response stated that the lands no longer belong to them, but have been handed over to the Custodian of Absentee Property. At stake are thousands of dunums of agricultural land on which the Palestinians grew olives and grapes throughout the years." It is not just agricultural land that would be lost to its owners, but all houses and properties. By some estimates "they could add up to half of all East Jerusalem property".[18] In the face of international and local protest, the government's legal adviser reversed this government decision on 1 February 2005. But the possibility that Israel will apply the absentee law in the future remains open.[19]

According to UN figures, summarized in the ruling of the International Court of Justice,[20] as a result of the construction of the wall, 237,000 Palestinians will be stranded outside it and disconnected from the West Bank proper. In addition, around 160,000 Palestinians would be included in the West Bank side of the wall, but would reside in almost completely encircled communities, cut off from their farmland, their jobs, universities and schools. Altogether, then, 400,000 Palestinians are affected by the wall. Similar figures have also been cited in the Israeli media.[21]

On 20 February 2005, following several rulings by the Israeli Supreme Court, the Israeli cabinet approved a modified route for the wall, thereby reducing by 2.5 per cent the amount of Palestinian land to be effectively annexed. The reductions were mainly in the area of South Hebron, where work on the wall had barely commenced (which means in practice that the route could still change and take in more territory as work progresses on it). There were smaller adjustments in other areas, with the result that some of the encircled villages retained some of their land. However, this does not materially affect the total number of Palestinians encircled by the wall.[22]

The current route of the wall thus cuts off 400,000 Palestinians from their sources of livelihood, and imprisons them in isolated enclaves. What will happen to these people, whose land is being annexed by Israel? With no means of subsistence, they will eventually be forced to leave the enclaves in which they find themselves, in order to seek employment on the peripheries of West Bank cities and towns. In this way, sections of the West Bank that border Israel will be ''cleansed'' of Palestinians. In the northern West Bank towns of Qalqilya and Tulkarm, where the wall was completed in 2003, this is already happening. Qalqilya used to be a flourishing local centre of commerce and agriculture. The wall separated it from its lands and encircled the town on all sides, leaving a bottleneck controlled by the army as the only exit connecting it to the West Bank. Now it is a dead city: many of its inhabitants have fled to seek subsistence on the edges of other West Bank towns; those who remain have succumbed to the despair and decline that characterizes prisoners.

Qalqilya is right on the "Green Line", the 1967 border with Israel. It would have been possible to build the Wall on its Israeli side, as the original plan proposed. This would have been a much shorter route, easier to guard and protect than the present line, which surrounds the town on all sides and cuts through West Bank territory. But the devisers of the wall's present route were guided not by security considerations but rather by the old Israeli vision of redeeming the land and "cleansing" it of Arabs.

On 9 July 2004, following months of research and discussion over the wall, the International Court of Justice (ICJ) issued a ruling, "Legal Consequence of the Construction of a Wall in the Occupied Palestinian Territory".[23] It determined that Israel "has the right, and indeed the duty, to . . . protect the life of its citizens" but that "the measures taken are bound nonetheless to remain in conformity with applicable international law". The court found the current route of the wall to be a serious and egregious violation of international law.

The first reactions in Israel were of worried concern regading the possible ramifications of the court's ruling. In mid-August 2004, Attorney General Menachem Mazuz presented the government with a report issued by a team of prosecutors. In his statement he wrote: "It is hard to exaggerate the negative ramifications the International Court ruling will have on Israel on many levels, even on matters that lie beyond the separation fence. The decision creates a political reality for Israel on the international level, that may be used to expedite actions against Israel in international forums, to the point that they may result in sanctions.'[24] The Attorney General recommended "the government make a supreme effort to make plans for the route of the separation fence comply with the ones specified in the High Court of Justice ruling."[25]

On the ground, however, the construction of the wall continued. By 2006, with the lifting of international pressure following the Gaza disengagement and the election of Hamas, Israel is determined to complete the wall, and even its route to the east, as specified in Olmert's plan, which, as we have seen, has become the blueprint for Israel's new government to follow. Israel is no longer hiding its intentions to turn the wall into a permanent fact. But liberal Israeli discourse now fully endorses it. A *Ha'aretz* editorial even pleaded with Olmert to speed up the wall's completeion, in order to speed up the realization of the new consolidation, or convergence plan:

> Interim Prime Minister Ehud Olmert must place the completion of the fence at the top of his agenda – first, in order to maintain security and save civilian lives . . . Second, completion of the fence is prerequisite for implementing the convergence plan vis-a-vis the West Bank. It is difficult to conceive a withdrawal to a new security line and the evacuation of tens of thousands of settlers from their homes without a physical barrier between Israel and the territories – just as the fence around the Gaza Strip facilitated the withdrawal from there. If Olmert wants to implement the redeployment in the near future, he must accelerate the fence's construction.[26]

Listing the numerous articles of the fourth Geneva Convention flouted by the present route, the ruling observes that "there is also a risk of further alterations to the demographic composition of the Occupied Palestinian Territory resulting from . . . the departure of Palestinian populations from certain areas".[27] In simpler language, the court is warning of "transfer".

The word "transfer" evokes the collective memory of the *nakba*, trucks arriving in the middle of the night to transport

Palestinian villagers across the border, which happened in a number of places in 1948. Transfer on that model is not possible in today's world, but the idea of cleansing the Palestinians trapped in the enclaves that Israel intends to annex remains vivid in the consciousness of the Israeli army. On 2 April 2003, the Israeli army produced a scene from this script: at 3 a.m., a large force raided the refugee camp of Tulkarm, blocked all the roads and paths with barbed wire and announced on loudspeakers that all males aged between fifteen and forty must go to a certain compound at the centre of the camp. At 9 a.m., the army began to transport the gathered males to a nearby refugee camp. This time it was only a staged scene, and the residents were allowed to return after a few days. But the producers of this particular show made sure that its significance would not escape the participants and the audience. They took special care to ensure that the evacuation was carried out with trucks – an exact re-enactment of the 1948 trauma. As one of the residents described his feelings when he got into the truck, "all the memories and childhood stories of my father and grandfather about the *nakba* came back."[28]

As I wrote at the time in *Yediot Aharonot*, "many interpret this show as a 'general rehearsal' for the possibility of a future transfer. There is no doubt that the current government is mentally prepared for transfer, but it is not certain that the 'international conditions' are ripe for executing this in the way that had been staged in the Tulkarm camp. But "transfer" is not just carried out with trucks. In the Israeli history of "land redemption" there is also another, more covert and sophisticated model. In the "Judaization of Galilee" project that began in the 1950s, the Palestinians that remained in Israel were robbed of half their lands, isolated in small enclaves, surrounded by Israeli settlements; gradually, they lost the bonds that held them together as a nation. This kind of internal transfer is now taking place in the occupied territories.'[29]

Right now, 400,000 Palestinians are destined for a slow and

invisible transfer away from their land. They are being pushed out of their towns and villages into the four big West Bank enclaves that Israel has allocated for Palestinian residence. If the world lets this happen, and if the process is completed, Palestinians will reside in these crowded enclaves surrounded by walls and electric fences, as they currently do in Gaza. Moreover, the Israeli "land redeemers" may envision even these prison enclaves as just an interim stage. They may believe that, weakened, impoverished, reduced to despair by prison life, many Palestinians will eventually move away altogether. Perhaps they are awaiting the international conditions conducive to the "creative" solutions of settling the Palestinians somewhere else entirely, as Sharon had proposed in the 1980s. Then, it was Jordan; now "transfer" circles are talking about Iraq, or an "extended" Jordan that would include parts of Iraq.[30] The short-term aim, however, is to concentrate as many West Bank Palestinians as possible in the four enclaves that will be controlled in the same way as the Gaza Strip.

In 1969, the Israeli philosopher Yeshayahu Leibovitz anticipated that in the occupied territories "concentration camps would be erected by the Israeli rulers . . . Israel would be a state that would not deserve to exist, and it will not be worthwhile to preserve it."[31] How far from Leibovitz's prophecy is the fenced-in Gaza Strip? In the West Bank, the situation is still different. The imprisonment of the Palestinians is not yet completed, and it can be stopped. Along the route of the wall, the internal struggle of Israeli society is now taking place – a conflict between the self-proclaimed "land redemptionists" who, no matter how much land they have, will always want more, and those who want to live in a state that deserves to exist.

8

The Struggle: Expanding the Prison Cells

WITH ISRAEL TURNING THE WEST BANK into a system of prisons, the most immediate question is how this process can be resisted, stopped and reversed. As Noam Chomsky has said, in many areas of the world today the struggle is to expand, or sometimes even just to maintain the size of the prison cells.[1] For years now the Palestinians have lived in a prison system monitored by Israel, but, as we have seen, Israel's policy under Sharon and his successors is to shrink the area of the cells still further. Now, the focus of the struggle is on preventing the completion of this prison system – on pushing away the narrowing prison walls. Largely unknown and unreported, since 2003 a new form of popular resistance has developed along the route of the wall in the West Bank. Palestinian farmers whose land is being robbed, together with Israeli opponents of the occupation, stand day after day in front of the bulldozers and the Israeli army. Along this route, the story of the other Israel–Palestine is being born. It deserves a book of its own, but I would like to tell here just some of its inspiring history, focusing on how it has developed on the Israeli side.

1. 2003 – Crossing the lines

Right from the very beginning of Israel's oppression of the Palestinian *intifada* in October 2000, there emerged from the core of the Israeli left many anti-occupation groups that stood up immediately against the new phase of the occupation. Among them were various draft resistance movements: the Coalition of

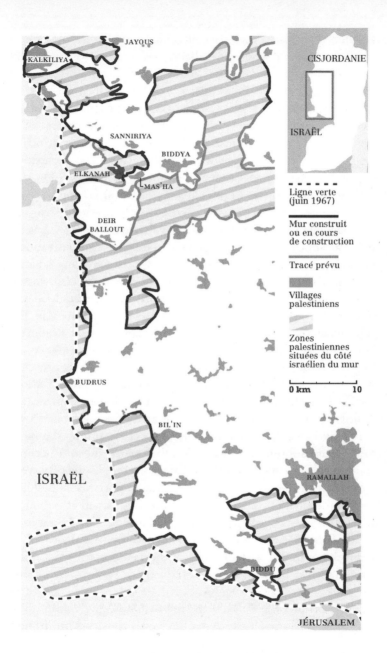

CISJORDANIE

ISRAËL

- - - Ligne verte
(juin 1967)

Mur construit
ou en cours
de construction

Tracé prévu

Villages
palestiniens

Zones
palestiniennes
situées du côté
israélien du mur

0 km ———— 10

JAYOUS

KALKILIYA

SANNIRIYA

BIDDYA

ELKANAH

MAS'HA

DEIR
BALLOUT

BUDRUS

BIL'IN

ISRAËL

RAMALLAH

BIDDU

JÉRUSALEM

Women for Just Peace, which comprises several women's organizations and whose members were demonstrating in Tel Aviv as early as 1 October 2000; Ta'ayush Arab–Jewish, a movement of Israeli Palestinians and Jews which focuses on solidarity work with the Palestinians in the occupied territories; the veteran movement Gush Shalom, and many others.[2] For many of these groups, most notably Ta'ayush, a basic principle has been that the struggle for peace and against the occupation should comprise joint Israeli–Palestinian resistance. On the Palestinian side, there were growing voices calling for a return to a popular and civil uprising, and away from armed struggle. Right from the start of the second Palestinian *intifada*, Israelis and Palestinians have co-organized peaceful demonstrations, extending hands to each other across the Israeli army's barricades and checkpoints. Ta'ayush and other groups also started regular solidarity convoys to the territories, delivering food and medicine. Activists in many groups have participated in the Palestinian olive harvest, in order to protect the Palestinians from attacks of the settlers. In one outstanding instance, in October 2002, Ta'ayush maintained a round-the-clock presence of two weeks in the village of Yanun near Nablus, whose residents started leaving because of the constant harassment of the settlers – to which the Israeli army turned a blind eye.

But by 2003 there was a feeling, especially among the new, young generation of Israeli activists that joined the anti-occupation struggle during the *intifada*, that these acts of solidarity were not sufficient. While they were of crucial importance in building the anti-occupation movement and directing Israeli attention to the realities of the occupation, they did not develop into a joint Israeli–Palestinian political struggle, led by the Palestinians themselves. By the end of 2002, the construction of the West Bank wall had begun. There was a feeling, particularly among the young, that the struggle needed to enter a new phase in order to protect the Palestinian land that was, and continues to be, grabbed. To be able to resist the wall's construction, Israelis had to cross the lines – to stand along with the Palestinians in their non-violent struggle over their land, against their own army. Given the political atmosphere in Israel at the time, for many Israelis, including anti-occupation activists, this was a difficult step to take.

At the same time, however, another model of support for the Palestinian struggle had been developing in the occupied territories. In spring 2001, a group of international activists joined Palestinians to establish the International Solidarity Movement (ISM).[3] (One of its Israel/Palestine founders was Neta Golan, an Israeli living in Ramallah.) Since then, hundreds of volunteers from around the world have travelled to Palestine and maintained a constant presence in Palestinian villages and towns, to provide as much protection to the Palestinians as they can, to document human rights violations, to prevent house demolitions and the uprooting of trees, and to perform other tasks necessary for the survival of Palestinian communities across the West Bank and the Gaza Strip. These were people who could not be viewed as sharing the responsibility for the oppression of the Palestinian people; they did not belong to the occupying people. Nevertheless, they chose to come and join the Palestinian struggle, driven by a sense of justice and humanity.

A handful of young Israeli activists decided to join the ISM individually, often without exposing their identity as Israelis. In 2002, they started travelling in all areas of the West Bank, learning about the situation there, and looking for the best way to resist the occupation. One of them was Yonatan Pollak, then twenty, from Tel Aviv, who would later become the symbol of the Israeli anti-wall struggle. In September 2002, Pollak went with the ISM to the village of Jayous, where 75 per cent of the community's farmland was destined to be annexed to the Israeli side of the wall. "I was shocked. I was completely astonished," he later said, "because [what I saw] was in absolute contradiction to what we were taught about this wall."[4] The weeks of struggle in Jayous, where people were trying to stop the bulldozers with their bodies, were a formative experience for the small group of Israelis who participated. As Pollak later explained, it was the first time they moved from protest to resistance. "Instead of holding a sign in front of Israel's Ministry of Defense, the Israeli activists were in the West Bank with Palestinians, trying to save Palestinian land from destruction and confiscation. It was the first opportunity for us as Israeli activists to create relationships with Palestinians . . . based on solidarity, not normalizing relations under occupation," he said.[5]

In early 2003, on the eve of the Iraq war, there was a growing apprehension among Palestinians and the Israeli left that the worst-case scenarios might take place. Given that the Israeli media had made mention of how Palestinians could be settled in Jordan, which itself might be given parts of the new "liberated" Iraq,[6] some feared that an act of transfer might even take place under the cover of war. But the chief fear, which turned out to be well founded, regarded what would happen in the areas along the wall's route. With the world's attention focused on Iraq, Israel could try to intensify construction of the wall – and brutally oppress any attempts of resistance. That March, the Israeli army started attacking the ISM activists who were in the territories witnessing the atrocities and forcing a degree of military restraint through their presence alone. On 16 March, Rachel Corrie, a twenty-three-year-old student from Olympia, Washington, and an artist with a deep faith in humanity and justice, was run over and killed in cold blood by an Israeli bulldozer in Gaza. On 6 April, Brian Avery from North Carolina was shot in the face by an Israeli tank in Jenin. (Avery survived, after months of facial reconstruction in hospital.) Six days later, the Englishman Tom Hurndall was shot in the head by Israeli snipers in Rafah. He died from his injury on 14 January 2004. Other ISM activists were arrested and deported. The army appeared determined to be unopposed in its work of destruction.

At the beginning of March 2003, a Palestinian Emergency Committee (PEC), was formed, comprising NGOs and human rights groups. It extended a call to the Israeli anti-occupation forces to stand together and to plan shared acts of protection. In response, representatives of sixteen Israeli anti-occupation groups met in Tel Aviv on 12 March, and a week later there was a joint meeting with the PEC. Of the many initiatives agreed on, I will follow here just one, which pertains to the future development of the joint Palestinian/Israeli struggle against the wall. In fact, following the meeting, there was some debate in the Israeli anti-occupation camp which it is important to pay attention to precisely because it regarded the very definition and concept of a Palestinian-led joint struggle. The debate took place in emails to the mailing list of the Coalition of Women for Just Peace (CWJP), where many of the other anti-occupation groups are also represented. Since this was a closed mailing-list exchange, I will omit the names of the participants, but I can disclose that I identify with A.

A few days after the Tel Aviv meeting, the coordinator of the CWJP list sent a message: "We have a request from Ta"ayush: Is the Coalition willing to donate money for food to the Palestinians in the territories? . . .' This solicited the following response from A.

Fri, 21 Mar 2003 18:49:54 +0100
Subject: Re: [CWJP] funding for food?

Dear all,
I attended the meeting of March 12 of all anti-occupation organizations at Gush Shalom's office. This was a response to the appeal by the Palestinian Emergency Committee to the Israeli organizations. Y.H. presented the summary of a previous meeting with the committee, and the "list" of their requests from us. One very explicit thing they said is that at the present emergency stage, they don't need food. They prepared for the emergency locally, and they feel this front is covered. What they need from us is political support.

A request they attached much importance to was that there would be also Israelis among the international solidarity people in the territories, particularly in this dangerous period.

I believe there is a deeper reason for their request for us not to focus now on food, a reason which I deeply share. If we continue to focus on food donations, this suggests that our responsibility to what is going on is that of a charity organization . . . (Of course I don't mean to imply that people should not donate – only that we shouldn't feel we are doing any form of struggle this way) . . . The challenge the Palestinian Emergency Committee posed to us is a real one. Being present in towns and villages which face most danger at this time is taking real responsibility. It is difficult, even dangerous. Obviously the army is trying to intimidate the international solidarity people, with Rachel Corrie dead, and Eric Hawanith, 21, from Chicago wounded in Nablus yesterday. But I don't believe they will dare apply the same means to Israelis. The fact that we are invited gives us the guarantee of safety from the Palestinian side. As it is now an emergency situation, perhaps we can think of ways to act along these lines?

A.

Through the responses and discussion that followed, it became apparent that there were two fundamental questions on which the participants could not achieve consensus. One concerned whether food convoys were still a meaningful form of struggle at the time. The other was the concept of the joint struggle, with A representing the position that it should be the Palestinians who lead the struggle and propose its focus and strategies. The following reply from a member of Ta'ayush addressed the first question, explaining the importance of maintaining the food convoys:

Date: Sat, 22 Mar 2003 23:01:39 +0200
To: "Coalition of Women for a Just Peace" <CWJP@ya-hoogroups.com>
Subject: A's email

Dear All,
I must disagree with A.

First the facts. According to the World Bank the effects of the siege are stupendous. Twenty-seven months after the outbreak of the intifada, 60 percent of the population of the West Bank and Gaza Strip live under the international poverty line of $2 per day. The number of poor has tripled from 637,000 in September 2000 to nearly 2 million today . . . Per capita food consumption has declined by 30 percent in the past two years and there is severe malnutrition in the Gaza Strip, equivalent to levels found in some of the poorer sub-Saharan countries, as found in a recent Johns Hopkins University Study. So, despite what some people say, there appears to be an acute need for food.

As to politics. I share with A. her fear that Israeli activists will underplay the politics of resistance and underscore in its stead a humanitarian approach. But this again is not the case regarding the food campaign.

In South Hebron, for example, one of the locations to which we delivered food this week the local population is fighting daily with their teeth to hold on to the land, despite the harassment, constant intimidation and violence of the settlers and Israeli military. The food supply and solidarity visit we held there earlier this week is crucial for their struggle, which is actually our struggle. Indeed, the food supply is meant to strengthen the Tzumud [sticking to the land] of the Palestinians, who are fighting against all odds, trying to hang on while Sharon and the Israeli government constantly and systematically destroy their infrastructure of existence.

Second, the activities Ta'ayush organizes, including the food campaign, manage to do a few other things. First, by going to closed military areas we break the military siege, the political, physical, and psychological barriers that are at the basis of Sharon's policies. This week we brought hundreds of people to the Salfit area which was under strict closure, including many Israelis who were in the occupied territories for the first time . . .

Third, the food campaign is used to mobilize the Israeli and international public, by exposing once again the oppression and subjugation of the Palestinian people. In and of itself the exposure of the dire poverty in the occupied territories, particularly during a period in which the media cares about nothing but the war against Iraq, is an extremely important political act . . .

Best,

B.

The discussion continued, with most participants siding with B. and adding further arguments as to the importance of food convoys. No one was doubting the importance of humanitarian work and aid to suffering people. However, A.'s perspective was that such aid cannot replace political struggle. Focusing on just a battle for the survival of the oppressed means, indirectly, accepting that the situation cannot be reversed. Where hope lies is in the next phase of resistance and struggle. In any case, the crucial factor at the time was that the initiative to shift the focus away from aid and solidarity work came from the Palestinians. This second question, on the meaning of a joint struggle, was largely ignored in the discussion. A. replied to B. and others:

Date: Sun, 23 Mar 2003 20:00:12 +0100
Subject: [CWJP] Facing the Palestinian emergency appeal

Dear all,
Trying to figure out the way the discussion of the Palestinian emergency appeal has developed, I think two issues have been

conflated. The one that most responses related to is our daily and long-term strategies facing the atrocities of the occupation and the suffering of the Palestinians, and the other, which I have been trying to focus on, is our response to the appeal of the Palestinian Emergency Committee (PEC).

As far as I can see, none of the responses pro food donations in the present discussion addressed the specific statement of our Palestinian partners. The discussion remained an internal assessment of what the Israeli anti-occupation forces believe is good now for the Palestinians, or for the political struggle of Israelis.

The appeal of the PEC to the Israeli organizations is something of a historical precedent, and, in my opinion, it deserves more attention . . .

Regarding [the PEC's request for] presence in areas of danger: The last days, a group of us has been forming, who would like to work on this front. The basic concept shaped through further consultation with PEC and ISM, is that in the West Bank, the area in most danger is the North – areas around the new "fence" (Qalqilia, etc) . . .

A.

The debate continued for several days, and then died out without reaching an agreement. Those who eventually answered the Palestinian call were at the time the activists of the young generation (most of whom did not concern themselves with this old-guard email debate). There was at that stage, a difference in views between the younger generation, which was ready to cross the lines and join the Palestinians in their struggle, and the established anti-occupation groups who were more cautious (but who would eventually join in). At about the same time, I had signed (together with around a hundred thousand people from around the world) a Znet-initiated petition that emerged in response to the threat of a new era of US-led war. The signatories committed themselves to a grassroots struggle for peace and justice, in solidarity with oppressed peoples through-out the world.[7] I decided to join the younger generation of Israeli activists in their pursuit of a meaningful grassroots struggle.

On 5 April 2003, as the US was bombarding Baghdad, the first anti-wall camp was founded in the village of Mas'ha, just south of the northern West Bank town of Qalqilya (see Figure 3, p.175[8]). ''Under the haze of the war on Iraq, the deception of 'security', and the silence of the media,'' said the first flyer put out by the camp, ''the apartheid wall is being built distant from the green line, confiscating thousands of dunams of agricultural land and water sources of entire villages.'' And the information sheet of the camp explained the background:

> The bulldozers have arrived to the village Mas'ha, adjacent to the Israeli settlement Elkana. Elkana is about 7 kilometers away from the green line, but the route of the fence, approved in the government meeting of June 24, 2002, was changed so that it will include Elkana as well in the Israeli side. The bulldozers have started to separate Mas'ha, in effect, from its only remaining source of livelihood after two and a half years of closure. 98% of the lands of Mas'ha will be placed on the Israeli side of the fence – between the fence and the green line, together with thousands of dunams of Bidia, Sanniriya and other villages in the area. Along with the lands that will be cut off the villages, the fence disconnects the road from Jenin to Ramallah, a segment of which will now be on the Israeli side of the fence, thus establishing further the isolation of the Palestinian enclaves from each other.

The initiative to establish the camp came from the village's farmers, who were losing their land. The driving force was Nazee Shalabi, a father of seven, who was determined not to give up his land without a struggle. He gathered together a group of equally determined fellow villagers, among them Tayseer Ezzedden and Ra'ad Amer, and together with Riziq Abu Nasser, the head of the Land Defense Committee in the Salfit region, they mobilized the village council, organized demonstrations and made contact with international activists in the area. The international women's group IWPS (International Women's Peace Service), based in the nearby village of Hares, responded immediately. Yonatan Pollak and other young Israeli activists, who were at the time travelling along the route of the wall in the northern West Bank and making contact with Palestinians, as well as members of the ISM and IWPS, were welcomed in Mas'ha and became partners in the struggle against the wall.

The Mas'ha camp was erected close to the path of the wall, with the aim of documenting, protesting, focusing Israeli and world attention, but strictly avoiding confrontations with the Israeli bulldozers or army. It was obvious that any attempt to physically disrupt the work on the wall would immediately lead to the military sealing off the area and dismantling the camp. By adhering to its principles of non-violent resistance, the camp lasted for four months, with the Israeli army unable to find an excuse to destroy it.[9]

A constant twenty-four-hour presence in the camp was maintained, with a minimum of two Israelis, two Palestinians and two internationals sleeping there every night, and often many more. On the Israeli side, the camp quickly attracted a wide spectrum of young activists, ranging from environmental and animal rights activists, to anarchists, students and high school kids. This was the new generation of the anti-occupation struggle – youth that got their political education through alternative internet zines, and who were themselves involved in forming the Israeli Indymedia. Some were graduates of the Prague and Genoa anti-corporate demonstrations, and viewed themselves as part of the generation of globalist rebels; others were just driven by an intuitive search for justice.[10] Of the veteran anti-occupation groups, the one that lent its support from the start was Gush Shalom, with Oren Medics as one of the camp's organizers, and Uri Avnery often speaking in the camp's demonstrations. Other individual veterans who joined in included Dorothy Naor and myself.

The Mas'ha camp quickly became the centre of the struggle against the wall, with bigger groups spending a day there on activities ranging from demonstrations and non-violent resistance training, to meetings and discussions that went on long into the night. The principles shared by the young activists were those of the global movements: direct democracy and grassroots struggle. Significantly, this was the first time in the entire history of the occupation that a real joint Israeli–Palestinian grassroots struggle was forming. Previously, Israeli–Palestinian cooperation had been the product of coordination between the ''leaderships'' in Ramallah and Tel Aviv, often ending in nothing more than the issuing of a joint petition. In Mas'ha, the spirit of direct democracy prevailed: decisions on the actions and policies of the joint struggle were taken in meetings at the camp by those present, rather than made by some remote leadership. For many of the Israelis, this was the first time that they had encountered the other side, while the Palestinians had only known Israelis as employers or soldiers. ''Until you arrived,'' Nazee Shalabi said once, ''I didn't have any idea that there were Israelis who want to live with us in peace.'' In the midst of the discourse of blood and terror that has prevailed in Israel for so long, people in Mas'ha were building new forms of coexistence in struggle.

The American activist and writer Starhawk,[11] who visited Mas'ha as part of her trip with the ISM, captured vividly its spirit in her piece 'Next year in Mas'ha':

> On the eve of Passover, after a month I spent in the occupied territories of Palestine working with the International Solidarity Movement, a month that saw one of our people deliberately run over by a bulldozer driven by an Israeli soldier, and two young men deliberately shot, one in the face, one in the head, I found myself unable to face the prospect of

a Seder, even with my friends in the Israeli peace movement. I couldn't sit and bewail our ancient slavery or celebrate our journey to the promised land. I was afraid that I might spew bitterness and salt all over any Seder table I graced, and smash something. So I went to the peace encampment at Mas'ha. Mas'ha needed people, and the moon was full, and I thought I could just lay down on the land under the moonlight and let some of the bitterness drain away . . .

To be at Mas'ha is to be on the absolute edge of the conflict. The road block that separates the village from the settlement is the divide between two realities. I got to Elkanah from Tel Aviv on the settlers' bus, full of elderly women who could have been my aunts and old men that could have been my uncles . . . We drove through one settlement to let people off and I got a tour of what looks like a transplanted Southern California suburb, complete with lush gardens and new houses, all with an aura of prosperity and complacent security — provided by armed guards and razor wire and the Israeli military . . . From Elkanah, I walked down the road a few hundred yards and climbed over the road block bulldozed to keep Palestinians out of Israel. I was in a dusty village of old stone and new cement houses and shuttered shops, backing onto open hillsides of ancient olives.

The camp at Mas'ha is on a knoll, two pink tents set up in an olive grove on stony ground studded with wildflowers, yellow broom, and prickly pear. The olives give shade and sometimes a backrest. If you look in one direction, the groves are spread out below the hilltop for miles of a soft gray green with blue hills in the back ground and small villages beyond, But encircling the hill, and cutting a gray swath across the hillsides, is the zone of destruction, a wide band of uprooted trees and bare subsoil, where a giant backhoe is wallowing like some giant, prehistoric beast, grabbing and crushing stones, gouging the earth, filling the air with dust and the mechanical bellowing of its engines . . .

A young man is sitting under a tree as I arrive, writing on stones with a black marker. He's a farmer, he tells me. In Arabic, he writes, "Dont cut the trees." He thinks for a moment, and adds another graceful line. I ask him to translate. He gives me a sweet smile, and points to the ground. "What is this?" "Earth?" I ask . . . "The earth speaks Arabic," he tells me.

All the Israelis but one have gone, to celebrate Pesach with their families. There are only two of us from the ISM and one woman from IWPS who stay over, along with two of the Palestinians, to guard the camp. As the full moon rises, I lie on the stones and meditate. I am hoping to find some peace or healing, but the earth is tortured here and all I can feel is her anguish. Down and down, through layers and centuries and epochs, I hear the ancestors weeping. The land is soaked in blood, and generations have faced ruthless powers and been cut down, and why should we be any different? I am woken up at three AM to take my shift on watch. I sit by the fire, exhausted, and finally drift back into sleep, waking again in the morning feeling sick at heart.

But people begin to arrive, for a midday meeting. The women from the IWPS, and the men from the village, and dozens of Israelis. We sit under the tent with its sides raised, talking about building an international campaign against the wall. One of the men, a stonemason, makes miniature buildings out of the stones at our feet as we talk. "Maybe we can't stop it here," one man from the village says, "But maybe we can stop it other places."

The Israelis who come are mostly young. They are anarchists and punks and lesbians and wild-haired students, and it strikes me that the mayor of Mas'ha and the village leaders in a very socially conservative society might actually have more in common with the Orthodox Jews who hate them than with these wild, social rebels. But the village accepts them all with good grace and a warm-hearted

Palestinian welcome. One woman is from the group "Black Laundry", which requires a somewhat complicated three-way translation of a Hebrew play on words. [In Hebrew, the word for *laundry* is *kvisa*, and the word for *sheep* is *kivsa*. So the name of the group – *black laundry* suggesting exposure of evil, creates an association with *black sheep* – standing for those viewed by the consensus as deviant.] She explains that it is a lesbian direct action group, and asks our translator if that's a problem. "Not for me," he says with a slightly quizzical shrug, and the meeting goes on.

Later we meet with the village women, who want to know if we can help them in any way. They are about to lose their source of livelihood: is there anything we can do? We have a long discussion about what we do in the ISM, and promise to research organizations that do community development work.

Back at the camp, all the young shabab – the term for young, unmarried men – have come out for the evening. We sit around the fire while two of the men prepare us dinner, laughing and talking. And suddenly I realize something wonderful is happening. The Israelis and the Palestinians can talk to each other, because most of the young men speak Hebrew. They are hanging out around the fire and talking and telling stories, laughing and relaxing together. They are hanging out just like any group of young people around a fire at night, as if they weren't bitter enemies, as if it could really be this simple to live together in peace.

So it was a strange Seder this year, pita instead of Matzoh, the eggs scrambled with tomato, hummous instead of chicken soup, water instead of wine, and instead of the maror, the bitter herbs which I have already tasted, a slight sweet hint of hope.

I can't ever again say "next year in Jerusalem." I can no longer believe in the promise of a land which requires the building of concrete walls and guard towers and ongoing murder to defend it . . . But I would like to believe in the promise of Mas'ha, in the example of a people who, faced with utter destruction of everything they need and hold dear, opened their hearts to the children of the enemy and asked for help. I would like to believe in the Israel reflected in the eyes of those who answer that call. That somehow, on this chasm between the conquerors and those who resist being finally conquered, the bridges and connections and meetings are happening that can tear down the walls of separation.

By next year, the camp at Mas'ha will most likely be gone. Already the contractors who work for the Israeli military have begun blasting a chasm that will soon cut the olive groves off from the village. An international campaign to stop the building of the wall has begun, but the reality is that they have the capacity to build it faster than we can organize to stop it.

And yet I say it again, as an act of pure faith:

Next year in Mas'ha.

By mid-June 2003, about a thousand Israelis had visited the camp or stayed overnight, and the core of regular Israeli activists was approaching three hundred people. The camp was beginning to attract some media coverage, thereby focusing attention on the wall, which until that point had hardly had any public debate in Israel. For the most part, the Israeli media continued to view the wall as a justified and vital security issue, but the actual reality of the wall was slowly penetrating international consciousness.

From the start, the Mas'ha camp faced an apparently unexpected obstacle – the Palestinian Authority. Not only did the PA district representatives not back the village's grassroots organization; they also exerted all kinds of pressure against the camp. The reasons behind such behaviour are complex and painful. As we have seen, following the Oslo Agreements the local grassroots network established during the first Palestinian *intifada* in the late 1980s was completely destroyed and replaced by an administration tightly controlled by Arafat and his close circle.[12] Much is known by now about the corruption of these administrative bodies of control, but what has received less attention is the fact that they were working in close collaboration with Israel, from the level of security cooperation to that of the local administration of towns and villages. In each area there was a Palestinian "District Coordination Office" (DCO), working in coordination with its Israeli counterpart. The charitable explanation of the district administration's opposition to the Mas'ha camp is that it could not give approval to grassroots activity outside its jurisdiction. The other, more painful explanation (true only of a few of the local administrators) is that they were carrying out Israeli instructions.

We should note that even three years after work on the wall had started, the Ramallah headquarters of the PA had still done nothing to protest against it, or to support the struggle of the people living along the path of the wall. In December 2004, eighteen months after the events of Mas'ha, when protest had already spread all along the wall's route, Ha'aretz reported on a demonstration by dozens of Palestinians outside the Palestinian cabinet meeting in Ramallah. They accused the cabinet of doing nothing to stop the wall: " 'The ministers don't care about the barrier, it doesn't affect them. They get VIP treatment at checkpoints and send their children to study abroad,' Salameh Abu Eid, 25, from Biddu village told Reuters . . . 'We ask you, Qureia, to stop supplying cement for the wall!' they shouted . . . The furious demonstration attested to growing popular discontent with the perceived incompetence and corruption of the Palestinian Authority, which has contributed to a surge in popularity of Islamist militants."[13] Sometimes, the Palestinian Authority's measures against the struggle were disturbingly comparable to Israeli ones. In May 2005, in a similar demonstration organized by the popular committee of the village of Bil'in, to whose struggle I return, a demonstrator from the village was severely beaten by the Palestinian Authority police.[14]

The Mas'ha camp started as an initiative of the entire village, with the mayor and village council speaking at the opening demonstration. But the district authorities (DCO of the Salfit region) succeeded in persuading them to disassociate themselves from the camp, and the village Fatah party also withdrew its support. The only political parties to resist this pressure were the communist People's Party, which had some influence in the village, and the smaller DFLP party (Democratic Front for the Liberation of Palestine). From the outset, their members viewed the resistance to the wall as a popular struggle of farmers trying to hold on to their land – a classic historical struggle. They formed part of the Palestinian core that initiated the camp, and were determined and courageous enough to continue in the face of considerable district authority pressure.

The Fatah and DCO authorities also showed much ingenuity in their effort to discourage the Israeli activists from getting involved. On one occasion, rumours spread that Hamas was threatening to attack the Israelis at the camp; it later transpired that a Fatah member had spread these baseless rumours in order to scare the Israelis away. This did not dissuade the young Israeli activists from participating in the camp; however, the DCO was more successful with Ta'ayush. Ta'ayush, by then known and highly respected in the area through its many demonstrations and food convoys, had a strict policy of coordinating its activity with the local PA. The District Cooperating Liaison for the Salfit District, Nawaf Souf (also known as Abu Rabia), informed Ta'ayush that he would not support the camp, and that Fatah would not participate in it. This had an immediate impact: Ta'ayush announced that it would not extend its backing to the camp, and would not collaborate in "irresponsible" activity supported only by a faction of the Palestinian people – that is to say, the People's Party and the DFLP. This in turn led to a catch-22: throughout the whole period of the Mas'ha camp, the Palestinian activists kept trying to encourage Fatah's participation, but were told that Fatah would not cooperate with an activity that Ta'ayush did not endorse.

Gradually, the Palestinian participation in the camp dwindled to a small group of the most determined. Rumours were spread about them, including accusations against Nazee Shalabi of past collaboration with Israel. This is a known strategy used by the PA against its opponents. When someone is accused of being a collaborator, he is isolated from his community, and is thus more vulnerable to persecution. On 16 June 2003 I wrote in a personal letter: "Yesterday, in the activist meeting in Mas'ha, it seemed as though the Palestinians would not be able to stand the pressure of their own PA anymore. They seemed despairing, thinking of giving up. I am afraid the camp is going to collapse. As the camp had become so big and renowned, while strictly non-confrontational, the army did not try to evacuate us forcefully. Why should it? It can use its henchmen to destroy us quietly. I don't really know what else can be tried. It is all so closed, locked. The internationals are being chased out and killed. The Palestinians are squeezed between the occupiers and their own collaborators . . ."

Nevertheless, the camp did not collapse. It continued for two more months, with a smaller daily presence but with regular weekly meetings at which protest activities in neighbouring areas were planned. In early August 2003, the protest concentrated on the case of one house on the edge of Mas'ha. The wall's route was designed so that the house of Hani and Munira Amer and their six children would be completely sealed in: enclosed on three sides by the wall, and by the fence of a nearby settlement on the remaining side. Once the wall was completed, the Amer family would need permission to leave their own house through a gate in the wall controlled by the army. There was pressure on the family to agree to leave with compensation, but they refused. The camp activists decided to confront the bulldozers. They moved the camp (including a tent), into the Amer family's yard. On 3 August, as the bulldozers came to destroy the family's barn, about sixty activists sat in front of it and managed to postpone the work. At dawn the next day, the bulldozers returned with the army. Forty-seven of the activists were arrested, including Nazee Shalabi, many internationals and twenty-four Israelis. The tent was removed, and the Amer yard was declared a closed military zone.

The battle of Mas'ha was lost. The village lost its lands, its wells and its olive groves to the wall; the gates to these lands are locked most of the time. Currently, Mas'ha is squeezed in a narrow corridor between the already-completed section of wall, and the new wall which is planned (See Figure 3). Mas'ha has joined the fate of Qalqilya (discussed in Chapter 7), with feelings of despair and isolation replacing its spirit of struggle. The Israeli activists kept contact with the village, and meetings continued to be held there, but the camp did not return to what it was. In December 2003, it was decided to refound the camp in the neighbouring village of Dir Balut, where the construction of the wall was just starting and local resistance was forming. Nevertheless, Mas'ha's resistance marked the beginning of what was to become a long and enduring joint Palestinian–Israeli–International struggle all along the route of the wall, which was proceeding steadily southwards. The core of the Palestinian activists in the Mas'ha camp continued down the planned route of the wall, to join other struggling villages. From the perspective of the Israeli struggle, this was a period of mobilization – gathering and organizing people who were prepared to cross the lines and to join the Palestinian struggle. In the process, a number of the camp's Israeli activists formed themselves into a movement devoted to a grassroots joint struggle against the wall, called "Anarchists Against the Wall". When the Palestinian popular struggle later spread to other areas, there was a core of organized Israeli activists ready to lend their support.[15]

In one of the first protest acts of the new camp in Dir Balut, the activists decided to return to Mas'ha on 26 December 2003, to take direct action, in which they would open one of the locked gates to the village's fields and olive groves. For about two weeks previously, internationals and Israeli activists from the camp had been monitoring the main gates of Mas'ha, which were supposed to be opened for thirty minutes three times a day to allow farmers to go to their fields. Instead, the gates remained permanently closed. In a press release dictated by phone from the action site the activists wrote: "No to the ghetto that's being built by Jews! No to walls between people! Stop the occupation! . . . At this very moment, Friday afternoon (seventh candle of Hanukah) dozens of activists are breaking down the gate of the apartheid wall which is also known as the "separation fence," to enable a free passage for the people of Mas'ha to their lands. The gate has remained closed since the wall was built two months ago. The farmers, whose land is on the other side of the fence, were told that they would be able to cross through the gate to work their lands. That promise turned out to be a methodical, crude and cruel lie. All throughout the suffocating wall the gates remain blocked and the Palestinian residents remain with no access to their only source of income . . .'

But the army decided to treat this action with the harshest of measures, perhaps to send a signal to Israeli activists to stay out of the Palestinian struggle. The soldiers immediately started firing live rounds. A sniper, identified in *Ha'aretz* as N.,[16] aimed carefully at the knee of one of the protestors, Gil Na'amati; Na'amati was shot in the knee, and the thigh of his other leg. This careful targeting of the smallest parts of the body, like the knee, requires extensive training and it is part of a technique developed by the Israeli army in the occupied territories since the early stages of the present *intifada*. It is designed to severely injure and disable people, without killing them.[17] Another American demonstrator at the protest sustained a shrapnel wound.

The army's brutality – applying live fire, rather than simply arresting the protestors – shook many in Israel. The following evening, 27 December, a big protest demonstration took place in front of the Defense Ministry offices in Tel Aviv. In its report of the demonstration, Gush Shalom recounted what happened:

> We've just come back from a fiery demonstration in protest of yesterday's shooting at peace activists. The story of the seriously-wounded Gil Na'amati in particular continues to make headlines. The 22–year old kibbutznik had to be raced to hospital after he lost consciousness through heavy bleeding. Both his legs were operated on to remove bullets; in one leg the knee was involved. The non-violent though militant protest at the Separation Fence was his first demonstration after he finished his three years of military service only two weeks ago. (His father said on TV that Gil had become so rebellious exactly because of what he had seen and had to participate in at the roadblocks in the West Bank.)
>
> This Saturday evening hundreds of furious demonstrators, many of them young, blocked the road in front of Tel Aviv's Defense Ministry for hours . . . The police came with far too small a force, but managed to arrest eleven protesters – among them David Tartakover, graphic artist and laureate of the prestigious Israel Prize. The others just continued their sit-in on the road.
>
> While blocking the road slogans were chanted: ''We won't kill nor be killed for the settlements'' . . . and placards displayed: ''When they shot at Palestinians we were silent!'' (from Anarchists Against the Wall); ''Purity of arms – a contradiction in terms!'' (the anti-militaristic group Profile Hadash); ''The Evil Wall Must Fall!'' (Gush Shalom). The gay peace group Kvisa Schora was also represented, but what especially attracted media attention was the presence of Knesset Member and Leader of the Meretz party Ran Cohen.
>
> When out of nowhere the prominent anarchist activist Yonathan Pollack[18] suddenly appeared – straight from the Ariel Police Station where he had been held overnight – it was decided to end the demonstration and march collectively

to the Tel Aviv (Yarkon) Police Station and demand the release of the detained activists.

The police station was pretty much besieged, and through the mediation of lawyers Yoni Lerman and Leah Tzemel it was agreed to lift the siege in return for the release of all activists.

Paradoxically, the army's attempt to scare the Israeli activists, and put an end once and for all to their presence in the Palestinian villages, gave considerable momentum to the struggle against the wall in Israel. This was the first time the army had used live ammunition against Israeli demonstrators – and this in a situation where there was absolutely no danger to the soldiers. There was a widespread feeling that a line had been crossed. Though Israeli society tolerated such violence against Palestinian demonstrators, and even remained relatively passive over the cases of the various internationalists shot earlier in the year, this episode could not so easily be ignored. The event, the anarchist participants, their parents and the subsequent protests, were covered heavily in the Israeli media. It came up for discussion in the Knesset, and eventually an investigation into the shootings was launched.[19] As a result of this coverage, the question of what these young demonstrators were doing in a Palestinian village came to the fore, and the cruel reality of the wall started penetrating more minds in Israel.

On 31 December 2003, Ta'ayush sent the following announcement to its mailing list:

Following last weekend's events, and marking the end of the activities at the protest tent against the Apartheid Fence in Dir Balut, Anarchists Against the Wall, the people of Dir Balut and Ta'ayush will hold a joint demonstration this Saturday, 3/1/04, protesting the continuing erection of the Apartheid Fence, and the outrageous shooting policy of the Israeli Army in 3 years of Intifada, which was suddenly "discovered" by many Israelis only this weekend. We would like to seize the new public discussion and media interest in what is happening behind the Green Line, and therefore we act with such a rush.

In the months to come, virtually all the anti-occupation groups of Israel were to join the Palestinian struggle along the route of the wall.

2. 2004 and On – The Struggle Continues

On the Palestinian side, the turning point in the popular struggle was the resistance that emerged around the time the Mas'ha camp was dismantled. It took place in the village of Budrus, further to the south of Dir Balut in the central (Ramallah) district of the West Bank and close to the Green Line (Israel's pre-1967 border). At the end of November 2003, the farmers of Budrus were notified that the path of the wall would run through their land, separating the village from nearly 1,000 dunams of its fruit and olive orchards.[20] Budrus started organizing, together with neighbouring villages, and when the bulldozers arrived in the end of December they found a united community ready for the struggle. As in the case of Mas'ha, the villagers invited Israelis and internationals to join them. On 29 December, three days after the traumatic events at the Mas'ha gate, Yonatan Pollak sent an urgent message to the Mas'ha Camp mailing list:

Today the bulldozers have reached the village of Budrus, which will lose much of its lands and end up enclosed and imprisoned on all sides by the wall, along with the villages of Niyalin, Midya and Kibya. The inhabitants of these villages, along with several international as well as Israeli activists, have managed to stop the bulldozers today, but army forces have promised to return tomorrow. People are urgently needed to stay and help at the site.

In January 2004, the focus of the Palestinian-led joint struggle moved to Budrus. Over the next three months, villagers – men and women, old and young – joined by Israeli and international activists, conducted dozens of non-violent demonstrations, often obstructing the construction of the wall by placing their bodies in front of the bulldozers.

The people of Budrus did manage to organize, unite and sustain the struggle, despite the lack of support, and even obstacles, put in their way by the Palestinian Authority. Indeed this time, unlike in Mas'ha, the village's Fatah party joined the struggle. Budrus provided the first successful model for a popular grassroots struggle in the West Bank, clearly defining the principles of non-violent civil resistance. It was also the first time that the Palestinian struggle along the wall really managed to capture world attention. In one of the many articles about Budrus, Mitch Potter of the *Toronto Star* wrote:

> When the Israeli backhoes and bulldozers first threatened this picturesque Palestinian hamlet, the people of Budrus had to think fast. The heavy machinery, they were told, would soon be scraping clean 1,000 dunams (about 250 acres) of olive groves from the edge of town, clearing a path for the separation barrier to follow. The town was in shock. ''We knew we had t'o do something. But we didn't have a lot of time to think about it. It was a crisis,' remembers Ayed Morar [Murrar], 42.
>
> From Budrus to Rantis, faction leaders from the nine Palestinian villages northwest of Jerusalem, whose land was most endangered by the infamous fence, converged for an emergency summit. Their stark choice: how to fight the seemingly inevitable. A decision was taken that day that might seem unlikely, given the ferocity of the past 3 years of bloody Intifada. The factions agreed to battle with words, not weapons. This corner of the uprising would raise no guns in its war against the Israeli barrier. So began a campaign of

peaceful protest that has made Budrus the talk of the West Bank, with a fame that far exceeds its tiny population of 1,200 people.

The Popular Committee to Resist The Wall was struck, with one representative from each of the nine villages, and Morar was named its leader. The nearly daily demonstrations that have drawn increasing television coverage in the months since that fateful decision are reminiscent of a more benign intifada, much like the one that played out long before suicide bombs and the aftermath of Sept. 11 turned the conflict on its ear. Mass rallies saw the whole of Budrus, everyone from toddlers to grandparents, gathering in the targeted fields after daybreak each morning, often staying until sundown. They linked arms and used their bodies as a human fence against the steel-and-razor wire version trying to plant itself in their place . . . "I am so proud of my people," said Morar. "We chose non-violent protest knowing we had to have absolute unity. And we got it. All the people of Budrus are together on this.'

On temporary leave from his job as a manager with the Palestinian Authority Interior Ministry, Morar cannot contain his disgust with the lack of support for the rump movement from his own government. "We started this on our own, but once it got rolling we had support from everywhere," he said. "International protesters have joined us, along with many peace supporters from Israel. We even had a member of the Swedish parliament here at one point. But through all that, not a single Palestinian minister has come to see what is happening. It is shameful. We ask them for nothing but moral support. And we don't even receive that.' Morar, who is familiar with the teachings of Mahatma Gandhi, said the lack of official Palestinian support underscores the failure of leadership. "It is a mistake even to say we have an intifada," he said. "What we have is nothing. Our weapons bring us the greatest misery." . . . But Morar said the Budrus movement is nevertheless beginning to trickle out to other communities to the south of Jerusalem that fear facing the future path of the fence as it wends its way south.[21]

Another aspect of the struggle that was clearly defined in Budrus and shaped the way the resistance would develop in the years to come concerned the respective roles of Palestinians and Israelis in the joint struggle. From Budrus on, it became clear that resistance must be led by the Palestinians, who mobilize their villages and determine the strategies. The Israeli and the internationals, meanwhile, would be partners in providing support. In an interview with Gideon Levy, Morar explained:

> In the north, from Jenin until Budrus, there were Israeli and international demonstrators, supported by Palestinians. But here, we think that it's our problem and that we have to defend our land and do something, and the Israelis and international protesters are only supporting us. First the Palestinians, and then the internationals. We are very grateful for Israeli and international support, but the Palestinians have to make a stand.[22]

During three months of protest in Budrus, the Israeli army killed one seventeen-year-old Palestinian, injured nearly 300 people with rubber bullets, rubber-coated steel bullets, or excessive use of tear gas. Thirty-three people were arrested, including Ayed Morar and two of his brothers. But the people persisted and won. In March 2004, the Israeli government decided to move the wall in the Budrus area to the Green Line. Instead of losing 1,000 dunams, the village lost 14.

After Budrus, the struggle spread along the route of the wall: from the northern Salfit district along the route of the Ariel settlement wall, to the central Ramallah district and towards the direction of Jerusalem (see map). Not every village had the spirit of Budrus. In some, infighting, or conflicts with the local PA leadership, has weakened the resistance, as happened in Mas'ha. The struggle has also carried with it a heavy price. The Israeli army and government were quick to grasp the potential obstacle posed to the Wall's construction by the growing popular struggle. To oppress the new non-violent Palestinian uprising, they used increasingly harsh means of repression. Palestinians were killed in peaceful demonstrations and hundreds were wounded. It takes an enormous spirit and courage to stand in protest against the Israeli military machine. Still, the struggle against the wall has already produced several symbols of resistance.

The next village to become the focus for the anti-wall struggle, in early 2004, was Biddu, south of Budrus. Its enduring and courageous resistance drew even more Israelis to partici-pate.[23] I described Biddu's struggle in *Yediot Aharonot*:

> Biddu is a beautiful Palestinian village, surrounded with vines and fruit orchards, a few miles to the east of the Israeli border of 1967. In the last couple of months, the village, that has lived in peace with its Israeli neighbors even during the present *intifada*, has become yet another symbol in the history of Israel/Palestine.
>
> The misfortune of this village is that its lands, as well as the lands of the other small Palestinian villages nearby, border the "Jerusalem corridor" – a sequence of Israeli neighborhoods to the North of Jerusalem. Israeli control of this land would enable territorial continuity "clean of Palestinians" from this corridor to the settlement of Givat Zeev, built deep inside the occupied West Bank, close to Ramallah. In the massive annexation project of Sharon and the Israeli army, this is the kind of land one "does not give up." For this reason, Israel is imprisoning the villagers inside a wall, and is grabbing their land. Biddu, and the ten villages around it, are allowed only one option – to sit quietly and watch as the fruit orchards that they have nourished from one generation to another, turn into the real-estate reserves of the Jerusalem corridor.

But rather than obeying, the village of Biddu united with the other nearby villages to defend their land. In the new model of popular resistance that has developed along the line of the wall in the West Bank, the whole village – men, women and children – are going out to put their bodies between the bulldozers and their land. A basic principle in this form of struggle is that of non-violence. Use of arms is strictly forbidden, and there is also visible effort on the part of the communities to restrain the youth from throwing stones. A second principle of the resistance is that it is a joint struggle of Palestinians and Israelis, whose fate and future are inter-twined. Like in other areas of the wall, the people of Biddu have called on the Israelis to join them. ''Raise the voice of reason, the voice of logic, above the sound of the bullets and the sound of the oppression . . .'' they wrote in an open letter to the settlements and the Israeli neighborhoods around them.

Indeed, Israelis have answered the call – from the young activists against the wall, to the neighbors from the Mevaseret Tzion neighborhood in the Jerusalem Corridor. Thirty of the latter have also joined an appeal that the villages submitted to the High Court of Israel, against the appropriation of their land. But in the eyes of the army, this new model of Palestinians and Israelis demonstrating together is the most dangerous. In Biddu the army has already posed snipers on the roofs, used live ammunition and killed five Palestinians. Dozens of others have been wounded. Following the media coverage and the protest, the army's use of live fire has decreased, but its violence has not. On April 17, Rabbi Arik Asherman was arrested in Biddu, when he tried to protect a Palestinian child strapped on to the hood of a military jeep.

In response to the violence of the army, the women of Biddu called for a quiet and small protest demonstration of women only, on Sunday, April 25th. About 30 Israeli women answered the call – women of diverse ages and from a wide array of occupations. In Biddu, we met with Palestinian women, and with women from the international organizations active in the occupied territories. A quiet protest walk started – less then a hundred women, carrying posters. There was no man in sight, nor children, who could potentially throw stones. We constituted no threat whatsoever. But for the army, this does not matter. "We will not allow this demonstration," a voice in uniform announced. Tear gas and stun-grenades directly followed. Paralyzed where I stood, I watched a hallucinatory scene. In the midst of the fog of smoke and tear gas, there were still a few women standing, silently lifting their posters in front of the soldiers. But then, out of the fog burst warriors on horses and charged into the women holding the posters. I have seen cops on horses before, but this was a different sight. It was dead clear that their batons were meant for breaking bones. Molly Malekar, the director of the Bat-Shalom organization, ended her quiet protest against the army's violence with a broken shoulder, and a severe blow to her head.

The army blocks any route of protest. It is no longer permitted even to stand silently with posters. And this does not hold only for Palestinians. From the army's perspective, we Israelis are also given only one option – sit silently and watch as our country loses its human face. But since Israel is still, officially, a democracy, it is not permissible for the army to be the body that determines the limits of the freedom of protest. It is necessary to form an independent committee of inquiry into the army's violence in Biddu, and to bring those responsible to justice.[24]

No inquiry committee was formed, of course, and the army violence continued. Nevertheless, the struggle of Biddu ended in a substantial victory. The Israeli High Court of Justice ruled on 30 June 2004 that the state should reroute 30 kilometres of a 40–kilometre stretch of the wall in this area, thus giving back to the Palestinian villagers a considerable part of their lands. The High Court was careful not to set a precedent against the wall in general. In anticipation of the International Court of Justice ruling that was scheduled to be announced in a few days, its decision began with the declaration that building a fence in the West Bank for security reasons is legal. Nevertheless, the court accepted the petitioners' claim that the planned route of the wall would cause disproportionate harm to local residents. "The current route," it wrote, "will make access to residents" agricultural lands almost impossible, thereby sabotaging farmers' livelihoods; it will also interfere with residents' freedom of movement and access to nearby cities, including access to medical care, schools and universities.'[25] Israel had to reroute the wall, also replacing segments that were already completed.[26]

Following the High Court ruling, Ayed Morar of Budrus wrote: "Legal decisions are always only a partial reflection of the reality on the ground, which is the main thing for us. The popular struggle has itself led to the decisions of the court – not the other way round. And so, before the popular struggle started expanding, when the construction of the Wall started, the inhabitants had tried to act on the legal front. Prior to the popular resistance, petitions to the courts faced rejection and a general unwillingness to intervene. It is the popular struggle that caused the change in the public debate, bringing about the change in the attitude of the Supreme Court in its last decision."[27] The International Court of Justice ruling on the wall, which followed on 9 July,[28] gave a considerable boost to the struggle, which continued to grow steadily on the Palestinian side, backed by growing Israeli support and participation.

Israeli participation in the Palestinian demonstrations has had a substantial contribution in bringing the Palestinian struggle to Israeli consciousness. Facing diminishing support from the Israeli public, the army developed brutal measures to discourage the Israelis from participating in the resistance, mainly targeting the young activists from Anarchists Against the Wall, who have been wounded, arrested and harassed daily. On 12 March 2004, Itai Levinsky was shot in the eye by a rubber bullet. As Aviv Lavie reported in *Ha'aretz*:

It was Levinsky who, last December 26, saved the life of Gil Na'amati after Na'amati was shot by an IDF sniper near Mas'ha. While the soldiers ignored the demonstrators' pleas to summon an ambulance, Levinsky organized a quick evacuation of the bleeding Na'amati in a Palestinian car, and at the checkpoint an Israeli ambulance joined them. Na'amati lost a great deal of blood and arrived at the hospital in a serious condition. The doctors told his father, Uri, the head of Eshkol Regional Council, that if the evacuation had been delayed they would probably not have been able to save his son's life. Almost three months later, on March 12, it was Levinsky who ended up in hospital. "I went to demonstrate at Hirbata," he recalls. "The army's reaction was violent to the extreme this time. They simply fired rubber bullets like crazy, even though most of the people quickly lay down on the ground among the rocks. Naturally, when you're lying down, there's no difference whether they fire at your head or your legs, because it's all at the same height. I was standing in front and talking to the soldiers via the megaphone, to make them understand that there were Israelis there, too, which sometimes makes them calm down a little. It's scary, but what can you do?" This time, though, the megaphone and the Hebrew weren't an insurance policy . . .[29]

Levinsky was hospitalized for ten days, and had to have nose and eye surgery. "The truth is that I was really lucky," he told Lavie, "because a rubber bullet that enters the eye can reach the brain. It's total chance that I'm alive. For both me and Gil it's pure luck that we weren't killed." In the same article Lavie reports a conversation he had with Yonatan Pollak, himself wounded several times:

One evening during the intermediate days of Pesach, I got a phone call from Yonatan Pollak, who sounded distraught. Pollak, 21, the son of the highly regarded actor Yossi Pollak, is considered the Israeli leader of the struggle against the fence (though as an anarchist, he disowns that description). Tall, charismatic, confident of his path, Pollak . . . does to the soldiers – who encounter him on an almost daily basis – what a red rag does to a bull.

"I called because within a few days there were two incidents in which Israeli demonstrators were almost killed . . ." Pollak said. "I called because if anything can stop the deterioration of the situation, it's media publicity. Let's leave the political aspect aside for the moment and talk about what's happening on the ground almost every day. There is a gradual but relentless escalation on the part of the army toward civilians taking part in demonstrations, which fundamentally are nonviolent. I spend a lot of time in the territories, and I've seen how riots and demonstrations are suppressed plenty of times, but what's happening here is something new. The feeling is that there are no procedures. They fire rubber bullets and throw tear gas freely, and they fire at the feet and at the head . . . At every demonstration I talk to the soldiers via a megaphone and tell them that this is a peaceful demonstration of Palestinians, Israelis and internationals – and the bullets whistle past my ears. At first we thought the cameras would deter them, then we thought the presence of Israelis would be a deterrent, but now there is nothing that deters the soldiers. I tell you: Someone is going to die out there."

Maybe it's time to stay home for a while?

Pollak: "I am a political person and I go to demonstrate. It's inconceivable that the state's response should be that I have to sit at home. Even if the army is convinced that what we are doing is a provocation – though from my point of view, of course, the provocation is the building of the fence on Palestinian land – in a democracy you can create provocations without being shot at.''

Are you afraid?

"Very much. That's why I'm talking to you. But that doesn't mean we are going to stop the demonstrations. We will continue, but I don't think that's a reason for any of us to die.''[30]

Indeed, the army did not manage to deter the Israeli activists. In the months to come, more of them joined in. Through 2004, the popular Palestinian struggle continued to spread to many more villages, and in most of the demonstrations the Israelis were also present, led at that time by Anarchists Against the Wall. In mid-2004, I wrote in *Yediot Aharonot*:

The breathtaking scenery of the Ariel district has been sliced up by the new roads that the rulers have built for their own exclusive use. Beneath them lie the old roads of the vanquished. There, on the lower level, is where the other Israel–Palestine treads. Israeli youths arrive in settlement buses and then make their way on foot and in Palestinian taxis among the checkpoints. They trek between the villages in groups or alone. Some sleep in the villages. Others will travel the same route the next day to reach the demonstration. Everywhere they go they are greeted with blessings and beaming faces. "Tfaddalu" the children in the doorways say, as if they had never heard of stone-throwing. Like the inhabitants of other Palestinian villages along the route of the fence, those in the Ariel area have opened their hearts and their homes to the Israelis who come to support their non-violent resistance to the barrier that is robbing them of their land . . .

The Israelis who stand with the Palestinians in front of the army went to the West Bank because they know there is a law that is higher than the army's laws of closed military zones: there is international law, which forbids ethnic cleansing, and there is the law of conscience. But what brings them back, day after day, is the new covenant that has been struck between the peoples of this land, a pact of fraternity and friendship between Israelis and Palestinians who love life, the land, the evening breeze. They know that it is possible to live differently on this land.[31]

Nevertheless, the experience of 2004 showed that the numbers of Israeli activists and resources were not sufficient to join in the daily Palestinian struggle along the whole route of the wall and to protect the Palestinians from the wrath of the Israeli army. For the Palestinians, what was needed was a centre for the struggle, a focal point that would hold long enough to attract the attention of the world, and which would also serve as a coordinating centre for the struggle of the surrounding villages, as Budrus and Biddu had previously done. From February 2005 onwards, the village of Bil'in has formed such a focal point. Situated in the central Ramallah district of the West Bank, about midway between Budrus and Biddu, Bil'in, with 1,600 inhabitants, lies near the big Israeli settlement cluster of Upper Modi'in, which juts out from the Green Line into the West Bank. Part of Bil'in's land had already been expropriated to enable the expansion of this settlement cluster; but now, according to the planned route of the wall, Bil'in would lose 60 per cent of its remaining lands to the so-called "Israeli side" of the wall. As disclosed in *Ha'aretz*, "The lands taken from the residents of Bil'in, some of which are privately owned, are mostly intended to expand existing settlements, but also to build a new settlement called Nahlat Heftziba."[32]

As I write this chapter, in April 2006, Bil'in is still the heart of the popular struggle in the centre region of the West Bank, after a full year of enduring, courageous and imaginative struggle. During this year, a tradition was founded of weekly demonstrations every Friday. These demonstrations continue to take place, week after week, month after month. A small presence of

Israelis and internationals is maintained in the village all week, but the Friday demonstrations also attract Palestinian villagers from neighbouring villages, internationals staying in other areas of the West Bank, and Israelis from a wide spectrum of society, including many who only joined the struggle in 2005. By now, the demonstrations have a fixed routine. After Friday prayers, a march heads towards the construction area where the wall is being built. On the initiative of the Bil'in villagers, there are often attempts to lend a creative flavour to the protest; sometimes, artistic installations and performances are prepared for the event during the week. But only rarely does the army let the protest proceed. On a quiet day, the demonstrators are dispersed with tear gas. But the army has invented many more sophisticated violent means to disperse them, including a new weapon nicknamed "the Scream" – a sound machine blasting the demonstrators with high frequencies that affect the inner ear, causing nausea, dizziness and potentially hearing damage.[33] Eventually, the bulk of the demonstrators retreat back to the village. The more militant Palestinian youth, robbed of the chance of a quiet political protest, stay near the construction area and throw stones at the soldiers, who respond with more force.

When conditions permit, demonstrations are followed by activist meetings, where the events of the day are analysed, and future protests are planned. The village has an internet site, which includes information about activities and samples of the huge Israeli and international media coverage that the struggle of Bil'in has attracted.[34] Throughout this whole period, demonstrations and protests have continued in many other villages, sometimes several on the same day, and usually with Israeli and international participation. At times another village is selected as a focal point for resistance, but the Friday demonstrations and meetings in Bil'in never cease.

Virtually all Israeli anti-occupation groups participate in this struggle, with the most persistent being Anarchists Against the Wall, Gush Shalom and Ta'ayush.

It takes substantial stamina to endure the demonstrations. The midday heat in Palestine is intense, and the tortured landscape does not give much shade, as people stand exposed to tear gas and army violence. I am often bewildered at how the Israelis, young and old, keep coming. The Friday demonstration that I attended on 6 May was considered relatively quiet and uneventful. On that "quiet" day, as the demonstrators were retreating through the olive groves, seeking shelter from the tear gas that burns your lungs, the poet Aharon Shabtai and Jacob Katriel, Professor Emeritus of the Technion Institute in Haifa, who were in completely different areas of the olive groves, were both hit in their right elbows by an unidentified object that at first felt like a stone. It was nothing very serious, nothing that required hospitalization – just a swollen hurting elbow for a week. It didn't even seem worth reporting – and indeed it was not. However, it requires considerable precision and effort to hit someone's elbow from a distance. (Neither Shabtai nor Katriel managed to see the person who shot at them.) It is hard to avoid the chilling thought that next time, the sniper who hit Shabtai and Katriel could aim at your eye instead. There, amidst the olive trees, escaping from the tear gas and unidentified flying objects, I met two students of mine, for whom this was their first demonstration in the occupied territories, and perhaps even the first demonstration of their lives. They looked lost and shocked – but, by the end of the semester, I heard that they had returned more than once. It would be impossible to tell here the full history of Bil'in's year of struggle. Instead, I will recount the events of just one, fairly typical, week from this year.

On Friday 2 September 2005, during the last week of the Gaza pullout, the Israeli army decided to put an end to the weekly demonstrations in Bil'in. "One hour before the beginning of the weekly demonstration, a squad of roughly a hundred soldiers invaded the village and proceeded to take over. In an unprecedented move, snipers set up posts on rooftops, jeeps and humvees patrolled the streets as a large group of soldiers positioned themselves outside the mosque, where the demonstration was scheduled to begin. Once the prayer was over, the people leaving the mosque were violently dispersed, without even a single stone having been thrown. A curfew was imposed immediately, and one of the commanders went on to announce that 'there will be no more demonstrations in Bil'in'.''[35] Later that day, the army used live fire, along with the standard rubber bullets. By the end of the day, twelve people were wounded and fourteen arrested.

By this point, Bil'in and its struggle were vivid in the Israeli consciousness. In response to this event, *Ha'aretz* devoted an editorial to the army's violence in Bil'in:

> After proving their sensitivity and intelligence in dispersing the demonstrations in Gush Katif, the Israel Defense Forces and police could have been expected to apply the same policy in handling the demonstrators against the separation fence in the village of Bil'in. The IDF and police did not fire at the protesters on the roof in Kfar Darom [in the Gaza Strip], even when the latter threw dangerous substances at them, and they refrained from using force even against violent protesters. Similarly, it could have been hoped that the soldiers would hold their fire when facing left-wing and Palestinian protesters. Instead, outrageous images are published week after week of soldiers kicking left-wing demonstrators and firing salt or rubber-coated bullets – showing their general contempt for the right to legitimate protest. Three different judges have recently castigated the defense forces for the excessive use of force in Bil'in. Despite this, they once again fired at the demonstrators, this time – last Friday – even before they had left the village area toward the fence. The demonstrations of the West Bank villagers, whose lands have been confiscated for the construction of the separation fence, have been taking place for the past two years. Together with the petitions to the High Court of Justice, they are a

legitimate and sometimes effective means of protest against the annexation of land intended to expand settlements, under the pretense of building the fence . . .'[36]

Bil'in's popular committee and the Israeli anti-occupation groups responded to the army's attack with a call for a mass demonstration in Bil'in the following Friday:[37]

> The village of Bil'in rises as a proud symbol of resistance for the people of Palestine and for all oppressed people world-wide, for its resistance to the wall. But its struggle symbolizes much more. It reveals the purpose of the wall – annexation and dispossession . . .
>
> We, Palestinians and Israelis, view the recent measures taken by the military as a substantial escalation in violent repression and as an additional infringement on our progressively eroding right to protest and resist the stealing of our lands and the denial of basic human rights. We will be holding a massive demonstration this coming Friday (Sept 9), and we call on you all to step up your efforts, spread the word widely, and join us in Bil'in as we deliver our message that the popular resistance to the wall and the occupation will not be crushed, that the protest against the crimes of occupation will not be silenced. Especially now, as the military is denying, through brute force, our right to protest, we urge you all to come out and raise your voice against the ongoing dispossession and violation of the basic human rights of the people of Bil'in and Palestine in general.
>
> The demonstration will begin at the Mosque in Bil'in at 13:00. Transportation details to follow shortly.

The announcement did not deter the IDF, which invaded the village at dawn on 9 September, determined to prevent the demonstration. As Greta, an ISM activist, reported that day, "at 5 am, the military came into Bil'in and said it was a closed military zone, and curfew would be enforced. At 6 am . . . the commander told Abdullah he had 15 minutes to tell the internationals and Israelis [staying in his house] to leave. Hours later, no one had obeyed that command, and internationals and Israelis remained throughout the day . . . At 7 am, Palestinians, Internationals, and Israeli activists went to the rooftops and invented their own music, complete with percussion drummed out on heaters and water tanks . . . The mood was festive in spite of 20 soldiers and several jeeps parked in front threatening the mood. We clapped and shouted and danced on the tops of the buildings, shouting back and forth to each other, trying to postpone any kind of violent confrontation with the military. The demonstration wasn't due to begin until 1 pm, and we had much to do to delay the Israeli military violence in those six hours.'' But the plan to delay the military violence did not fully succeed, as Greta went on to relate: ''Apparently, the Israeli military became nervous listening to the music, and started lobbing tear gas and stun grenades at the Palestinians. Within a few minutes, a Palestinian man was shot in the leg.'' Through the morning, five Israelis, three internationals and one Palestinian were arrested. Nevertheless, at 1 p.m. the Palestinians and the remaining Israelis and internationals headed to the main square, in violation of the curfew.[38]

At the same time, 300 people from the Israeli side answered the Popular Committees' call and started their hazardous journey into the besieged Bil'in. What follows are extracts from Coalition Against the Wall's report on that day:

The army sealed off all roads to Bil'in, but the demonstrators arrived through the ultra-Orthodox settlement of Upper Modi'in. Through the building site, where a new settlement neighborhood is being added, the protestors gained access to the olive groves and canyons in Bil'in village . . . Walking several kilometers in difficult terrain during the hottest hour of the day, the demonstrators succeeded in getting to the construction site from the western ("Israeli") side. Military and police forces which waited there started shooting tear gas and tried to arrest them. The demonstrators divided into small groups and most of them succeeded in entering the Bil'in built-up area, with soldiers and police chasing them through the village's back alleys. The Bil'in people received the Israelis with great enthusiasm, offering refuge in their homes – and cold water. Some 25 Israelis were arrested in that process, among them Dr Anat Matar of the Tel-Aviv University, Philosophy Department, and veteran Meretz activist Latif Dori.

At 1pm, about a hundred demonstrators succeeded in getting through to the main square of Bil'in in front of the mosque, where they joined a large number of Palestinian curfew breakers. Also present were many international activists, most of them US citizens. A bit later there arrived more Israelis, who had fallen behind but not given up, among them former Knesset Member Uri Avnery of Gush Shalom who on this very day marks his 82nd birthday, Yakov Manor of Ta'ayush and Dorothy Naor of New Profile.

For about an hour, Israeli and Palestinian demonstrators stood in the main square, facing the soldiers and Border Police, chanting slogans . . . Some called at the soldiers: "Why don't you embrace us as you did with the settlers?" The Bil'in leaders invited Israelis and internationals to join them in dancing and clapping while singing "we will win, we will win, here in Bil'in, here in Bil'in, Christian Muslim hand in hand, Israeli movement with us will stand" . . . After an hour, the soldiers resumed shooting and the village square was soon covered with clouds of tear gas. Environmental activist Advocate Dov Chinin got a rubber bullet in his leg. The demonstrators found refuge in the backyard of a nearby home . . . It was decided to hold after all, and in spite of the army's opposition, the weekly march towards the site of the wall. So the demonstrators conducted the march, chanting "after all the wall will fall" and then returned to the village center. Shortly after the army and Border Guard forces left Bil'in followed by calls of derision from the protestors.[39]

On the following Friday, 16 September, the weekly demonstration was preceded by a Beethoven concert by the Dutch pianist Jacob Allegro Wegloop. (Much effort was invested in getting the piano, contributed by Yonatan Pollak's parents, into the village, and Wegloop himself was smuggled in at early dawn, before the army arrived.) David Rovics, a political folk singer touring the West Bank, also contributed to the musical side of the demonstration. The Israeli demonstrators again had difficulties reaching the village through the sealed-off roads, but most of them made it. There was too much Israeli and international media presence for the military to risk taking excessive measures of revenge for the events of the previous week. So the army instead "just" used tear gas to disperse the demonstration march that followed the concert. This is how the Bil'in struggle continues to date.

In over two years of the struggle against the wall, there have been some successes. In a few more cases than I have mentioned here, Israeli High Court injunctions have stopped the bulldozers. But these are still just drops in the ocean. In the areas bordering the wall, Israel continues its massive project of driving the Palestinians off their land. As we saw in the previous chapter, if the wall is completed, 400,000 Palestinians will lose their land and livelihood; many of them may eventually become refugees in the Palestinian enclaves that Israel has designated for them. In the Palestinian *nakba* (catastrophe) of 1948, 730,000 Palestinians were driven from their villages. But rather than waiting for the history books to tell the story of the second Palestinian *nakba*, the Palestinians along the wall are struggling to stop the narrowing of their prisons. Armed only with the extraordinary spirit of people who have clung on to their land for generation after generation, they stand in the path of one of the most brutal military machines in the world.

This daily struggle is our hope. It has become possible with the help of individuals from all over the world who come to protect and support the non-violent Palestinian resistance. They face harassment – many are being stopped and deported – but still they keep coming. As long as more people join them, even for a short time, as long as they are supported by many others at home who are unable to travel there, the struggle will go on, offering hope where governments fail.

In February 2006, Mohammed Khatib, a leading member of Bil'in's Popular Committee Against the Wall and the secretary of its village council, wrote:

We refuse to be strangled by the wall in silence. In a famous Palestinian short story by Ghassan Kanafani, "Men in the Sun," Palestinian workers suffocate inside a tanker truck. Upon discovering them, the driver screams, "Why didn't you bang on the sides of the tank?" In Bilin, we are banging, we are screaming . . . Please stand with us.[40]

Notes

Introduction

1 An earlier version of this book appeared in French in April 2006 as *L'Héritage de Sharon*, *Détruire La Palestine, Suite*, (Paris: La Fabrique).

2 Tanya Reinhart, *Israel/Palestine – How to End the War of 1948*, (New York: Seven Stories Press, 2002). Expanded second edition, 2005.

3 *Israel/Palestine*, Introduction, pp. 7–8.

4 In 1982, then Defense Minister Ariel Sharon led Israel into war in Lebanon with the ambitious goals of creating a "new order" in the Middle East, destroying the Palestinian Liberation Organization – which had developed in the Palestinian refugee camps in Lebanon – and gaining permanent control over Southern Lebanon, which borders with Israel. The attack left over 11,000 Lebanese and Palestinians dead (Robert Fisk, *Pity the Nation—Lebanon at War*, Oxford: Oxford University Press, 1990, p. 323). Even though Israeli society perceived the war with Lebanon as a failure, the Israeli military stayed in the conquered land of Southern Lebanon until May 2000.

5 *Israel/Palestine*, ch. 2, pp. 21–60.

6 Amir Oren, *Ha'aretz*, 19 October 2001.

7 Ora Coren, "Israel Ranks among Most Corrupt in West", *Ha'aretz*, 8 April 2005. The World Bank report appeared also in *Business Data Israel (BDI)*, the day before.

8 On 28 March 2004 Israel's chief prosecutor officially recommended Sharon's indictment for allegedly taking hundreds of thousands of dollars in bribes when he was foreign minister, in a case known as the Greek Island Affair. However, on 14 June 2004, Israel's attorney general cleared the prime minister of receiving bribes "and in doing so removed an obstacle that has prevented the opposition Labor Party from joining the government" (Joshua Brilliant, "Attorney General clears Sharon of Bribery", *United Press International*, 15 June 2004).

9 Gil Hoffman, " 'National Responsibility' Name of PM's New Party", *Jerusalem Post*, 23 November, 2005.

10 For a survey of the Algiers resolution, See *Israel/Palestine*, ch. 1, pp. 14–15.

11 For a survey of the polls till 2002, see *Israel/Palestine*, ch. 10, pp. 223–6. More recent polls will be mentioned in this book. The real will of the majority was exposed at the time of the Gaza pullout, when about 70 per cent of Israelis supported the evacuation of the settlements in the polls.

12 For example, on 12 April 2002, following Israel's atrocities in the Jenin refugee camp, *Ha'aretz* innocently reported what "military sources" had told the paper: "The IDF [Israeli army] intends to bury today Palestinians killed in the West Bank camp . . . The sources said that two infantry companies, along with members of the military rabbinate, will enter the camp today to collect the bodies. Those who can be identified as civilians will be moved to a hospital in Jenin, and then on to burial, while those identified as terrorists will be buried at a

special cemetery in the Jordan Valley" (Anat Cygelman, Amos Harel and Amira Hass). Apparently, no one in Israel was particularly concerned at the time about issues of international law, war crimes and mass graves. The evening before, Israeli TV even showed refrigerator trucks that were waiting outside the Jenin camp to transfer bodies to "terrorist cemeteries". It was only after international attention began to focus on Jenin that this information was quickly concealed and reinterpreted using any absurd reasoning to explain that nothing of the sort had ever happened. This is how the respectable analyst Ze'ev Schiff of *Ha'aretz* later summarized the event: "Toward the end of the fighting, the army sent three large refrigerator trucks into the city. Reservists decided to sleep in them for their air conditioning. Some Palestinians saw dozens of covered bodies lying in the trucks and rumors spread that the Jews had filled trucks full of Palestinian bodies" ("Back to Jenin", *Ha'aretz*, 17 July 2002).

13 *Yediot Aharonot*, Israel's largest-selling paper, and the one with the best connections with military and governmental sources, has parallel internet editions in both English and Hebrew (Ynet), which I also quote at times. These, however, are independent editions, rather than a translation of the daily Hebrew paper. *Jerusalem Post*, which is also quoted, is an Israeli English-language paper.

1. Spring 2003: The Road Map Era

1 Arnon Regular, Gideon Alon and Aluf Benn, *Ha'aretz*, 30 April 2003.

2 Amos Harel, *Ha'aretz*, 30 April 2003.

3 The two events were apparently not related. A statement issued by the Hamas-related Al-Qassam Brigades assumed responsibility for the Tel Aviv explosion, saying it was carried out in revenge for Israel's assassination of Ibrahim Almakadma, a senior member of their organization, in the Gaza Strip two months ago (Roni Singer and Amos Harel, *Ha'aretz*, 1 May 2003).

4 Aluf Benn and Arnon Regular, *Ha'aretz*, 1 May 2003.

5 The document, published in *Ha'aretz* on 1 May 2003, is entitled "Elements of a Performance-Based Road Map to a Permanent Two-State Solution to the Israeli–Palestinian Conflict, Draft December 2002", hereafter RM. All direct quotations from the Road Map are taken from this version.

6 The Israeli authorities and media attributed the failure of the Camp David negotiations to the Palestinian's insistence on the "right of return". By now it is pretty well known that this is not true, and that the right of return was barely discussed in Camp David (see for a survey my *Israel/Palestine*, Ch. 2, "The Right of Return," pp. 51–60). Since then, further confirmation that the negotiations did not fail over the right of return has come from senior Israeli security officials. An extensive survey of their revelations was provided by Akiva Eldar, "Popular Misconceptions," *Ha'aretz*, 11 June 2004. From Eldar's summary it becomes evident that an agreement could have been reached in Camp David, had Israel wanted it. For example, Amos Malka, head of Israeli Military Intelligence (MI) from mid-1998 to the end of 2001, insists that the official Israeli version has no backing in any research document: "We [MI] assumed that it is possible to reach an agreement with Arafat under the following conditions: a Palestinian state with Jerusalem as its capital and sovereignty on the Temple Mount; 97 percent of the West Bank plus exchanges of territory in the ratio of 1:1 with respect to the remaining territory; some kind of formula that includes the acknowledgement of Israel's responsibility for the refugee problem and a willingness to accept 20,000–30,000 refugees. All along the way . . . it was MI's assessment that he had to get some kind of statement that would not depict him as having relinquished [the right of

return], but would be prepared for a very limited implementation . . . No one . . . argued that Arafat's expectations included Israeli agreement to take in 300,000 to 400,000 refugees in the framework of the right of return' (ibid.). Arab affairs specialist Mati Steinberg, who was at the time of the Camp David negotiations a special advisor on Palestinian affairs to the head of Israel's Shin Bet security service, also confirmed that the negotiations did not fail "over the issue of the right of return, which was barely discussed at that summit and was born retrospectively in Israel in order to create the internal consensus" (ibid.).

7 RM, *Ha'aretz*, 1 May 2003.
8 RM, *Ha'aretz*, 1 May 2003.
9 RM, *Ha'aretz*, 1 May 2003.
10 *Israel/Palestine*, ch. 7, pp. 146–7.
11 Aluf Ben, *Ha'aretz*, 10 March 2002.
12 Amos Harel, *Ha'aretz,* 30 April 2003.
13 'Israel's Road Map Reservations,' *Ha'aretz,* 27 May 2003.
14 Ibid.
15 See my *Israel/Palestine*, ch. 9, pp. 194–6.
16 Chris McGreal, *Guardian*, 23 August 2003.
17 The *Altalena* was a ship carrying ammunition from France to Israel in June 1948 under the command of the Etzel (Irgun) and in direct challenge to the authority of the Hagana. The *Altalena* was destroyed by the Hagana in Tel Aviv harbour (author's note).
18 Mahmoud Dahlan is the head of the Palestinian Preventive Security forces in the Gaza Strip (author's note).
19 Aluf Benn, *Ha'aretz,* 2 May 2003.
20 Arnon Regular, *Ha'aretz,* 25 May 2003.
21 Aluf Ben, *Ha'aretz*, Hebrew edition, 2 June 2003. In the English-language version of *Ha'aretz*, mention of Sharon's rejection of a ceasefire was removed, the headline only announcing Sharon's willingness to evacuate outposts.
22 RM, *Ha'aretz*, 1 May 2003.
23 "Israel's Road Map Rreservations," *Ha'aretz*, 27 May 2003.
24 Gideon Alon, *Ha'aretz*, 28 May 2004.
25 Abraham Burg, *Yediot Aharonot*, 5 June 2003.
26 Arnon Regular, *Ha'aretz*, 3 June 2003.
27 Arnon Regular, Aluf Benn and Nathan Guttman, *Ha'aretz*, 26 June 2003.
28 Amos Harel and Associated Press, *Ha'aretz*, 26 June 2003.
29 Arnon Regular, Aluf Benn and Nathan Guttman, *Ha'aretz*, 26 June 2003.
30 Ibid.
31 The text of the Palestinian ceasefire declaration can be found in *Ha'aretz*, 30 June 2003.
32 Amos Harel, *Ha'aretz*, 28 July 2003.
33 Aluf Benn, *Ha'aretz*, 2 May 2003.
34 Daniel Sobelman and Amos Harel, *Ha'aretz*, 30 June 2003.
35 Amos Harel, *Ha'aretz*, 15 August 2003; Chris McGreal, *Guardian*, 23 August 2003.
36 Amos Harel, *Ha'aretz*, 15 August 2003.
37 Aluf Benn, *Ha'aretz*, 15 August 2003. See also Amos Harel, *Ha'aretz*, 21 August 2003.
38 Aluf Benn, *Ha'aretz*, 15 August 2003.
39 For a survey of this policy in the first two years of the Palestinian uprising, see my *Israel/Palestine*, ch. 7, pp. 138–42.
40 Suzanne Goldenberg, *Guardian*, 22 August 2003. See also Ze'ev Schiff, *Ha'aretz*, 26 August 2003.
41 See for example Inigo Gilmore's report in the UK *Daily Telegraph*, 24 August 2003.
42 Ze'ev Schiff, *Ha'aretz*, 26 August 2003. See also Amos Harel, *Ha'aretz*, 21 August 2003.

43 Chris McGreal, *Guardian*, 22 August 2003.

44 Amos Harel and Daniel Sobelman, *Ha'aretz*, 26 June 2003.

45 Aluf Benn, *Ha'aretz*, 24 August 2003.

46 Arnon Regular, *Ha'aretz*, 8 October 2003.

47 Ibid.

48 Arnon Regular, "Hamas Pleads for Help from Arab World," *Ha'aretz*, 16 September 2003.

49 Ibid.

50 This was several weeks after Sharon had announced already his "disengagement" plan to withdraw from Gaza, thereby consolidating what was perceived as his metamorphosis from hawk to dove.

51 Quoting myself, "Ahmed Yassin viewed himself as struggling against the occupation. As reported in *Yediot Aharonot*, his demand was a full withdrawal of the Israeli army from the occupied territories, back to the borders of 1967. In 1993, Hamas agreed to the principles of the Oslo accords, but did not believe that Rabin would translate these principles into action, and urged the Palestinian people to remember that the occupation was not yet over. During the iron-fist period of Barak and Sharon, Yassin proposed a long term *hudna* (ceasefire), but he also believed that Israel would never end the occupation of its own will. 'The only language the enemy understands is that of war, bombs and explosives', he preached to his followers, declaring that 'every Israeli is a target for us' . . . ." ("As in Tiananmen Square," *Yediot Aharonot*, 30 March 2004, translated from Hebrew by Netta Van Vliet).

52 Robert Fisk, *Independent*, 23 March 2004.

53 Suzanne Goldenberg, *Guardian*, 24 March 2004.

54 Tanya Reinhart, "As in Tiananmen Square," *Yediot Aharonot*, 30 March 2004, translated from Hebrew by Netta Van Vliet.

2. Winter 2004: The Disengagement Plan

1 Yoel Marcus, *Ha'aretz*, 3 February 2004.

2 Gideon Alon, *Ha'aretz*, 28 May 2004 (quoted in Chapter 1).

3 Aluf Benn, *Ha'aretz*, 24 November 2003. See also Paul Harris and Kamal Ahmed, *Observer*, 18 April 2004. Sharon confirmed this information again in interviews in *Ha'aretz* and *Yediot Aharonot*, on the eve of the Jewish New Year in 2004, see below.

4 Amotz Asa-El, Herb Keinon and Gil Hoffman, "My Algeria Is Here," interview with Ariel Sharon, *Jerusalem Post*, 9 September 2004.

5 Ari Shavit, "The Big Freeze," interview with Dov Weisglass, *Ha'aretz Magazine*, 8 October 2004.

6 See Chapter 1 above.

7 Sidney Blumenthal, *Guardian*, 14 November 2003.

8 Agencies, *Guardian*, 22 October 2003.

9 Shlomo Shamir, *Ha'aretz*, 19 October 2003.

10 I discuss the wall project and the ICJ ruling in Chapter 7 below.

11 Chris McGreal, *Guardian*, 27 November 2003

12 Janine Zacharia, *Jerusalem Post*, 5 October 2003.

13 Chris McGreal, *Guardian*, 27 November 2003.

14 Interview with Nahum Barnea and Shimeon Schiffer, *Yediot Aharonot* Saturday Supplement, 15 September 2004. Sharon was asked how his disengagement plan differed from a proposal by the former Israeli opposition leader Amram Mitzna, who suggested in his election campaign that Israel should restart peace talks with the Palestinians by withdrawing from the Gaza Strip, including the isolated settlement of Netzarim. Sharon replied: "Under Mitzna's

plan, we would start with the evacuation of Netzarim and then continue to evacuate according to the Road Map.''

15 Aluf Benn, *Ha'aretz*, 14 September 2004. Sharon disclosed the same information also in the *Yediot Aharonot* interview (see previous note).

16 Sidney Blumenthal, *Guardian*, 14 November 2003, quoted above.

17 For a detailed survey of these negotiations see my *Israel/Palestine*, ch. 3, pp. 61–77. I argue there, based on analysis of the available documents, that in these lengthy negotiations, optimistically described in the media, neither Rabin nor Barak ever actually committed to withdraw in the future from any area of the Golan Heights, and certainly not in the Shepherdstown document brokered by Clinton.

18 ''Interview with Syria's President,'' *New York Times*, 30 November 2003, p. 1. For an analysis of the interview, see Zvi Bar'el, *Ha'aretz*, 2 December 2003.

19 Aluf Benn, *Ha'aretz*, 3 December 2003.

20 Amos Harel, *Ha'aretz*, 24 December 2001.

21 Aluf Benn and Daniel Sobelman, *Ha'aretz*, 3 February 2002.

22 Ed Vulliamy, *Observer*, 13 April 2003.

23 Barbara Slavin, *USA Today*, 8 October 2003.

24 Brian Whitaker, *Guardian*, 17 May 2004.

25 Agencies, *Guardian*, 7 October 2003.

26 Barbara Slavin, *USA Today*, 8 October 2003.

27 Merle D. Kellerhals, Jr, usinfo.state.gov (Washington File), 14 November 2003.

28 Aluf Benn, *Ha'aretz*, 14 September 2004.

29 Ari Shavit, ''The Big Freeze,'' Interview with Dov Weisglass, *Ha'aretz Magazine*, 8 October 2004.

30 See for example, Professor Ephraim Ya'ar and Dr Tamar Hermann's report on the poll of the Tami Steinmetz Center for Peace Research at Tel Aviv University, *Ha'aretz*, 10 December 2002, where the percentage was 71. Other polls showed similar findings.

31 I survey these stable polls findings in my *Israel/Palestine*, Ch. 10. In the report of Ya'ar and Hermann (see previous note), 20 per cent are ready to evacuate all settlements in the West Bank, and additional 52 per cent are ready to evacuate the settlements outside the big settlement blocks in the center of the West Bank (which would enable the evacuation of 90 per cent of the West Bank). So at the time of the elections, it can be said that 72 per cent of Israelis were willing to dismantle the settlements in most of the occupied territories.

32 See above, Chapter 1.

33 Anat Cygielman, *Ha'aretz*, 2 November 2003.

34 Before this public announcement, Sharon had presented an outline of the plan in a speech at the Herzliya conference on 18 December 2001 (Aluf Benn and Gideon Alon, *Ha'aretz* correspondents and agencies, *Ha'aretz*, 21 December 2003).

35 Yoel Marcus, *Ha'aretz*, 3 February 2004.

36 Ari Shavit, ''The Big Freeze,'' Interview with Dov Weisglass, *Ha'aretz Magazine*, 8 October 2004 (quoted above).

37 Aluf Ben, *Ha'aretz*, Hebrew edition, 6 February 2004.

38 *Yediot Aharonot* Saturday Supplement, 20 February 2004.

39 Itamar Eichner and Nehama Duek, *Yediot Aharonot*, 19 April 2004.

40 Yosi Yehushua, *Yediot Aharonot*, 19 April 2004.

41 ''Sharon and George W. Bush's Letters in Full'', *Ha'aretz*, 15 April 2004.

42 I discuss these plans in *Israel/Palestine*, ch. 2, pp. 21–26.

43 I explore these issues further in Chapter 7.

44 ''The Disengagement Plan of Prime Minister Ariel Sharon, Key Principles'', *Ha'aretz*, April 16 2004, hereafter ''Disengagement Plan.'' The published plan is available at: http://www.haar-

etz.com/hasen/pages/ShArt.jhtml?itemNo=416024&contrassID=1&subContrassID=1&sb-SubContrassID=0&listSrc=Y.

45 Disengagement Plan, Section III, *Security Reality after the Evacuation*, clause A1.
46 Disengagement Plan, Section XII, *The International Crossing Point*.
47 Disengagement Plan, Section III, *Security Reality after the Evacuation*, clause A3.
48 Amotz Asa-El, Herb Keino and Gil Hoffman, ''My Algeria Is Here,'' interview with Ariel Sharon, *Jerusalem Post*, 9 September 2004.
49 Disengagement Plan, Section I, Overview, Clause F.
50 Aluf Benn, *Ha'aretz*, 18 March 2004.

3. Israel's Plans for Gaza

1 The ''Gaza first'' plan had been advocated since the 1980s by Labor politicians such as Shimon Peres and Yossi Beilin. In 1992 some Likud members like Roni Milo expressed their support. See, for example, Amos Karmel, *hakol politi (It's All Politics)* (Tel Aviv, 2001), p. 862.
2 Dr Haidar Abd-el Shafi, born in Gaza in 1919, is a physician and a highly respected independent Palestinian leader.
3 *Ha'aretz*, 3 November 1993.
4 Alternatively, the Dugit settlers sought a site inside Israel's borders, to which they could relocate. They said: 'We never wanted to live in the Gaza Strip. We just wanted a place near the sea, and this is the only site the Likud Government was willing to give us.' (*The Other Israel*, May 2004, Issue 64, http://www.israelipalestinianpeace.org/issues/61toi.htm actions).
5 As discussed in detail in my *Israel/Palestine*, ch. 9, pp. 188–98.
6 Karmel, *hakol politi*, p. 64 (see also note 1, above).
7 Amnon Kapeliouk, Yitzhak Rabin interview, ''1983: New Opportunities for Peace,'' *Trialogue*, Winter 1983, quoted in Noam Chomsky, *The Fateful Triangle* (Cambridge, Mass.: 1983, 1999), p. 48.
8 See my *Israel/Palestine* for more details, ch. 9, pp. 188–98.
9 See above, Chapter 2.
10 *Yediot Aharonot* Saturday Supplement, 9 March 2001.
11 Ibid.
12 See http://www.pchrgaza.org/special/statisics_intifada.htm.
13 PUBLIC AI Index: MDE 15/053/2004. See also Amnesty International report *House Demolition and Destruction of Land and Property*, AI Index: MDE 15/033/2004.
14 PUBLIC AI Index: MDE 15/053/2004.
15 Sara Roy, ''A Dubai on the Mediterranean,'' *London Review of Books*, 29 October 2005.
16 See ch. 8, pp. 116–28; ch. 8, pp. 170–81.
17 Amira Hass, *Ha'aretz*, 9 June 2004.
18 Nir Hasson, *Ha'aretz*, 2 August 2004.
19 UN Relief and Works Agency for Palestine Refugees in the Near East Headquarters, Gaza, press release no. HQ/G/06/2004, 1 April 2004; website: www.unrwa.org.
20 Aluf Benn and Arnon Regular, *Ha'aretz*, 21 January 2005.
21 *Reuters*, 20 January 2005 (cited in *Ha'aretz online*, http://www.haaretzdaily.com/hasen/spages/529513.html). See also Chris McGreal, *Guardian*, 20 January 2005.
22 Arnon Regular, Aluf Benn and Amos Harel, *Ha'aretz*, 17 October 2004.
23 *UNRWA Gaza Field Assessment of IDF Operation Days of Penitence*, 20 October 2004, http://www.un.org/unrwa/news/incursion_oct04.pdf
24 Amira Hass, *Ha'aretz*, 19 January 2005.

25 Chris McGreal, *Guardian*, 20 May 2004.

26 Amos Harel, *Ha' aretz*, 20 May 2004.

27 Amos Harel, *Ha'aretz*, 20 January 2005.

28 Alex Fishman, *Yediot Aharonot* Saturday Supplement, 19 March 2004.

29 Amir Oren, *Ha'aretz*, 14 May 2004.

30 Disengagement Plan, Section III, clause A3.

31 Ze'ev Schiff, *Ha'aretz*, 27 December 2005.

32 This will be discussed below in Chapter 6.

33 Disengagement Plan, Section VI, *The Border Area between the Gaza Strip and Egypt ("Philadelphi Route")*.

34 Amos Harel and Yuval Yoaz, *Ha'aretz*, 26 January 2005.

35 Amos Harel, *Ha'aretz*, 10 February 2005.

36 Amos Harel and Yuval Yoaz, *Ha'aretz*, 26 January 2005.

37 Amost Harel, *Ha'aretz*, 11 March 2005.

38 For more details see my *Israel/Palestine*, ch. 3, pp. 61–8.

39 Conal Urquhart, "Israel to Seal off Gaza with Underwater Wall," *Guardian*, 18 June 2005.

4. Winter 2004–5: The Post-Arafat "Period of Calm"

1 Aluf Benn, *Ha'aretz*, 7 December 2004.

2 See Chapter 2 above.

3 Conal Urquhart, *Observer*, 9 January 2005.

4 Roni Shaked, Itamar Eichner et al., *Yediot Aharonot*, 7 January 2005.

5 Aluf Benn, *Ha'aretz*, 16 January 2005.

6 See above, Chapter 1.

7 Amos Harel, *Ha'aretz*, 14 January 2005.

8 Pace report, Voice of America news (voanews.com), 31 December 2004.

9 Press release no. 10, Presidential Campaign of Dr Mustafa Barghouthi (http://www.mustafabarghouthi.ps), 1 January 2005.

10 Nir Hasson, *Ha'aretz*, 5 January 2005.

11 Conal Urquhart, *Guardian*, 5 January 2005.

12 Palestinian Labor Minister Ghassan al-Khatib quoted in *Al Jazeera*, 14 January 2005.

13 *Ha'aretz*, 16 January 2005.

14 Amos Harel, *Ha'aretz*, 16 January 2005.

15 For example Harel reported then that "military Intelligence told the political echelon . . . that the new Palestinian government headed by Prime Minister Mahmoud Abbas (Abu Mazen) has no intention of uprooting the terrorist infrastructure" (Amos Harel, *Ha'aretz*, 30 April 2003, quoted in Chapter 1).

16 Ibid.

17 Arnon Regular, Aluf Benn and Amos Harel, *Ha'aretz*, 18 January 2005.

18 Arnon Regular, *Ha'aretz*, 23 January 2005.

19 Arnon Regular, *Ha'aretz*, 19 January 2005.

20 Ibid.

21 Ze'ev Schiff, *Ha'aretz*, 25 January 2005.

22 See my *Israel/Palestine* for Ya'alon's role in the years 2000–2.

23 Akiva Eldar, *Ha'aretz*, 25 April 2005.

24 Molly Moore, *Washington Post*, 31 October 2003. According to this report, "Ya'alon also criticized the government"'s decision to expand the barrier being built between the West Bank and Israel deep into Palestinian territory to encompass more Jewish settlements and cut off tens of thousands of Palestinians from their agricultural lands and families.'

25 Ibid.

26 However, Ya'alon's "dovish" tendencies should not be exaggerated. The same *Washington Post* article also mentions that "a civilian government official accused Ya'alon of hypocrisy, alleging that the military commander carried out many of the orders that hampered Abbas without raising objections. Some military analysts and officials also note that Ya'alon has supported some of the armed forces" most controversial tactics in the Palestinian territories, including targeted killings' (*Washington Post*, 31 October 2003). There is also some evidence that Ya'alon has continued to support a big military offensive in Gaza before the pullout. Like Sharon, he kept insisting that Israel "would not be satisfied with police deployment and PA talks to persuade the heads of terror groups, but expects Abbas to disarm Hamas and Islamic Jihad" (Gideon Alon, *Ha'aretz*, 16 February 2005). The cabinet debate described above is consistent with several other occasions during his term, when Ya'alon stressed the importance of sensitivity to the international atmosphere at the time of the operation, and of waiting for the right time.

27 *Jerusalem Post*, 24 October 2000.

28 Senior security analyist Alex Fishman reported that the operation had crushed an initiative of the Hamas and Tanzim (a Fatah-related militant organization) to declare a full unilateral ceasefire. "The Tanzim communique – calling for an end to suicide bombings, to the shooting of mortar shells and missiles and to any other activity against Israeli civilians – was due to be published . . . [on 23 July 2002] as an article in the *Washington Post* and simultaneously in the Palestinian and Israeli press. The US administration was also briefed on this initiative, though in essence it was internationally sponsored by the EU.' ("Tanzim Intended to Halt Terror" [Hebrew], *Yediot Aharonot*, 23 July 2002); the same was reported in *Ha'aretz* (Hannah Kim, "Between the Lines/Liquidating an Initiative," *Ha'aretz*, 26 July 2002). Akiva Eldar reported that "Yossi Beilin, back this week from talks in Washington, says that the cease-fire attempt and the Gaza bombing were the talk of the town wherever he went – the National Security Council, the State Department and Congress. He says that he was asked if it was an accident that for a third time, Sharon ordered such an operation just as the chances for a cease-fire begin to take shape." ("If There's Smoke, There's No Ceasefire," *Ha'aretz*, 30 July 2002).

29 Ze'ev Schiff, *Ha'aretz*, 25 January 2005.

30 This is explored fully in Chapter 5 below.

31 Chris McGreal, *Guardian*, 25 January 2005.

32 Chris McGreal, *Guardian*, 24 January 2005.

33 Chris McGreal, *Guardian*, 24 January 2005.

34 Ibid.

35 *New York Times*, 25 January 2005.

36 See above, Chapter 1.

37 Reported on Ynet, 8 November 2005. Dates cover September 2004 to September 2005.

38 Chris McGreal, *Guardian*, 8 February 2005.

39 Conal Urquhart, *Guardian*, 4 February 2005.

40 Aluf Benn, Arnon Regular and agencies, *Ha'aretz*, 9 February 2005.

41 Ibid.

42 "Excerpts of Sharon's Speech," *Ha'aretz*, 9 February 2005.

43 News agencies, *Ha'aretz*, 9 February 2005.

44 As the *Guardian* reported, the Arab media was far less enthusiastic: "Lebanon's leftist *As-*

Safir newspaper ran the headline: "Sharm el-Sheik summit crowns Sharon a man of peace . . . for nothing." Sahar Baasiri, of Lebanon's leading *An-Nahar* newspaper, said the summit provided "the service of cleaning up Sharon's image . . ." "The whole world classifies him [Sharon] as a war criminal, and yet he was welcomed and given a place at a round table as if his hands were clean of Palestinian blood," wrote Abdul-Wahab Badrakhan of the widely read pan-Arab *Al Hayat* daily. But some said the summit had to be held if the four-year conflict – which according to an Associated Press count had left 3,458 people dead on the Palestinian side and 1,027 on Israeli side – was to end. "Peace is made with enemies," said *Al Hayat*'s editor-in-chief, Ghassan Charbel. "The other choice is violence and extremism, car bombs and suicide bombers" (David Crouch and agencies, *Guardian*, 9 February 2005).

45 Ibid.

46 *Ha'aretz*, 10 February 2005. In another incident on 9 January, a Hamas militant died in what both PA and Israeli security sources described as a "work accident", i.e. "he was killed when explosives he had exploded prematurely" (Ze'ev Schiff, *Ha'aretz*, 13 February 2005). This has been for years the formula used when either of these sources chooses not to take open responsibility for the killing. In this case, it appears that this was the work of Palestinian security forces.

47 Al Jazeera and agencies, "Second Palestinian Killed after Summit', aljazeera.net, 10 February 2005.

48 "Who Broke the Ceasefire (First)?," MIFTAH, 12 February 2005, http://www.miftah.org. The Palestinian Initiative for the Promotion of Global Dialogue and Democracy, MIFTAH, as described in its home page, "is a non-governmental non-partisan Jerusalem-based institution dedicated to fostering democracy and good governance within Palestinian society through promoting public accountability, transparency, the free flow of information and ideas, and the challenging of stereotyping at home and abroad. Established in December 1998, with Hanan Ashrawi as its Secretary-General, MIFTAH's aim is to serve as a Palestinian platform for global dialogue and cooperation guided by the principles of democracy, human rights, gender equity, and participatory governance."

49 Ibid.

50 Amos Harel, *Ha'aretz*, 15 April 2005.

51 Arnon Regular, Aluf Benn and Nathan Guttman, *Ha'aretz*, 26 May 2005.

52 Amira Hass, *Ha'aretz*, 8 February 2005.

53 Amos Har'el, *Ha'aretz*, 9 February 2005.

54 *Palestinian Monitor* (http://www.palestinemonitor.org), 16 February 2005.

55 Amos Harel and Arnon Regular, *Ha'aretz*, 15 April 2005.

56 See my *Israel/Palestine*, ch. 10, pp. 181–8. See also note 46, above.

57 Amos Harel and Arnon Regular, *Ha'aretz*, 30 May 2005.

58 Arnon Regular and *Ha'aretz* Service, *Ha'aretz* (Hebrew edition only), 3 May 2005.

59 Roni Singer, Aluf Benn, Amos Harel and Arnon Regular, *Ha'aretz*, 27 February 2005. Israel blamed Syria and Hizbollah for initiating the Islamic Jihad attack, and there were reports that the Palestinians did as well. But Planning Minister Ghassan Khatib "denied the PNA [PA] had accused Lebanon's Hizbollah guerrilla group of involvement in the Tel Aviv bombing, saying the media 'should be careful not to take news related to the Palestinian side from Israeli sources' (Palestine Media Center, 28 February 2005).

60 Arnon Regular, *Ha'aretz*, 4 March 2005.

61 Amos Harel, *Ha'aretz*, 4 March 2005.

62 Mark Lavie, Associated Press, 28 February 2005.

63 Palestine Media Center, 28 February 2005.

64 Arnon Regular, *Ha'aretz*, 18 March 2005

65 Ibid.

66 Ibid.

67 The PLO is a coalition body of Palestinian organizations that was founded in 1964 (before the Israeli occupation). Since 1967, the dominant organization in the PLO has been Fatah, and in 1969 Fatah's leader Yasser Arafat was elected the chair of the PLO. Over the years, the PLO has been recognized by the Arab League and large parts of the international community as the official representative of the Palestinian people. (The Palestinian Authority – established in 1994 following the Oslo Agreements with the approval of the PLO – is a body functioning as an autonomous government and representing only the Palestinians in the occupied territories.)

68 Danny Rubinstein, *Ha'aretz*, 11 April 2005.

69 The report is cited in *International Middle East Media Center – IMEMC* (http://www.imemc.org), 14 July 2005.

70 Ibid. According to this report, during those four months, Palestinian groups in Gaza fired 434 shells (197 of which did not reach an Israeli target but landed in Palestinian areas instead). This is a substantial reduction compared to the rate of 100 shells per week in the period of tension before the calm (quoted above, Chapter 3, p. 00).

71 The military tribunal eventually acquitted the commander on 15 November 2005 (author's note).

72 Chris McGreal, "Snipers with Children in Their Sights," *Guardian*, 28 June 2005.

5. Summer 2005: The Gaza Pullout: The Role of International Pressure

1 Tanya Reinhart, "A Pacifier for the Majority," *Yediot Aharonot*, 17 March 2004.

2 Yosi Verter, *Ha'aretz*, 8 October 2004.

3 Gideon Alon, *Ha'aretz*, 2 March 2005.

4 Lily Galili, "Prisoner of his Gush Katif Home," *Ha'aretz*, 30 March 2005.

5 Alex Fishman, *Yediot Aharonot*, Saturday Supplement, 18 March 2003.

6 Tanya Reinhart , "The Israeli Left Is Opting for Suicide," *Yediot Aharonot*, 23 March 2005, translated from Hebrew by Mark Marshall.

7 "Prisoner of his Gush Katif Home," *Ha'aretz*, 30 March 2005.

8 Ofer Petersburg, *Yediot Aharonot*, 8 April 2005.

9 Uzi Benziman, "What Does Condoleezza Know?," *Ha'aretz*, 15 May 2005.

10 Aluf Benn, "Sharon Aides: The Public Is Being Misled about Pullout Preparations," *Ha'aretz*, 9 June 2005.

11 Ibid.

12 Ronen Bergman and Yuval Karni, *Yediot Aharonot* Saturday Supplement, 5 August 2005.

13 The official reason given for postponing the evacuation was that this was in order that it should happen after the Jewish Tisha B'Av fast (the ninth day of the month Av in the Jewish calendar), which in 2005 happens to be on 15 August – as, of course, was known before (author's note).

14 Amir Oren, "The Evacuation Is Only on the Horizon," *Ha'aretz*, 10 May 2005.

15 Aluf Benn, Gideon Alon and Nathan Guttman, *Ha'aretz*, 7 June 2004.

16 Aluf Benn, *Ha'aretz*, 7 June 2004.

17 It may be argued that the reason why Sharon did not pass the evacuation resolution in the 6 June 2004 cabinet meeting was that at the time he did not have a sufficient majority to do so. (Prior to the cabinet discussion, the Likud "rebels," Benjamin Netanyahu, Limor Livnat and

Silvan Shalom, who objected to the plan, were forming a partnership on this issue with ministers of the extreme right National Union.) But the fact of the matter is that on the eve of the cabinet meeting, it was widely reported that "Prime Minister Ariel Sharon fired National Union ministers Avigdor Lieberman and Benny Elon on Friday morning in a bid to win a cabinet majority on the revised disengagement plan which will be presented to the cabinet for a vote on Sunday" (Aluf Benn, Mazal Mualem, Gideon Alon and Nadav Shragai, *Ha'aretz*, 4 June 2004). Sharon therefore had a clear majority with which to pass the actual decision on evacuation; nevertheless, he sided with the Likud "rebels" in the meeting and postponed this decision. "During the meeting, Justice Minister Yosef Lapid called his Shinui faction colleagues for a consultation to demand that Sharon include in the cabinet decision a mention of the exact date when settlement evacuation would begin. However, it was decided that Sharon would just announce the March 1 2005 date for the end of preparations for evacuation," after which the decision to evacuate would be discussed (Aluf Benn, Gideon Alon and Nathan Guttman, *Ha'aretz*, 7 June 2004).

18 Aluf Benn, *Ha'aretz*, 7 June 2004.

19 The first session of this special committee, headed by PMO Director-General Ilan Cohen, took place on 26 July 2004. Cohen told the press that "Sharon told him 'not to compromise over security needs.' Gaza Regional Council Chairman Avner Shimoni won approval for 26 bullet-proofed buildings in Gush Katif. The new buildings are meant for residences, and school rooms are meant for Kfar Darom, Netzarim and Neveh Dekalim. So far, some 350 development projects have been submitted to the committee" (Aluf Benn and Nir Hason, *Ha'aretz*, 27 July 2004).

20 Yuval Yoaz, *Ha'aretz*, 26 October 2004.

21 Aluf Benn, Mazal Mualem and Amos Harel, *Ha'aretz*, 20 February 2005.

22 Aluf Benn, "Sharon as Gorbachev," *Ha'aretz*, 21 February 2005.

23 See above, Chapter 4.

24 See Chapter 1.

25 Aluf Benn, *Ha'aretz*, 15 April 2005.

26 Amos Harel, *Ha'aretz*, 11 April 2005.

27 Ibid.

28 Aluf Benn and Nathan Guttman, *Ha'aretz*, 11 April 2005.

29 Aluf Benn, *Ha'aretz*, 15 April 2005.

30 Ibid.

31 Arnon Regular, Aluf Benn and Nathan Guttman, *Ha'aretz*, 26 May 2005.

32 Ibid.

33 Akiva Eldar and Arnon Regular, "Sharon to Discuss Keeping Hamas out of Elections," *Ha'aretz*, 17 June 2005.

34 Ibid.

35 *Agence France Presse*, 6 October 2005.

36 Aluf Benn and Gideon Alon, "Israel Seeks Support Abroad for Blocking Hamas in PA poll," *Ha'aretz*, 3 October 2005.

37 For a detailed survey of the destruction of Palestinian institutions and the return of the military rule, see my *Israel/Palestine*, ch. 8, pp. 148–52. For a survey of what motivated this spree of destruction, see ibid., ch. 9, pp. 181–207.

38 Aluf Benn, *Ha'aretz*, 2 October 2005.

39 For example, in September 2005, "Prime Minister Ariel Sharon said . . . that he had asked European leaders and UN Secretary-General Kofi Annan to press for the disarming of Hamas militants and the abolition of their covenant, which calls for Israel's destruction. Sharon told a conference of American Jewish leaders that Israel would not cooperate in Palestinian elections scheduled for January unless those two conditions were met. Israeli assistance is

considered vital for smooth elections . . . An aide to Sharon said not providing support would mean no easing of Palestinian access to polling stations in the area dotted by Israeli military checkpoints, and no help in arranging voting in East Jerusalem" (News agencies, *Ha'aretz*, 20 September 2005).

40 Aluf Benn, "Opposing PLC Elections Is Flawed, U.S. Says," *Ha'aretz*, 18 September 2005.

41 *Ha'aretz* staff and agencies, Israel, "U.S. at Odds Over Timing of Disarming Palestinians," *Ha'aretz*, 24 October 2005.

42 Yitzhak Benhorin, "Israel Changes Stance on Hamas," Ynet, 3 November 2005.

43 Arnon Regular, "U.S. Pushes for PA Election To Be Held on Schedule," *Ha'aretz*, 4 January 2005.

44 Report of the Defence Science Board Task Force on Strategic Communication, September 2004, http://www.acq.osd.mil/dsb/reports/2004-09-Strategic_Communication.pdf. The report was summarized by Neil Mackay, investigations editor, "Pentagon Report Reveals Catalogue of Failure," *Sunday Herald* (Scotland), 5 December 2004, as well as the BBC site http://news.bbc.co.uk/go/pr/fr/-/2/hi/americas/4040543.stm.

45 Hannah K. Strange, UPI, published in Washington *Time*, 20 January 2005. The poll was conducted by the Program on International Policy Attitudes together with GlobeScan. A total of 21,953 people were interviewed in countries from every area of the globe, including Australia, Japan, South Africa, Mexico and Canada. Between 500 and 1,800 people were surveyed in each country in face-to-face or telephone interviews between 15 November 2004 and 5 January 2005.

46 Report of the Defence Science Board Task Force, p. 40 (see above, note 44).

47 Thomas Fuller, *Herald Tribune*, 31 October 2003; Ahto Lobjakas, Radio Free Europe, 3 November 2003. 7,500 people across the European Union were polled. The poll sparked outrage in Israeli government circles, followed by criticism and attacks on the Commission that ordered it, from the international pro-Israel lobby. In the US, a survey conducted for the Jewish Anti-Defamation League showed that 43 percent of Americans believe Israel is a threat to world peace (Jonathan M. Katz, *Guardian*, 18 December 2003).

48 Report of the Defence Science Board Task Force, p. 3 (see note 44, above).

49 Jon Henley, *Guardian*, 4 June 2005.

50 Thomas Fuller, *Herald Tribune*, 31 October 2003.

51 Seymour M. Hersh, "The Coming Wars," *New Yorker*, issue 31, 24 January 2005.

52 For example, according to *Ha'aretz* the German weekly magazine *Der Spiegel* disclosed that "Israel is prepared to launch an attack on Iran's nuclear sites in order to paralyze them and prevent them from being operational". It also related that "the *Los Angeles Times* reported that U.S. and Israeli officials say Israel has modified U.S.-made Harpoon cruise missiles so it can launch nuclear warheads from submarines. The State Department and Pentagon declined to comment on the report, as did an Israeli military spokesman, in line with that nation's policy of refusing to say if it has nuclear weapons." *Ha'aretz* added that this information was leaked "amid heightened tensions in the region and concern over Iran's atomic program" (Reuters and Haaretz Service, *Ha'aretz*, 'IDF Planning to Attack Nuclear Sites in Iran', 12 October 2003). In March 2005 *Ha'aretz* reported that, according to the London *Sunday Times*, "Israel has drawn up plans for a combined air and ground attack on Iranian nuclear installations if diplomacy fails to halt Tehran's atomic program . . . The newspaper said Prime Minister Ariel Sharon and his inner cabinet had given 'initial authorization' for a unilateral attack on Iran at a private meeting last month . . . The *Sunday Times* reported that Israeli forces had been simulating attacks on a mock-up of Iran's Natanz uranium-enrichment plant in the last few months" ('*Sunday Times*: Israel Plans to Hit Iran Nuke Plant, by Reuters, *Ha'aretz*, 14 March 2005).

53 Amir Oren, "Inside Track," *Ha'aretz*, 11 February 2005.

54 Aluf Benn, "Sharon Urged Bush: Step Up Pressure to Prevent Iran Getting Nukes," *Ha'aretz*, 13 April 2005.

55 Aluf Benn, "Variations on Iran"'s Nuclear Point of No Return,' *Ha'aretz*, 11 May 2005.

56 David Hirst, *Guardian*, 21 December 2004.

57 Nathaniel Popper, "U.S.-Israel Tensions Rising on Eve of Disengagement," *Forward*, 12 August 2005.

58 See Chapter 4 above.

59 A glimpse into the schemes of deception prevailing in the thinking of Israeli military circles can be found in a March 1982 memo from Ehud Barak to Sharon that was leaked to *Ha'aretz* in January 1999 (discussed in detail in *Israel/Palestine*, ch. 4, pp. 78–87). Barak, who was at the time head of the Israeli army's Planning Division and a favourite of then Defense Minister Sharon, urges Sharon to widen the planned war in Lebanon to a full-scale strike on Syria, exposing along the way his perception of diplomacy and democracy. (He recommended, for example, that the plan be concealed from the political echelon.) As for the US, he explains that Washington would be dealt with through "highly complex and delicate preliminary discussions, which will in no case reveal the full extent of our intentions" . . . (Amir Oren, *Ha'aretz*, 8 January 1999).

60 Robert Fisk, "Ariel Sharon", *Independent*, 6 January 2006 including excerpts from Robert Fisk, *The Great War For Civilisation: The Conquest of the Middle East* (London: Fourth Estate, 2005).

61 Aluf Benn, *Ha'aretz*, 20 October 2002.

62 See above, Chapter 1.

63 Israeli analysts agreed that such demands were hardly difficult to fulfil. See Aluf Benn, *Ha'aretz*, 20 October 2002.

64 Yoav Stern and Gideon Alon, "61 Outposts Built on Non-Israeli Land," *Ha'aretz*, 10 March 2005.

65 *Ha'aretz* staff, *Ha'aretz*, 5 August 2004.

66 Ibid.

67 Aluf Benn, *Ha'aretz*, 6 August 2004. The Hebrew heading of this item was "Israel: US Won't Pressure to Freeze Settlement in Election Time". In the English version it was changed to "Sharon Promises US Envoy he'll Remove Illegal Outposts".

68 See for example Amos Harel and Nir Hasson, "Dozens of Buildings Erected in Outposts in Last Three Months", *Ha'aretz*, 6 June 2005.

69 See for some examples *Israel/Palestine*, ch. 9, pp. 198–207.

70 Steven Erlanger, "U.S. Presses Israel to Smooth the Path to a Palestinian Gaza", *New York Times*, 7 August 2005.

71 Ze'ev Schiff, "A Cold Wind Blowing from the CIA," *Ha'aretz*, August 29 2004.

72 Shmuel Rosner, *Ha'aretz*, 5 August 2005.

73 Julian Borger, *Guardian*, 22 April 2005.

74 E.J. Kessler, "Indictments Shed Light on Aipac 'Spying' Probe," *Forward*, 12 August 2005.

75 Ze'ev Schiff, "Something Is Bothering the FBI," *Ha'aretz*, 24 June 2006.

76 Nathaniel Popper, "U.S.–Israel Tensions Rising on Eve of Disengagement," *Forward*, 12 August 2005.

77 Scott Wilson, "Israel Set to End China Arms Deal Under U.S. Pressure," *Washington Post*, 27 June 2005. A more detailed version of how the conflict erupted in August 2004 was given the following December by Alex Fishman, senior security analyst of *Yediot Aharonot*, who wrote that "as early as 2000, close to the eruption of the Phalcon affair . . . Israel reported to the administration about a deal with China to sell the attack drone known by the trade name Harpy, produced by a subsidiary of Israel Aircraft Industries. The Americans didn't like the deal – but they also didn't express firm

opposition. The Israelis understood that as an okay. In the intervening years, the Americans continued to show interest in the topic, but not to the point of creating a crisis . . . In March 2004, director general of the Defense Ministry Amos Yaron was asked by Pentagon officials whether Israel still stood by its commitments and wasn't working on an additional deal to sell Harpy-class attack drones to China. He checked and discovered that in 2002, Israel had indeed sold – at China's request – [spare] parts of the Harpy. He also learned that in 2004 there was an additional Chinese order for seven more Harpy kits. Yaron ordered that the Chinese request not be honored. This was reported to the Americans last July. The moment the report was received, a furor broke out . . . The United States fundamentally does not believe Israel's reports. The Americans collect information, from their own sources, about military developments in China . . . Now there is an examination under way surrounding the Harpy: The Americans are sending questions and the Israeli defense establishment is answering, hoping that they will suffice and the affair will calm down." At the present, the Americans are "worried that under the guise of spare parts, Israel is performing upgrades that fundamentally transform a weapons system, making it even more deadly" (*Yediot Aharonot* Saturday Supplement, 24 December 2004; the English translation quoted here appeared in *Forward*, 7 January 2005).

78 See for a survey of the US demands, Ze'ev Schiff and Ha'aretz service, "U.S. Orders Israel to Increase Control of Security Exports", 12 June 2005.

79 Ibid.

80 Ze'ev Schiff, "U.S.Sanctions Still in Place, Despite Deal over Security Exports", *Ha'aretz*, 28 August 2005.

81 Ze'ev Schiff, "Taking on U.S. over China – A Lost Cause," *Ha'aretz*, 14 June 2005.

82 Ibid.

83 Shmuel Rosner and Aluf Benn, "U.S., Israel Sign Deal on Defense Exports," *Ha'aretz*, 17 August 2005.

84 Ze'ev Schiff, 'U.S. Sanctions Still in Place, Despite Deal over Security Exports', *Ha'aretz*, 28 August 2005.

85 Aluf Benn, "U.S. Keeping Israel out of Prestigious Fighter Plane Program", *Ha'aretz*, 12 October 2005.

86 Shmuel Rosner and Amos Harel, 'U.S. Brings Israel Back on Board for Fighter Plane Development Project', *Ha'aretz*, 6 November 2005.

87 As *Ha'aretz* summarized this period in mid-July, "Hamas cells operating out of the . . . West Bank have not been involved in terrorist attacks for an extended period of time thanks in large part to its commitment to an Egyptian-brokered cease-fire among militant groups (Amos Harel, Nir Hasson and Arnon Regular, *Ha'aretz* correspondents, *Ha'aretz* Service and Agencies, "8 Rockets Land in Sderot Area"; "IDF Readies for Gaza raid,, *Ha'aretz*, 16 July 2005.)

88 See above, section 2.

89 I mentioned one such case (on May 29 2005) in Chapter 4. Another took place on 18 May 2005. See "Agencies in Gaza", *Guardian*, 19 May 2005.

90 Chris McGreal, *Guardian*, May 20 2005.

91 See above, Chapter 1.

92 For example, shortly after the escalation of mortar attacks following the killing of the three boys on 9 April, senior Israeli intelligence official Yossi Kuperwasser informed the Knesset Defense and Foreign Affairs Committee that "Palestinian leader Mahmoud Abbas is attempting to halt the rocket and mortar fire in the Gaza Strip" (Ilan Marciano, "Calm Not Over Yet", Ynet, 11 April 2005). Though the PA was usually attempting to stop escalation through negotiations with the militant groups, Palestinian security forces in Gaza

were also active in forcefully preventing mortar launching: in the period between February and March 2005, they prevented directly fourteen Qassam launches, and carried out twenty-one joint operations with the Israeli army to prevent such attacks (Alex Fishman, "Iron Fist at End of the Summer," *Yediot Aharonot* Saturday Supplement, 6 May 2005; quoted below).

93 Amos Harel, "Analysis: The End of the Period of Calm Is Fast Approaching," *Ha'aretz*, 16 July 2005.

94 Amos Harel, Nir Hasson and Arnon Regular, *Ha'aretz* correspondents, *Ha'aretz* Service and Agencies, *Ha'aretz*, "8 Rockets Land in Sderot Area; IDF Readies for Gaza Raid,' 16 July 2005.

95 ibid.

96 Amos Harel, "PA Declares State of Emergency in Gaza", *Ha'aretz*, 15 July 2005.

97 Conal Urquhart, "Israel Masses Troops along Gaza Border," *Guardian*, 18 July 2005.

98 Alex Fishman, "Iron Fist at End of the Summer," *Yediot Aharonot* Saturday Supplement, 6 May 2005.

99 Ibid.

100 Ibid.

101 Amir Oren, "The Fire Next Time," *Ha'aretz*, 26 March 2004.

102 Ibid.

103 Ibid.

104 For a detailed survey of Operation Defensive Shield and Jenin, see, among many other sources, my *Israel/Palestine*, ch. 8, pp. 148–170.

105 Amos Harel, "Mofaz Wanted a 'Blitz' in Gaza, Ben-Eliezer Wanted a 'Sting' ", *Ha'aretz*, 12 May 2002. Harel writes: "Thursday morning, as reservists showed up for induction at their bases, a few officers started to express doubts about the anticipated operation. Speaking among themselves, and to reporters, officers warned about a possible blood-bath. Others commented that for the first time during the intifada, the IDF was about to embark on a mission without a public consensus behind it. It appeared as though the Tuesday night attack in Rishon Letzion, which occurred after weeks of relative quiet, did not stir the level of public support for a strong IDF response as had emerged after the waves of lethal terror attacks in March."

106 Ibid.

107 Aluf Benn, "Rice Due Here This Week in Bid to Defuse Tensions," *Ha'aretz*, 17 July 2005.

108 AFP, 18 July 2005.

109 Reuters, "Deadline Looming for Pullout, Rice Warns Ahead of Her Visit," *Ha'aretz*, 20 July 2005.

110 Steven Erlanger, "U.S. Presses Israel to Smooth the Path to a Palestinian Gaza," *New York Times*, 7 August 2005.

111 Ibid.

6. *Winter 2005–6: A Return to the "Long War"*

1 Amira Hass, "Thousands Stuck in Gaza Strip until Rafah Crossing Reopens," *Ha'aretz*, 23 September 2005.

2 The Disengagement Plan of Prime Minister Ariel Sharon, Key Principles, Section XII, "The International Crossing Point", hereafter Disengagement Plan. The published plan is available at: http://www.haaretz.com/hasen/pages/ShArt.jhtml?itemNo=416024&con-traooID−1&oubContrassID−1&subSubContiassID−0&llst3rc−Υ.

3 Aluf Benn, "Israel to Build Israeli–Palestinian-Egyptian Terminal in South", *Ha'aretz*, 9 August 2005. Later that month Israel agreed that the Rafah terminal would remain open,

but only for outgoing traffic, while entering Gaza would be possible only through the new Kerem Shalom terminal.

4 Steven Erlanger, *New York Times*, 7 August 2005.

5 Michael A. Fletcher, *Washington Post*, 15 April 2005.

6 Amira Hass, "Quartet Envoy: Israel Acting as if Disengagement Never Happened," *Ha'aretz*, 24 October 2005.

7 Yoav Stern, "EU to Check Travelers under Rafah Plan," *Ha'aretz*, 2 November 2005.

8 The quotes are from the document of the crossings agreement, which can be found on the UN Reliefweb (http://www.reliefweb.int), entitled "Agreed Documents by Israel and Palestinians on Movement and Access from and to Gaza, S366/05," 15 November 2005.

9 Shmuel Rosner and Amos Harel, "U.S. Brings Israel Back on Board for Fighter Plane Development Project," *Ha'aretz*, 6 November 2005.

10 Roni Sofer, *Ynet* (Hebrew), 15 November 2005.

11 Akiva Eldar and Shmuel Rosner, "U.S. to Israel: Gaza Cargo Crossings Must Remain Open," *Ha'aretz*, 4 November 2005.

12 Ibid.

13 'Agreed Documents by Israel and Palestinians on Movement and Access from and to Gaza, S366/05', (http://www.reliefweb.int) 15 November 2005.

14 Akiva Eldar, "Israel Bows to Int''l Pressure: Convoys to Begin Next Week,' *Ha'aretz*, 15 December 2005.

15 Steven Erlanger, "No Buses Roll from Gaza to West Bank, Despite Deal," *New York Times*, 31 December 2005.

16 Ibid.

17 Ibid.

18 Ibid.

19 Ibid.

20 Amira Hass, "Go Study in Australia?," *Ha'aretz*, 14 December 2005.

21 Arnon Regular, "PA's Abbas, Dahlan Slam Israel for Unfinished Gaza Business," *Ha'aretz*, 12 September 2005.

22 For analysis of what drove US pressure on Israel, see above Chapter 5, section 2.

23 Aluf Benn, "Leaving Gaza – The Day After," *Ha'aretz*, 12 September 2005.

24 Amos Harel, Arnon Regular, Nir Hasson, *Ha'aretz* staff and Associated Press, "Security Cabinet Approves Response against Qassams," *Ha'aretz*, 25 September 2005.

25 Gideon Alon, *Ha'aretz*, 12 January 2005.

26 Amos Harel, Arnon Regular, Nir Hasson, *Ha'aretz* staff and AP, "Security Cabinet Approves Response against Qassams," *Ha'aretz*, 25 September 2005.

27 Ibid. The decision to enforce this buffer zone was ratified in a cabinet meeting on 26 December (Amos Harel, *Ha'aretz*, 27 December 2005.) At the same time it was decided to incorporate two large Palestinian towns – Beit Hanun and Beit Lahia – in the buffer zone, which is more than five kilometres deep (Zeev Schiff, "IDF Plans Aggressive Response to Qassam Fire," *Ha'aretz*, 27 December 2005).

28 On 2 April 2006, *Ha'aretz* reported that "the Israel Defense Force has been pounding the northern Gaza Strip with a massive artillery, air and naval attack for the past 48 hours . . . The IDF has already reduced the safe distance set for artillery aimed toward Palestinian residential areas. If the situation escalates, the General Staff has not ruled out steps that will cause people to flee from homes located . . . in Beit Hanun and Beit Lahia in the northern Strip" (Amos Harel, "Army, Navy Pound Gaza Launch Sites in Massive Assault").

29 Eyad El Sarraj, "Stunning Gaza!", Electronic Intifada (http://electronicintifada.net), 28 September 2005. Dr Eyad El-Sarraj from Gaza is the founder and director of the Gaza

Community Mental Health Programme (GCMHP) and the commissioner-general of the Palestinian Independent Commission for Citizens' Rights.

30 Chris McGreal, "Palestinians Hit by Sonic Boom Air Raids," *Guardian*, 3 November 2005.

31 Ibid.

32 Amos Harel, Aluf Benn and Nir Hasson, "IDF to Impose Aerial Siege," *Ha'aretz*, 23 December 2005.

33 Amos Harel , "U.S. Backs Israel as IDF Continues Gaza Air Strikes," *Ha'aretz*, 27 September 2005.

34 "US 'Understands' Israel's Need to Respond to Attack," *AFP*, 25 September 2005.

35 Amos Harel, Arnon Regular, Nir Hasson, *Ha'aretz* staff and AP, *Ha'aretz*, 25 September 2005.

36 Yossi Melman, "Israel Predicts Iran Will Pay 'Heavy Price' for Nuclear Defiance," *Ha'aretz*, 5 February 2006.

37 Aluf Benn, "Olmert: Israel Will Separate from Most Palestinians," *Ha'aretz*, 8 February 2006.

38 "Israel Bars East Jerusalem Voting for Palestinians," AFP, 21 December 2005.
Israel's official basis for objection was that East Jerusalem is sovereign Israeli territory (having been annexed in 1967). In previous Palestinian elections Israel had nevertheless permitted the voting in East Jerusalem, including the 1996 legislative elections and the January 2005 presidential election. "In the past, we have allowed Palestinians to vote in post offices but not this time," an official in Sharon's office explained to AFP.

39 Arnon Regular, "U.S. Pushes for PA Election to be Held on Schedule," *Ha'aretz*, 4 January 2006.

40 Aluf Benn, "Analysis/Olmert Faces Reality," *Ha'aretz*, 11 January 2006.

41 Shmuel Rosner, "U.S and the PA Election/Next Mission: Educating Hamas," *Ha'aretz*, 27 January 2006.

42 Ibid.

43 Ibid.

44 Amos Harel, "IDF: Hamas Will Abide by Ceasefire Even After PA Election," *Ha'aretz*, 21 January 2006.

45 Yediot Aharonot poll, *Yediot Aharonot*, 27 February 2003.

46 Professor Ephraim Yaar and Professor Tamar Hermann, Peace Index' January 2006; *Ha'aretz*, 8 February 2006.

47 Aluf Benn, "Israel Seeks Backing for Int'l Boycott of Hamas," *Ha'aretz*, 29 January 2006.

48 BADIL Resource Center for Palestinian Residency and Refugee Rights, press release, 27 January 2006 (E/02/06), www.badil.org.

49 Ibid.

50 *Israel/Palestine*, ch. 1, "The Oslo Years: False Expectations", pp. 13–20.

51 David Hirst, "Arafat's Last Stand?", *Guardian* (UK), 14 December 2001. For more on Arafat's failure see my *Yediot Aharonot* articles "Mandela He Ain''t,'" 25 May 1994; "Arafat's Return to Gaza," 7 July 1994, which can be found in www.tau.ac.il/~reinhart/political/politicalE.html.

52 To give just an instance of how the PA rulers have mingled with the occupiers in corruption, in April 1994, the Palestinian delegation signed in Paris an economical agreement with Israel that was disastrous to the Palestinians, guaranteeing Israeli control of every aspect of Palestinian economy. In 1997 *Ha'aretz* disclosed some of what went on behind the scene in these negotiations: Mohammed Rashid, the Kurdish millionaire who served as an economy counsellor of Arafat, closed a deal by which the taxes, which Israel collects on all oil imports to the territories and which should have returned to the PA for the use of the Palestinian

people, will return instead to a private account in a Tel Aviv bank ('Bank Leumi'), which is accessible only to Arafat and to Rashid. *Ha'aretz* reported that the money is reserved for "the evacuation of Arafat, his family, and some senior officials, in case of an upturning", and to cover some secret security services. As reported, Rashid closed the deal with no others but the former heads of the Israeli security services: the mediator was Yoseph Ginosar, formerly the head of the 'interrogation' section of the Israeli secret services (Shabak), which is in charge of the torture of Palestinian prisoners. Through Ginosar, Rashid promised the monopoly on oil sales to the territories to Dor company, another of whose directors is Shmuel Goren, formerly the 'military coordinator' of the territories. (Ronen Bergman and David Ratner, "The Man who Swallowed Gaza", *Ha'aretz* Saturday Magazine, 4 April 1997).

53 Amnesty International, Palestinian Authority: Silencing Dissent, AI Index MDE 21/020/ 2000 – News Service no. 162, 5 September 2000 (http://web2.amnesty.org).

54 Ramzy Baroud, "The Palestinian Authority: Losing Track of What Matters Most", http:// www.iviews.com, 13 September 2000.

55 BADIL Resource Center for Palestinian Residency and Refugee Rights, press release, 27 January 2006 (E/02/06), www.badil.org (quoted above).

56 A detailed research of the training of the Palestinian security forces by the CIA and other intelligence groups is found in Arnon Regular, "The Intelligence Pros: This Is How the CIA Operates in Israel and in the Teritories", *Kol Ha'ir*, Jerusalem, 24 November 2000, pp. 54– 60 (in Hebrew).

57 *Israel/Palestine*, ch. 9, "Arafat's Security Record", pp. 181–8.

58 Arnon Regular, "The Intelligence Pros", *Kol Ha'ir*, Jerusalem, 24 November 2000, pp. 54– 60 (in Hebrew); see also note 56, above.

59 Alex Fishman, *Yediot Aharonot* Saturday Supplement, 27 January 2003.

60 Robert Fisk, "The Problem with Democracy," *Independent*, 28 January 2006.

61 Ismail Haniyeh was born in 1962 in the Shati refugee camp in Gaza. He graduated from the Islamic University of Gaza with a degree in Arabic literature, and in 1993 was appointed dean of that university. In 1997, when Sheikh Ahmed Yassin was released from Israeli prison, Haniyeh was appointed to head his office, and became one of Hamas's political leaders, with a reputation as being moderate and pragmatic. He had spent three years in Israeli administrative detention (1989–92), and although he belongs to the political rather than the military wing of Hamas, he was put on the targeted list of the Israeli army, escaping a failed assassination attempt on 6 September 2003.

62 Arnon Regular, "Hamas to Appoint Moderates as PM, Speaker of PLC," *Ha'aretz*, 16 February 2006.

63 Ibid.

64 'We Do Not Wish to Throw Them into the Sea,' *Washington Post*, 26 February 2006.

65 Ibid.

66 Quadrennial Defense Review 2006, www.defenselink.mil/qdr.

67 Ann Scott Tyson, *Washington Post*, 4 February 2006.

68 Ibid.

69 Shmuel Rosner , "Congress Toes the Line of U.S. Public Opinion on Hamas," *Ha'aretz*, 16 February 2006.

70 E.J. Kessler, "Pro-Israel Activists Cheer Cheney," *Forward*, 10 March 2006.

71 Ibid.

72 Ibid.

73 Amira Hass, *Ha'aretz*, 28 February 2006.

74 Gideon Levy, "As the Hamas Team Laughs," *Ha'aretz*, 19 February 2006.

75 Arnon Regular, Amos Harel and Aluf Benn, "Karni Crossing Reopens, but Closes Again 40 Minutes Later", *Ha'aretz*, 21 March 2006.

76 PCHR, Palestinian Centre for Human Rights, press release, Ref: 6/2006, 19 March 2006 (www.pchrgaza.org).

77 Arnon Regular and Amos Harel, "Haniyeh: New Hamas Government Will Give Abbas" Peace Talks a Chance', Ha'aretz, 30 March 2006.

78 Tzadok Yehezkeli, "Dichter: Haniyeh is in Crosshairs," Ynet (English), 23 February 2006.

7. A System of Prisons: The Plans Behind the West Bank Wall

1 For a full discussion of this, see my Israel/Palestine, ch. 9, pp. 181–207.

2 Gideon Alon, Ha'aretz, 24 June 2002.

3 The report was summarized in Justin Huggler, UK Independent, 12 November 2003.

4 Akiva Eldar, Ha'aretz, 16 February 2004.

5 These are the pre-Oslo figures for 1993, as quoted in Haim Gvirzman, "Two in the Same Basin," Ha'aretz, 16 May 1993. According to the Palestinian Hydrology group, at present, out of the annual recharge of the western part of the Mountain Groundwater Basin, which is 362 million CM/year, the total Palestinian withdrawal is only 22 million CM/year (www.pengon.org, Report #1).

6 Haim Gvirzman, ibid.

7 The map in Figure 2, based on the Hebrew map in Yediot Aharonot, was prepared by Jan de Yong and appeared in Foundation for Middle East Peace (www.fmep.org), vol. 10, no. 4, July–August 2000.

8 See Amira Hass, "Israel Cuts off Jordan Valley from Rest of West Bank," Ha'aretz, 13 February 2006.

9 Meron Rappaport, "A Wall in the Heart," Yediot Aharonot, Seven Days Saturday Supplement, 23 May 2003 (translation by Daily Summary of the Hebrew Media).

10 Ibid.

11 Amnon Dankner and Ben Kaspit, "The Road Blast – Sharon's New Initiative", Ma'ariv, 2 January 2006 (Hebrew; www.nrg.co.il/online/1/ART1/027/938.html).

12 Aluf Benn and Yossi Verter, "Olmert to Offer Settlers: Expand Blocs, Cut Outposts," Ha'aretz, 10 March 2006. The full interview in which Olmert lays out his plans was published in Ha'aretz the same day.

13 Ibid.

14 Ibid.

15 See my Israel/Palestine, ch. 2, pp. 42–50.

16 Aluf Benn, "Olmert: Israel Will Separate from Most Palestinians," Ha'aretz, 8 February 2006.

17 Aluf Benn and Yossi Verter, "Olmert to Offer Settlers: Expand Blocs, Cut Outposts', Ha'aretz, 3 March 2006. In an analysis of Olmert's plan, Ha'aretz reported that if it were to take place, it would be done in the same way as the previous evacuation of three settlements in the north of the West Bank – Ganim, Kadim and Sanur, near Jenin (see map), which took place together with the disengagement from the Gaza Strip in the summer of 2005. As mentioned in Chapter 2 above, these isolated settlements, unlike those in Gaza, were evacuated because they were too costly to maintain, with their residents wishing to leave. But after the evacuation the area remained under strict Israeli military control and the Palestinians were not allowed access to the evacuated lands. Sources close to Olmert clarified that "the emerging model for the next disengagement is that of the northern West Bank: the evacuation of the settlers and the demolition of their homes, but with the land

retaining its present status – under Israeli security and civilian control. The Israel Defense Forces will continue to patrol and the Palestinians will not be allowed to establish new villages on the sites of the evacuated settlements. The territory will be handed over to them only as part of a political settlement and not without a quid pro quo" (Aluf Benn, "Toughing Out the Waiting Game," *Ha'aretz*, 23 February 2006.)

18 Meron Rappaport, *Ha'aretz*, 20 January 2005. See also his extended coverage in the *Ha'aretz Weekend Magazine* of the same day.

19 Yuval Yo'az, *Ha'aretz*, 2 February 2005.

20 For this ruling, see above p. 170.

21 Meron Rappaport, *Yediot Aharonot*, 23 May 2003; Akiva Eldar, *Ha'aretz*, 16 February 2004.

22 In Khirbet Jbara in the Tulkarm Governorate, the cabinet approved moving a 6-km section of the barrier closer to the Green Line. As a result, the Palestinian population in this area will no longer be located in a completely closed area, but rather on the West Bank side of the barrier. This will reduce the overall Palestinian population completely isolated from the West Bank by about 340 persons, according to a UNOCHA report of March 2005 on the preliminary analysis of the effects of the new wall route approved in February 2005. See www.ochaopt.org for details.

23 The International Court of Justice, seated in The Hague, is the principal judicial organ of the United Nations. Established in 1945, the court is composed of fifteen judges elected by the UN General Assembly and the UN Security Council. Its main functions are to settle disputes submitted to it by states and to give advisory opinions on legal questions submitted by the UN. The UN sent the issue of the separation wall to the ICJ in December 2003, asking it to prepare an opinion on "the legal ramifications of the construction of the wall inside Palestinian territory".

24 Yuval Yoaz, Hague fence ruling may lead to sanctions, *Ha'aretz*, August 19, 2004.

25 *Ibid.*

26 Ha'aretz editorial, Top priority for the fence, *Ha'aretz April 26, 2004*.

27 Paragraph 22 of the ruling. The full text of the ICJ ruling of can be found at http://www.icj-cij.org/icjwww/idocket/imwp/imwpframe.htm.

28 Arnon Regular, *Ha'aretz*, 4 March 2003.

29 Tanya Reinhart, "Sophisticated Transfer," *Yediot Aharonot*, 10 April 2003; translated from Hebrew by Irit Katriel.

30 For example, Alex Fishman wrote in *Yediot Aharonot* Saturday Supplement, 20 September 2002: "The revolutionary group in the Pentagon is processing the world perceptions of the RAND Institute into operative plans. The goal: change of the political map through military means . . . For example, in the working presentation at the Pentagon it was stated that Palestine is actually Israel. Otherwise said, the Palestinians will be able to realize their national aspirations mainly in a state like Jordan. Jordan takes on a key role. According to this plan, when the story of the Ba'ath regime in Iraq is over with, democratic Iraq will return to be part of the Hashemite Kingdom."

31 Yeshayahu Leibovitz, "Territories, Peace and Security, *Ha'aretz*, 3 November 1972, reprinted in Y. Leibovitz, *Judaism, the Jewish People and the State of Israel* (Jerusalem, 2005), p. 449 (Hebrew).

8. *The Struggle: Expanding the Prison Cells*

1 Noam Chomsky, interviewed by David Barsamian, says in *The Common Good* (Monroe, ME: Common Courage Press, 1998): "Some of the rural workers in Brazil have an interesting slogan. They say their immediate task is "expanding the floor of the cage". They understand

that they're trapped inside a cage, but realize that protecting it when it's under attack from even worse predators on the outside, and extending the limits of what the cage will allow, are both essential preliminaries to dismantling it. If they attack the cage directly when they're so vulnerable, they'll get murdered' (p. 85).

2 I survey some of their struggle between 2000 and 2003 in *Israel/Palestine*, ch. 10, pp. 226–35.

3 The ISM's site is: http://www.palsolidarity.org. Its goals, as developed in subsequent years and currently described on this site, are "to support and strengthen the Palestinian popular resistance by providing the Palestinian people with two resources, international protection and a voice with which to nonviolently resist an overwhelming military occupation force".

4 Sonia Nettnin, www.palestinechronicle.com, 24 October 2005.

5 Ibid.

6 For example, Alex Fishman, *Yediot Aharonot* Saturday Supplement, 20 September 2002 (quoted in Chapter 7).

7 "We Stand for Peace and Justice," *Z Magazine*, 27 March 2003, http://www.zmag.org/wspj/index.cfm.

8 Map shows detail adapted from B'Tselem, "The Separation Barrier in the West Bank, September 2005", www.btselem.org. (B'Tselem is the Israeli information centre for human rights in the occupied territories.)

9 It even happened on one occasion that soldiers guarding the construction of the wall later joined in the anti-wall struggle themselves.

10 The core of the Israeli activists at the founding stage included Raz Avni, Ronen Eidelman, Tal Jacobson, Liad Kantarovitz, Itai Levinsky, Yoni Masi, Na'ama Nagar, Yonatan Pollak, Aya Zamir and many others.

11 Starhawk (www.starhawk.org) is the author of *Webs of Power: Notes from the Global Uprising* and eight other books on feminism, politics and earth-based spirituality. She works with the RANT trainer's collective, which offers training and support for mobilization on global justice and peace issues.

12 See above, Chapter 6, section 2.

13 News agencies, "Palestinians Demonstrate over Lack of PA Action against Fence," *Ha'aretz*, 4 December 2004.

14 The event was reported briefly in *Ha'aretz*, 23 May 2005.

15 There is a documentary film about the Mas'ha camp, produced and directed by participants: "Temporary Inconvenience", Producer: Claudia Levin; directors: Daniel Sivan and Yoni Massi. It can be ordered at: claudia.levin@claudiusfilms.com.

16 *Ha'aretz* Service, "IDF Detectives to Question 3 in Shooting of Protesters," *Ha'aretz* online, 30 December 2003.

17 For a detailed survey of the Israeli army's policy of injuries, See *Israel/Palestine*, ch. 6, section 1, pp. 112–16.

18 Pollack had been arrested at the previous day's protest at Mas'ha (author's note).

19 *Ha'aretz* Service, "IDF Detectives to Question 3 in Shooting of Protesters," *Ha'aretz* online, 30 December 2003.

20 Map is from September 2005. By that time, the struggle for Budrus had been won, and the wall was moved back to the Green Line.

21 Mitch Potter, *Toronto Star*, 6 March 2004.

22 Gideon Levy, "The Peaceful Way Works Best," *Ha'aretz* Friday Magazine, 13 February 2004.

23 For more on Biddu's struggle and the army's violence, see Gideon Levy, "Twilight Zone/ Fighting the Fence," *Ha'aretz*, *Magazine*, 5 March 2004.

24 Tanya Reinhart, "Biddu: The Struggle Against The Wall" (different title in Hebrew), *Yediot Aharonot* and Ynet, 5 May 2004, translated from Hebrew by Netta Van Vliet.

25 Yuval Yoaz and Aluf Benn, "Court Nixes Route of Fence Near J'lem," *Ha'aretz*, 1 July 2004.

26 Again, map shows already the route of the wall after these changes.

27 Ayed Morar, "After the Hague: A Message from an Activist," Ta'ayush mailing list, 13 July 2004.

28 See above, Chapter 7, p. 169.

29 Aviv Lavie, "Picking their Battles," *Ha'aretz* Friday Magazine, 15 April 2004.

30 Ibid.

31 Tanya Reinhart, "Standing against the Claws of the Wall," *Yediot Aharonot* and *Ynet*, 23 June 2004, translated from Hebrew by Mark Marshall and Edeet Ravel.

32 *Ha'aretz* editorial, "Where's the Restraint in Bil'in?," *Ha'aretz*, 6 September 2005.

33 Associated Press, "IDF Disperses Riot with Sound Technology," Ynet (www.ynetnews.com), 3 June 2005.

34 See http://www.bilin-village.org.

35 From a leaflet of the popular committee (see pp. 213–17).

36 *Ha'aretz* editorial, "Where's the Restraint in Bil'in?," *Ha'aretz*, 6 September 2005.

37 Signatories to this statement were the Popular Committee Against the Wall, Gush Shalom, Ta'ayush, Coalition of Women for Just Peace, the Committee Against House Demolitions, and Anarchists Against the Wall.

38 Greta B, "You Can't Break Our Spirit," http://www.palsolidarity.org, 9 September 2005.

39 Coalition Against the Wall, press release, 9 September 2005, http://www.geocities.com/keller_adam/BilSept9_he.htm.

40 Mohammed Khatib, "We Refuse to Be Strangled by the Wall in Silence," http://www.bilin-village.org.

Index